LES PRIX NOBEL

THE NOBEL PRIZES

1992

Dear John,

With considerable admiration
Happy to know you
for so long!

Keep up your outstanding
work!

[signature]

NOBELPRISET

The Nobel Prize

LES PRIX NOBEL

THE NOBEL PRIZES

1992

NOBEL PRIZES, PRESENTATIONS, BIOGRAPHIES, AND LECTURES

Physics

GEORGES CHARPAK

Chemistry

RUDOLPH A. MARCUS

Physiology or Medicine

EDMOND H. FISCHER
EDWIN G. KREBS

Literature

DEREK WALCOTT

Peace

RIGOBERTA MENCHÚ TUM

Prize in Economic Sciences in Memory of Alfred Nobel

GARY S. BECKER

ALMQVIST & WIKSELL INTERNATIONAL
STOCKHOLM — SWEDEN

ISBN 91-85848-21-2

Printed in Sweden by Norstedts Tryckeri AB, Stockholm 1993

CONTENTS

THE NOBEL INSTITUTIONS

THE NOBEL FOUNDATION is the organization to which has been entrusted the fortune bequeathed by Alfred Nobel in order to enable a Prize to be awarded to the most deserving person in each of the following fields: Physics, Chemistry, Physiology or Medicine, Literature, and Peace. The Foundation is the administrative body of the institutions which award the Nobel Prizes. The essential task of its Board is to administer the funds and the other property of the Foundation. The institutions responsible for awarding the Prizes elect delegates who, in turn, elect the members of the Board with the exception of the president and the vice president. Despite the private nature of the Foundation, the latter are appointed by the Government. The electing institutions are as follows:

In Sweden:
THE ROYAL SWEDISH ACADEMY OF SCIENCES — for the Prizes in Physics and Chemistry;

THE NOBEL ASSEMBLY AT THE KAROLINSKA INSTITUTE (the full professors of the medical faculty) — for the Prize in Physiology or Medicine;

THE SWEDISH ACADEMY — for the Prize in Literature.

In Norway:
THE NORWEGIAN NOBEL COMMITTEE (five members appointed by the Norwegian Parliament) — for the Peace Prize.

The Swedish institutions set up special *Nobel Committees* which are instructed to prepare reports and to submit recommendations for the awarding of the Prizes.

In Norway, the corresponding preparatory work is entrusted by the institution that awards the Peace Prize, the Norwegian Committee, to its president, assisted by the secretary of the committee and by three experts in the fields of international law, political history and economic sciences.

Prize candidates put forward by those competent under the special statutes to present proposals are studied by the respective preparatory bodies, and explanatory reports are submitted to the institutions whose task it is to award the Prizes. The institutions then make their decisions, which are irrevocable. Traditionally, all the deliberations and recommendations of the committees are secret.

In 1992, the Swedish Nobel Committees were made up of the following members:

for Physics:
CARL NORDLING, Professor of Atomic and Molecular Physics at Uppsala University, *Chairman of the Committee;* BENGT NAGEL, Professor of Mathematical Physics at the Royal Institute of Technology, Stockholm; ERIK KARLSSON, Professor of Physics at Uppsala University; CECILIA JARLSKOG, Professor of Theoretical Elementary Particle Physics at Stockholm University; TORD CLAESON, Professor of Physics at Chalmers University of Technology, Gothenburg; *Secretary of the Committee:* ANDERS BÁRÁNY, Associate Professor of Theoretical Atomic Physics at the Manne Siegbahn Institute of Physics, Stockholm; *adjoint member:* PER CARLSON, Professor of Elementary Particle Physics at the Manne Siegbahn Institute of Physics, Stockholm.

for Chemistry:
SALO GRONOWITZ, Professor of Organic Chemistry at Lund University, *Chairman of the Committee;* STURE FORSÉN, Professor of Physical Chemistry at Lund University; BERTIL ANDERSSON, Professor of Biochemistry at Stockholm University; CARL-IVAR BRÄNDÉN, Professor of Molecular Biology at the Swedish University of Agricultural Sciences, Uppsala; BJÖRN ROOS, Professor of Theoretical Chemistry at Lund University; *Secretary of the Committee:* PEDER KIERKEGAARD, Professor of Structural Chemistry at Stockholm University; *adjoint members:* LENNART EBERSON, Professor of Organic Chemistry at Lund University; TORVARD LAURENT, Professor of Medical and Physiological Chemistry at the Uppsala Biomedical Centre (BMC); INGMAR GRENTHE, Professor of Inorganic Chemistry at the Royal Institute of Technology, Stockholm.

for Physiology or Medicine:
HANS WIGZELL, Professor of Immunology, *Chairman of the Committee;* GÖRAN HOLM, Professor of Medicine, *Deputy Chairman of the Committee;* BERTIL DANEHOLT, Professor of Molecular Genetics; STEN GRILLNER, Professor of Physiology; ANITA APERIA, Professor of Pediatrics; *Secretary of the Committee:* ALF LINDBERG, Professor of Clinical Bacteriology; *adjoint members:* GÖRAN AKUSJÄRVI, Professor of Microbial Genetics; BERTIL FREDHOLM, Professor of Pharmacology; GÖSTA GAHRTON, Professor of Medicine; BERTIL HAMBERGER, Professor of Surgery; ARNE HOLMGREN, Professor of Biochemistry; HANS JÖRNVALL, Professor of Medical Physiological Chemistry; ERLING NORRBY, Professor of Virology; RALF PETTERSSON, Professor of Molecular Biology; NILS RINGERTZ, Professor of Medical Cell Genetics; LARS TERENIUS, Professor of Experimental Dependency Research.

for Literature:
KJELL ESPMARK, Professor, *Chairman of the Committee;* STURE ALLÉN, Professor, *Secretary of the Committee;* ÖSTEN SJÖSTRAND, Writer; KNUT AHNLUND, Professor; LARS FORSSELL, Writer.

for the Peace Prize;

FRANCIS SEJERSTED, Professor, *Chairman of the Committee;* GIDSKE ANDERSON, Writer, *Deputy Chairman of the Committee;* ODVAR NORDLI, Governor and Former Prime Minister; KÅRE KRISTIANSEN, Former Member of Parliament; HANNA KVANMO, Former Member of Parliament; *Secretary of the Committee:* GEIR LUNDESTAD, Professor, Director of the Norwegian Nobel Institute.

THE PRIZE-WINNERS AND CITATIONS

THE ROYAL SWEDISH ACADEMY OF SCIENCES
decided on October 14, 1992, to award the Nobel Prize in Physics to

GEORGES CHARPAK
Ecole Supérieure de Physique et Chimie, Paris, France, and CERN, Geneva, Switzerland,

for his invention and development of particle detectors, in particular the multiwire proportional chamber.

On the same date, the Academy decided to award the Nobel Prize in Chemistry to

RUDOLPH A. MARCUS
California Institute of Technology, Pasadena, California, USA

for his contributions to the theory of electron transfer reactions in chemical systems.

THE NOBEL ASSEMBLY AT THE KAROLINSKA INSTITUTE
decided on October 12, 1992, to award to the Nobel Prize in Physiology or Medicine jointly to

EDMOND H. FISCHER and
EDWIN G. KREBS
University of Washington, Seattle, Washington, USA

for their discoveries concerning "reversible protein phosphorylation as a biological regulatory mechanism".

THE SWEDISH ACADEMY
decided on October 8, 1992, to award the Nobel Prize in Literature to

DEREK WALCOTT
Trinidad

for a poetic oeuvre of great luminosity, sustained by a historical vision, the outcome of a multicultural commitment.

THE NORWEGIAN NOBEL COMMITTEE
decided on October 16, 1992, to award the Nobel Prize for Peace to

RIGOBERTA MENCHÚ TUM
Guatemala

in recognition of her work for social justice and ethno-cultural reconciliation based on respect for the rights of indigenous peoples.

Candidates formally proposed for the various Nobel Prizes in 1992 totalled
for Physics, 255
for Chemistry, 304
for Physiology or Medicine, 226
for Literature, 156
for Peace, 113.

THE NOBEL CEREMONIES

Presentation of the Prizes in Stockholm

The Prizes in Physics, in Chemistry, in Physiology or Medicine, and in Literature, and also the Prize in Economic Sciences in memory of Alfred Nobel, were presented to the Prize-Winners as part of a traditional programme established by the Prize-Awarding Institutions and by the Board of the Nobel Foundation. The festivities were organized by the Executive Director of the Foundation, Mr. Michael Sohlman. The ceremonies took place in the Grand Auditorium of the Concert Hall in Stockholm.

Among the guests were the year's Prize-Winners, Charpak, Marcus, Fischer, Krebs, Walcott, and Becker (Prize in Economic Sciences), and their families, and also a number of Prize-Winners from previous years: Siegbahn (1981), Samuelsson (1982), Brodsky (1987), and Lederman (1988).

A number of members of the Government, including the Prime Minister, Mr. Carl Bildt, the heads of missions and other members of the diplomatic corps honoured the ceremony with their presence. In addition to the Nobel organizations in Sweden, various academies, a number of learned and literary societies, the universities, the Nobel family, the world of arts, industry and the press were also represented. The assembly also included high-ranking representatives of the civil service and the military.

At 4.30 p.m. His Majesty the King, Her Majesty the Queen, and Their Royal Highnesses Prince Bertil and Princess Lilian, the Duke and Duchess of Halland, entered the hall saluted by the Royal Anthem. The ceremony then proceeded as shown in the programme reproduced on the following page.

At the end of each address delivered by the speaker responsible for introducing the prize-winning work, H.M. the King presented the Prize-Winner with the *diploma,* the *medal,* and a *document* showing the amount of the Prize.

PROGRAMME

"Kungssången" (Royal Anthem)

"Rákóczy March" from Damnation of Faust . . . . *Hector Berlioz*

The Laureates take their seats on the stage

Speech by *Professor Lars Gyllensten,* Chairman of the Board of the Nobel Foundation

3rd movement from Symphony No. 8 F major op. 93   *Ludwig van Beethoven*

Presentation of the Nobel Prize in Physics 1992 to *Georges Charpak* after a speech by *Professor Carl Nordling*

Presentation of the Nobel in Chemistry 1992 to *Rudolph A. Marcus* after a speech by *Professor Lennart Eberson*

"The Maiden under the Lime Tree".
Soloist *Gösta Winbergh* . . . . *Wilhelm Peterson-Berger*

Presentation of the Nobel Prize in Physiology or Medicine 1992 to *Edmond H. Fischer* and *Edwin G. Krebs* after a speech by *Professor Hans Jörnvall*

"Una furtiva lagrima" from L'elisir d'amore.
Soloist *Gösta Winbergh* . . . . *Gaetano Donizetti*

Presentation of the Nobel Prize in Literature 1992 to *Derek Walcott* after a speech by *Professor Kjell Espmark*

"Rythm of Time" from Orpheus in Town. . . . . *Hilding Rosenberg*

Presentation of the Sveriges Riksbank (Bank of Sweden) Prize in Economic Sciences in Memory of Alfred Nobel 1992 to *Gary S. Becker* after a speech by *Professor Assar Lindbeck*

The Swedish national Anthem "Du gamla, du fria"

"Festivity March" from The Prodigal Son. . . . . *Hugo Alfvén*
Played while the guests are leaving the auditorium

Music performed by
The Royal Stockholm Philharmonic Orchestra
Soloist: *Gösta Winbergh,* tenor
Conductor: *Niklas Willén*

14

OPENING ADDRESS

By Professor Lars Gyllensten, Chairman of the Board of the
Nobel Foundation.
Translation from the Swedish text.

Your Majesties, Your Royal Highnesses, Ladies and Gentlemen,

On behalf of the Nobel Foundation I would like to extend to this year's laureates and other guests a warm welcome to the 1992 Prize Award Ceremony.

It is for us a pleasure and an honour to note the great interest in and the great and increasing respect for the Nobel Prize and the activities connected with it. For this, of course, our gratitude is mainly due to the laureates — but also to those awarding the prizes, who have been able to discharge their onerous duties with great address. This I can say without risk of being accused of boasting, for it is not the Nobel Foundation but the bodies awarding the prizes that are responsible for the deliberations leading up to the decisions about who is to receive them. Misunderstandings often arise on this point. It is extremely important to emphasize that those awarding the prizes enjoy complete independence not only from the Nobel Foundation, but from all other authorities and agencies as well. This autonomy is of essential importance for the objectivity and quality of the awards.

This year's laureates represent an elite among today's research workers and the creators of contemporary culture. It is my privilege to congratulate them and to bid them heartily welcome among colleagues, friends and admirers. These words also apply to the laureate, the functionaries and the guests in Oslo, where Alfred Nobel's prize for the advancement of peace is being awarded today.

This year has seen the celebration of the 500th anniversary of what has been called the "discovery" of America by Christopher Columbus. The word "discovery" is an instance of Western presumptuousness. The American continents had been discovered by their inhabitants several thousands of years before Columbus' voyage. What Columbus, his companions, and those who followed after him did was to open a route across the sea for the exploitation of a continent which had hitherto been spared this kind of outrage. Gradually not only violence and pillage was to be involved, but also peaceful growth and the development of culture.

What did Columbus and those who followed in his footsteps actually do? The answer consists of two paradoxes. He himself had, as we know, set his mind on finding an economically serviceable sea route to India and its treasures. For the rest of his life he was also to believe that this is what he had achieved.

The other paradox is more complex and controversial. The exploitation of the American continent was one of the first steps in the technological, economic and military growth of Western Europe and of colonialism. In this was seen an auspicious, expansive spirit and encouraging evidence of how progress can be created and rewarded.

What is the historical import of all this? Is there anything good about this increasingly arrogant pursuit of growth—anything beneficial for our future? We now know a great deal about what the technology and economics of the West and its expansion have entailed in the form of fatal risks and damage to the entire biosphere. Was then the spirit of Columbus' undertaking, and what it was to promote, of value to mankind? We do not know—any more than Columbus knew what he was doing. We do have a pretty good idea of what human technological and economic undertakings have achieved so far. But what this cultural attitude and its expansive patterns of life will lead to in the future is unknown to us. All is not well—and the long-term prospects for life on earth are far from promising.

Another anniversary is, to a certain extent, of a similar nature. I am thinking of the 50th anniversary of the activation of the first pile of uranium, in December 1942. This was to launch the practical exploitation of nuclear energy, both for the production of weapons of mass-destruction and for the production of power. Have these appalling weapons prevented major warfare and mass destruction on a global scale—leaving military history to restrict itself to what are called conventional weapons? And what will they lead to in the future? Will it be possible to regulate their use—or are we heading towards undreamt-of catastrophes, caused by accidents or criminal political regimes? Nobody knows. There are similar uncertainties concerning the use of nuclear power. It may be possible to limit the risks on the whole and to overcome the damaging effects on the environment involved in everything connected with its development, not least those related to the extraction and enrichment of uranium as fuel. Have the prospects of resources of energy which nuclear engineering seemed to offer been beneficial? Or do they lull us into a hopeful confidence which prevents us from altering the long-term destructiveness of patterns of living and consumption in the industrialised countries, so that a tolerable life can be created on earth? These are questions we cannot answer.

It is a truism to point out that most human undertakings contain different degrees of uncertainty, ignorance and doubt about their long-term consequences. This is true not least of technological and scientific undertakings. Dudley Herschbach, the Nobel Laureate in Chemistry in 1986, expressed this in a conversational aphorism. He observed that we—research workers—are working in areas where we do not quite know what we are doing. This is a reflection which could lead to pessimism and defeatism. But he added optimistically that it is pleasurable not to understand. It offers a possibility of learning something new and special. The truth awaits us. The point is that if we are to be mistaken, we should be mistaken in an interesting way.

16

This year's environmental conference in Rio involved an analysis of the ways in which humankind has been mistaken and acted mistakenly, and continues to act mistakenly, if, in the long run, we really do want to create a tolerable life on earth. It is an optimistic sign that this conference ever took place and that it aroused so much international commitment as it did. It should perhaps be regarded as a mistake that no binding, weighty undertakings were given. But deep inside, we should like to feel that in this case this is an "interesting mistake" — a pragmatic, deliberate step on the path that can lead to binding decisions and constructive, efficacious measures in the future.

THE NOBEL PRIZE IN PHYSICS

Speech by Professor Carl Nordling of the Royal Swedish Academy of Sciences.
Translation from the Swedish text.

Your Majesties, Your Royal Highnesses, Ladies and Gentlemen,

This year the Nobel Prize in Physics has been awarded to Georges Charpak, France, for his invention and development of particle detectors, in particular the multiwire proportional chamber. It is the tenth time in the history of the Nobel Prize that the word "invention" has been used in the citation for the award in physics.

None of us owns the kind of detector for which the prize is being awarded today, but we are all equipped with other forms of detectors. Our eyes are detectors of light, our ears detect sound, our noses detect odors and so on. The signals from these sense organs are sent to a computer—the brain. There they are processed, communicated to our consciousness and used as the basis of our actions and our conception of the world in which we live.

But we are not always content with this. Our curiosity about the world extends beyond our immediate sensory impressions. For this reason inventive people have constructed devices of various kinds which intensify our senses or replace them completely—if this is at all possible in principle. Galileo Galilei constructed telescopes, Zacharias Janssen invented the microscope etc.

Today's elementary particle physicists look deep inside matter using accelerators as microscopes. In these accelerators particles chosen as suitable projectiles, electrons for instance, are raised to high energies and then made to collide with each other. This produces new particles like the sparks from fireworks. In this invisible deluge of sparks, which can be discharged a hundred million times each second, there is information about the innermost constituents of matter and the forces with which they interact.

In order to acquire this information, enormous installations are built, which contain various kinds of detectors. Professor Charpak has invented the detector which has meant most for the progress in the area of elementary particle physics during the last few decades.

The list of qualities demanded of a detector of elementary particles is a long one. It must react quickly, must be able to cover large surfaces—hundreds of square meters—and must send its signals direct to a computer. It must be sensitive to position, i.e. it must not only be able to say *if* something has happened but also *where*, and it must also be capable of following the total length of the trajectory of a particle, often several meters. And it must be able to do all this even when it is placed in a strong magnetic field.

All of these requirements are fulfilled by the multiwire proportional chamber, the detector which Georges Charpak invented in 1968. This detector is used, in some form or other, in more or less every experiment within elementary particle physics today, and Georges Charpak has been at the centre of the development which has taken place since the original invention was made. Many important discoveries have been made using his detectors.

Charpak's research is an example of an advanced technological development within basic science. Its original purpose was to contribute to the development of nuclear physics and elementary particle physics in order to provide further facets of our conception of the world. This aim has been achieved, but Charpak's detector has also found applications well outside the field of elementary particle physics, for instance in medicine. In this development too, Charpak plays a central role.

Monsieur Charpak,
Le Prix Nobel de Physique de l'année 1992 vous a été decerné pour votre invention et développement de détecteurs de particules, notamment de la chambre proportionelle multifils. J'ai l'honneur de vous adresser les félicitations les plus chaleureuses de l'Académie Royale des Sciences de Suède, et je vous invite à recevoir votre Prix des mains de Sa Majesté le Roi.

THE NOBEL PRIZE IN CHEMISTRY

Speech by Professor Lennart Eberson of the Royal Swedish Academy of Sciences.
Translation from the Swedish text.

Your Majesties, Your Royal Highnesses, Ladies and Gentlemen,

The 1992 Nobel Prize in Chemistry is being awarded to Professor Rudolph Marcus for *his contributions to the theory of electron transfer reactions in chemical systems.* To understand the background of his achievements, we must transport ourselves back to the period around 1950, when chemistry looked completely different than it does today. In those days, it was still difficult to determine the structure of chemical compounds, and even more difficult to make theoretical calculations of the rate of chemical reactions.

Reaction rate is a fundamental concept in chemistry. A mixture of chemical compounds undergoes changes, or chemical reactions, at different rates. Today we can measure reaction rates using virtually any time scale from quadrillionths of a second to thousands of years. By the late 19th century, Sweden's Svante Arrhenius, later a Nobel Laureate, had shown that the rate of a chemical reaction can be described in terms of the requirement for a reacting system to cross an energy barrier. The size of this barrier was easy to determine experimentally. Calculating it was a formidable problem.

In the years after 1945, a new technique for determining reaction rates had been developed: the radioactive tracer technique. By substituting a radioactive isotope for a given atom in a molecule, new types of reactions could be studied. One such reaction was the transfer of an electron between metal ions in different states of oxidation, for example between a bivalent and a trivalent iron ion in an aqueous solution. This turned out to be a slow reaction, that is, it took place over a period of hours, something highly unexpected by the chemists of that day. Compared with an atomic nucleus, an electron is a very light particle. How could the slowness of its movement between iron ions be explained?

This problem led to lively discussion around 1950. Marcus became interested when he happened to read through some papers from a symposium on electron transfer reactions, where the American chemist Willard Libby had suggested that a well-known spectroscopic principle known as the Franck-Condon principle might apply to the movement of an electron between two molecules. Marcus realized that this ought to create an energy barrier, which might explain the slow electron transfer between bivalent and trivalent iron in an aqueous solution. To enable the two iron ions to exchange an electron, a number of water molecules in their surroundings must be rearranged. This increases the energy of the system temporarily, and at some point the electron can jump without violating the restrictions of the Franck-Condon principle.

In 1956, Marcus published a mathematical model for this type of reaction, based on classic theories of physical chemistry. He was able to calculate the size of the energy barrier, using simple quantities such as ionic radii and ionic charges. He later extended the theory to cover electron transfer between different kinds of molecules and derived simple mathematical expressions known as "the quadratic equation" and "the cross-equation." These could be tested empirically and led to new experimental programs in all branches of chemistry. The Marcus theory greatly contributed to our understanding of such widely varying phenomena as the capture of light energy in green plants, electron transfer in biological systems, inorganic and organic oxidation and reduction processes and photochemical electron transfer.

The quadratic equation predicts that electron transfer reactions will occur more slowly the larger the driving force of the reaction is. This phenomenon received its own name, "the inverted region." To a chemist, the phenomenon is just as unexpected as when a skier finds himself gliding more slowly down a slope the steeper it is. In 1965, Marcus himself suggested that certain chemiluminescent reactions ("cold light") might serve as an example of the inverted region. Only after 1985, however, could further examples of such reactions be demonstrated. The most improbable prediction in his theory had thereby been verified.

Professor Marcus,
In the space of a few minutes, I have tried to trace and explain the origins of the theory of electron transfer that carries your name. Your theory is a unifying factor in chemistry, promoting understanding of electron transfer reactions of biochemical, photochemical, inorganic and organic nature and thereby contributing to science as a whole. It has led to the development of many new research programs, demonstrating the lasting impact of your work. In recognition of your contribution to chemistry, the Royal Swedish Academy of Sciences has decided to confer upon you this year's Nobel Prize in Chemistry.

Professor Marcus, I have the honor and pleasure to extend to you the congratulations of the Royal Swedish Academy of Sciences and to ask you to receive your Prize from the hands of His Majesty the King.

THE NOBEL PRIZE IN PHYSIOLOGY OR MEDICINE

Speech by Professor Hans Jörnvall of the Nobel Assembly of the Karolinska Institute.
Translation from the Swedish text.

Your Majesties, Your Royal Highnesses, Ladies and Gentlemen,

This year's Nobel Prize in Physiology or Medicine is awarded for discoveries concerning reversible protein phosphorylation. What does that mean and how does phosphorylation work?

Let us start with proteins. They can be compared with workers in our tissues. We are composed of cells, each cell constituting a small community. Constant activity is a characteristic feature both of cells and ordinary communities. There are systems for transportation, energy generation, production, and waste handling. In society all this is handled by humans, in a cell proteins take our place. How do they accomplish their functions? Well, exactly like human workers, they operate by way of interaction with other components. Much in the same manner as a driver or pilot recognizes the controls, proteins recognize "their" partners, binding them to influence the reaction paths.

And now phosphorylation: one or several small phosphate groups are coupled to a protein, changing its properties. If the parallel with our human workers is pursued further, one could perhaps compare phosphorylation with ballet shoes. Despite their small size they have dramatic effects on their wearer! The shape of the foot is altered and after that, work is like a dance. Edmond Fischer and Edwin Krebs, this year's Laureates, described this principle in the fifties. They showed how muscles liberate an energy-rich form of sugar from its storage form by phosphorylation of a protein. After that, science gradually gained insight into the fact that this constitutes a general principle manifested in all cellular activities. Today, a considerable part of world bioscience involves protein phosphorylation.

Why this regulation via coupling of small groups? One advantage is that the process is reversible, i.e. the shoes can be taken off and put on, a process which can be repeated again and again. Thus, proteins can be regulated in both directions. Another is that the reactions can be carried out in successive steps, creating a cascade that amplifies the end effect. Much like the hydraulic amplification in a brake: a gentle touch of the pedal can stop even a heavy car. In the world of proteins, Krebs and his collaborators paved the way for this knowledge by studying also the preceding protein in the chain of phosphorylations, while Fischer concentrated his efforts along other lines and, as recently as some years ago, reported the purification of a special type of phosphate-removing protein.

Yet another advantage is that the regulation can be affected by different signals. The system that Fischer and Krebs first studied can be activated either by means of a stress hormone released when we become frightened and our muscles prepare us for escape, or by an act of will when we wish to run for other reasons. Phosphate groups are in these two cases attached in response to separate signals, much as they are in all other cellular response systems. What relevance does this have to medicine? The easiest answer is that we all know of the consequences in society from imbalances in economic chain reactions! We are now in a position to start perceiving how illnesses, including common diseases like hypertension and tumors, are accompanied by imbalances in phosphorylations. Relationships initially recognized in connection with glycogen storage in muscles and liver, have thus been proven to pertain to cellular regulatory processes in general. An excellent demonstration of the power of basic research and of the versatility of simple models. The protein system in glycogen storage has given rise, over the years, to several Nobel Prizes, in 1947 to Gerty and Carl Cori for the course of the catalytic conversion of glycogen, in 1971 to Earl Sutherland for mechanisms of action of hormones, and now to Fischer and Krebs for discoveries concerning reversible protein phosphorylation as a biological regulatory mechanism.

Edmond Fischer and Edwin Krebs,
I have tried to describe your field of research and elegant discoveries in your studies of reversible protein phosphorylation, going back to the initial detection of the activation mechanism of phosphorylase, and continuing with protein phosphatases. Over the years, your early observations on a particular system have contributed to the opening up of novel insight into basic protein regulations at all levels and in all cells. On behalf of the Nobel Assembly of the Karolinska Institute, I convey to you our warmest congratulations, and ask you now to step forward to receive your Nobel Prizes from the hands of His Majesty the King.

THE NOBEL PRIZE IN LITERATURE

Speech by Professor Kjell Espmark of the Swedish Academy.
Translation from the Swedish text.

Your Majesties, Your Royal Highnesses, Ladies and Gentlemen,

Trying to capture Derek Walcott's oceanic work in a formula would be an absurd enterprise—had he not himself come to our assistance, shrewdly hiding a few key formulations in his texts. His friend Joseph Brodsky lifts out one of them in his analysis of the work:

> I'm just a red nigger who love the sea,
> I had a sound colonial education,
> I have Dutch, nigger, and English in me,
> and either I'm nobody, or I'm a nation.

These lines in *The Star-Apple Kingdom* call to mind, in the first place, how Walcott unites white and black on his father's as well as on his mother's side but they also remind us of the fact that in his poetry he amalgamates material from different cultures, West Indian, African, and European.

It does not, however, stop at the mingled voices of heritage or the union of themes from different parts of the world. In his introduction to the first volume of plays, we find another Walcott word of great validity—"The mulatto of style." Walcott's art arises from the crossing of two greatly differing traditions, the first a tradition he allowed himself to be adopted by, the European lineage from Homer via Dante, the Elizabethans, and Milton to Auden and Dylan Thomas, an elaborate tradition discernible in lavish metaphor and luxurious sound and rhythm, the second a domestic ageless tradition, an elementary language where, like a new Adam, the poet gives things their names, perceiving how the speech sounds take shape—as in a passage in the autobiographical *Another Life:* "I watched the vowels curl from the tongue of the carpenter's plane, / resinous, fragrant..." Derek Walcott's extraordinary idiom is born in the meeting between European virtuosity and the sensuality of the Caribbean Adam.

But this very personal combination includes not only themes and languages. It is also a question of historical outlook. And here we are helped by yet another formula—"the New Aegean." The archipelago in focus is a reincarnation of the Aegean one: Greek antiquity finds a natural home in the Caribbean present. This can of course be most distinctly seen in Walcott's latest work, *Omeros,* his mosaic epic about the fisherman Achille and his ex-colleague the taxi driver Hector fighting for the favour of the fair housemaid Helen. But the Homeric pattern in this poem is not unique. In fact, *Omeros* has been emerging all through Walcott's production, appearing again and again in names and themes and continuously present in the Odyssean surging of the waves.

What carries the ancient murmur into today's Caribbean, what makes history present is the sea. "The Sea is History" — in a magnificent poem with that name, the sea can allow "the plangent harps of the Babylonian bondage" to sound in the West Indies, where slavery is still manifest in the memories of the skin.

Walcott's latest major poem abundantly exemplifies the combination of a vertiginous historical panorama and morning-fresh Caribbean now. But I should like to illustrate his art of capturing an enormous perspective of time in the tangible moment by means of a few lines in the previous volume, *The Arkansas Testament*. The associations of the poem's self-contemptuous ego at his shabby motel run to Saul on his way to Damascus:

> On the far side of the highway,
> a breeze turned the leaves of an aspen
> to the First Epistle of Paul's
> to the Corinthians.

This wind, which miraculously transforms the leaves of the tree into the pages with St. Paul's commandment of love, is more than an ingenious allusion to a moment where revelation changed history. The breeze pulling an age long since past into the now of the senses, captures, at the same time, a theme that has been sounding for a few decades in Derek Walcott's production — a Pauline empathy vigorous enough to cross centuries and continents.

Dear Derek Walcott,

In your last book, God allows one of your protagonists to be guided by a sea-swift across the ocean, back to his African origin. The quick divine movement of this pilot bird through space and time embodies the thrill given by your poetic art. As a great admirer of that art, I am happy to convey to you, on behalf of the Swedish Academy, the warmest congratulations on the Nobel Prize in Literature 1992 and to invite you to receive the Prize from the hands of His Majesty the King.

THE NOBEL BANQUET IN STOCKHOLM

After the formal presentation of the Prizes a distinguished company gathered in the Blue Hall of the Stockholm City Hall. Among those present were:

His Majesty the King and Her Majesty the Queen, Their Royal Highnesses Prince Bertil and Princess Lilian, the Duke and Duchess of Halland.

And also:

The 1992 Prize-Winners and the previous Prize-Winners mentioned earlier.

Also present were members of the Government and of Parliament as well as heads of the diplomatic missions of the countries of the Prize-Winners and a very large number of scholars, high-ranking Swedish officials and other distinguished persons.

The Chairman of the Foundation proposed a toast to His Majesty the King. The guests rose to drink this toast. Before the speeches of the Prize-Winners, His Majesty proposed a silent toast to the memory of the great benefactor and philanthropist Alfred Nobel.

SPEECHES BY THE LAUREATES

Georges Charpak

Your Majesties, Your Royal Highnesses, Ladies and Gentlemen,

The honour bestowed upon me by the Nobel Foundation appeared to me not to belong to the real world.

I should have found, at my side, everyone from CERN, the European Organization for Nuclear Research. But an incident, a few days ago, enlightened me concerning the surprising decision of the Jury: the official photographer informed me that I was the 137th Nobel Laureate of whom he has had to make a portrait. Certainly all of you know that 137 is a magic, quasi-mystical number in physics. It is equal to the velocity of light times the reduced Planck constant divided by the square of the electron charge! This number governs the size of all objects in the Universe. Some people claim that if this value were to be slightly different life would not be possible.

This information led me, through channels which I cannot reveal publicly, to the origin of the decision of the Jury: they have been inspired by the goddess Freja, the wife of Odin, a spiritual cousin of the goddess Venus, who has decided to choose me to deliver a message.

My very modest contribution to physics has been in the art of weaving in space thin wires detecting the whisper of nearby flying charged particles produced in high-energy nuclear collisions. It is easy for computers to transform these whispers into a symphony understandable to physicists.

But the whispers can also be produced by radiations widely used in biology or in medicine, such as electrons from radioactive elements or X-rays. In this last case it is possible to reduce, by a large factor, the doses of radiations inflicted on the patients. Despite its use still on a very small scale, the first results with wire chambers point clearly to the direction to be taken. The techniques being developed for matching the needs in radiation detectors of the future high-energy colliders foreseen at CERN or in the USA will clearly bring the ideal solution for the imaging of radiations: each quantum will be detected, one by one, with an accuracy of a few microns.

The message from the world of the goddesses Freja and Venus is clear: invest without hesitation in the future high-energy accelerators. You will have as a reward the best solution for the radiography of such fragile objects as women's breasts.

As a fallout, you will learn everything you want to know about the Higgs field, the hidden matter of the Universe, and marvellous new particles which are haunting the dreams of physicists and will become familiar notions to you. But please, do not consider that I am behaving like some lobbyist in Washington. The message comes from the world of Freja and Venus and I have been chosen as the passive medium.

Rudolph A. Marcus

Your Majesties, Your Royal Highnesses, Ladies and Gentlemen,

I deeply appreciate the great honor that Your Majesties and the Royal Swedish Academy of Sciences are bestowing on me today. I believe that it is the entire field of electron transfer, which reaches into many areas of chemistry and into biology, that is being recognized. Individuals in this room, and many others who are not here, have made tremendous contributions to this area of research. I did have the good fortune to learn about some important results at a relatively early stage in the development of this field, and to have the background to treat the problems. I'm not sure that I fully realized, until I saw the Academy's fine poster on electron transfer, how many areas of practical life those processes enter into.

I think that the award recognizes another aspect which sometimes occurs in science as well as in other fields — simplicity and beauty. The lay person may not recognize, as I did not recognize in mathematics until I spent a year or more at a mathematical institute, that the beauty which a scientist can experience after deriving a simple equation or executing an incisive experiment is just as real as that which the artist may experience in creating a work of art.

I believe, too, that there are many analogies between the sport of skiing, which I dearly love, and doing theoretical work in science — the challenge and sense of excitement when the slope is a little more difficult than one feels comfortable with, or the boredom if too easy, or the probable disaster if too difficult.

It is a pleasure to acknowledge my great debt to individuals in this room — Norman Sutin, John Miller, and Sven Larsson in the electron transfer field, Seymour Rabinovitch for his pioneering work in another area, unimolecular reactions, which has occupied almost half my time, and to my family — my wife Laura, whose positive outlook and companionship have been so important during our forty-three years of marriage, and our three sons, Alan, Kenneth, and Raymond, who have long outdistanced their father in skiing, and with whom we have shared so many happy experiences. I thank Your Majesties and the Academy for giving me the opportunity to share this great honor with you all.

Edmond H. Fischer

Your Majesties, Your Royal Highnesses, Ladies and Gentlemen,

On behalf of my colleague and closest friend of forty years, Edwin Krebs and myself, I would like to express our gratitude for the immense honor bestowed upon us today.

I thought I would reflect here on a theme most scientists enjoy recalling: the part luck played in their accomplishments. That was easy because, without question or false modesty, no success has owed more to serendipity than ours. First, we happened to have chosen the right enzyme to study at precisely the right time, and discovered that it was regulated by the simplest of reactions. Second, this simplest of reactions, rather than being restricted to that one system only, turned out to be involved in just about every aspect of cell regulation, from hormone action to gene expression to cancer. Of course, hundreds of scientists participated in these developments and this award really celebrates their collective contributions. But then comes the inevitable question: why were we singled out among so many brilliant colleagues.

It dawned on me that the answer was obvious: NAME RECOGNITION! Indeed, among previous science Laureates there have been no less than 3 other Fischers (all spelling their name correctly — with a "c") and one other Krebs, the late Sir Hans, a good friend of ours. With the two of us today, that makes a total of 6 which beats all other contenders by a mile. So, name recognition must have been very important. But just as important was the fact that, over the years, we have been blessed with the most superb group of collaborators.

It is commonly said that a teacher fails if he has not been surpassed by his students. There has been no failure on our part in this regard considering how far they have gone. We owe our success to them, and also to the fact that, as the saying goes, two "Eds" are better than one.

28

Derek Walcott

Your Majesties, Your Royal Highnesses, Distinguished Representatives of the Nobel Foundation, Honourable Members of the Academies, the Karolinska Institute and Election Committees, Students, Ladies and Gentlemen,

The honour that you pay me is accepted in the one name that comprises all of the supposedly broken languages of the Caribbean. They cohere in this moment, a moment that recognises their endeavour and one which I receive with pride and humility on their behalf. Pride in the continuing struggle of Antillean writers, humility in the glare of representing them by my own evanescent image.

Gary S. Becker

Your Majesties, Your Royal Highnesses, Ladies and Gentlemen,

I would like to express my gratitude to the Royal Swedish Academy of Sciences for the superb honor conferred on me. It is not necessary to have special reasons to be happy to be here, but I do feel especially pleased. This Prize gives recognition in the most influential way possible to all economists who endured many obstacles, criticisms, and even ridicule to study and analyze broader aspects of behavior than is traditional in economics.

During the first half of this century economics became more of a systematic science, but it also became increasingly isolated from the study of society, law and government. I was fortunate to have had outstanding teachers, several who later won this Prize. They supported my desire to use economic theory to try to understand discrimination against minorities and other questions that were much broader than those that had become the core of economics. I am grateful for their insights and encouragement.

I am not revealing any professional secrets when I state that not very long ago this type of research was not popular among most economists and other social scientists. But attitudes are changing, and there are now thriving schools of scholars in many fields using what is called the economic approach to analyze nonmarket and social behavior.

Economics is a very young science in comparison with the physical and biological sciences. Still, much is now known about economic and social life, although perhaps even more remains to be learned. For the economic and social world is mysterious, and it sometimes changes quickly and in surprising fashion. Every time we peel away some of the mystery, deeper challenges rise to the surface.

Economics surely does not provide a romantic vision of life. But the widespread poverty, misery, and crises in many parts of the world, much of it unnecessary, are strong reminders that understanding economic and social laws can make an enormous contribution to the welfare of people.

PRESENTATION OF THE PRIZE AND BANQUET IN OSLO

The Nobel Prize for Peace in 1992 was awarded to Rigoberta Menchú Tum of Guatemala. The presentation of the Prize took place on December 10 at a solemn ceremony in The City Hall in Oslo. Their Majesties King Harald and Queen Sonja honoured the ceremony with their presence. Mrs. Mitterrand of France and Mrs. Salinas of Mexico, representatives of the Norwegian Parliament and the Government, the heads of missions and other members of the diplomatic corps also attended the ceremony.

The Nobel Foundation was represented by Former Executive Director of the Nobel Foundation Baron Stig Ramel and his wife. Violinist Arve Tellefsen opened the ceremony with "A Mountain Vision" by Ole Bull. Then the Chairman of the committee, Professor Francis Sejersted, gave a speech in honour of the 1992 laureate. The 1992 Peace Prize Laureate Rigoberta Menchú Tum received the diploma and medal. Seven Marimba musicians from the Marima del Instituto Indigena Santiago played Guatemalan folksongs. Rigoberta Menchú Tum then gave her combined acceptance speech and Nobel lecture. Arve Tellefsen concluded the ceremony with Adagio from Sonata no.1, G-minor BWV 1001 by Johann Sebastian Bach.

THE NOBEL PRIZE FOR PEACE

Speech delivered by Francis Sejersted, Chairman of the Norwegian Nobel Committee, on the occasion of the award of the Nobel Peace Prize for 1992, Oslo, December 10, 1992.
Translation from the Norwegian text.

Your Majesties, Your Excellencies, Ladies and Gentlemen,

The Norwegian Nobel Committee decided to award the Nobel Peace Prize for 1992 to Rigoberta Menchú Tum. It is a particular pleasure for us to welcome you, Rigoberta Menchú Tum, here to Oslo to receive the award. Welcome to this little winter country in the far north, so far from your own country and your own world. The distance, both geographically and culturally, is vast, but the occasion of this award, in particular, should prompt us to think about nearness. Wherever in the world they take place, conflicts and wars have in our time become the whole world's concern. Even at this distance, we feel threatened by a local conflict in Guatemala, not militarily, but because it affects the world's future. The situation in Guatemala acquires a special significance because it is such a clear case of general problems that we must all contribute to solving. I refer to such matters as ethnic and racial segregation, the rights of aboriginal peoples, the environment and the sharing of resources, the gap between poor and rich. I refer to the role of women in society. The path Guatemala takes in all these respects is important to us. So we commit ourselves.

Nearness has another aspect to it, however, which a person like Rigoberta Menchú Tum obliges us to think about. It appears in the general humanity of our deepest needs, our dreams of peace and reconciliation, our longing for the good life, our right to live and to be respected. We have needs and we have rights simply by virtue of our humanity, across ethnic, cultural and geographical divides. A moment like the present also serves to remind us of this nearness, inherent in our common humanity. By maintaining a disarming humanity in a brutal world, Rigoberta Menchú Tum appeals to the best in all of us, wherever we live and whatever our background. She stands as a uniquely potent symbol of a just struggle.

Rigoberta Menchú Tum is a Quiché Indian. She was born in a poor Indian village in the Guatemala mountains, and grew up in the Indian culture, only learning Spanish as an adult. As she describes her childhood in her autobiography, it was marked by great closeness in the family and in the village, but also by extreme poverty. In order not to starve, she was forced as a child to join in the cotton-picking on the big plantations, where the Indians were treated little better than animals. "I started thinking about my childhood," she writes in the autobiography, "and I came to the conclusion that I hadn't had a childhood at all. I was never a child. I hadn't been to school, I hadn't had enough food to grow properly, I had nothing. I asked myself: 'How is this possible?'" This is her account of how at an early age awareness began growing on her of the road she must take in life. How will a world turn out that steals childhood from children? That is a question we must ask ourselves today. A few people nevertheless seem to be born with reserves of inner strength and humanity that defy the worst conditions. What such people have to tell us is worth listening to.

Rigoberta Menchú Tum was to experience the confiscation of Indian land. Her village was one of several hundred that were levelled with the ground. Massacres were normal. Guatemala acquired a civilian government in 1982, but even so innumerable massacres have been registered since then in rural districts. Several hundred mass graves are known. Since the beginning of this year alone, American and Canadian human rights organizations have registered 380 summary executions and 80 cases of torture. The guerillas, themselves a response to the brutal expulsion from the land, have in their turn been used as an excuse for a blind brutalisation of the whole society. That extreme brutalisation struck at Rigoberta Menchú Tum's own family. Her father, who was the elected leader of his village, was active in starting the CUC, the Committee of the Peasant Union, which soon won widespread support. He was burnt to death. Her mother and brother were bestially tortured and killed by the military.

It is five hundred years this year since Columbus "discovered" America, as we have been brought up to say, or since colonisation began. The celebration of the anniversary has at least produced one benefit, in the spotlight it has so effectively focussed on the worldwide problem of the rights of aboriginal peoples. Developments in America demonstrate the problem more clearly than anywhere else. This was a whole continent, the population of which in Columbus's day may have numbered as many as 100 million. Today only a fraction of those Indian peoples survive, and any truly Indian culture can only be found isolated in small pockets. Why was the Indian culture less able than others to resist the European pressure? Any processes elsewhere resembling the one in America have only taken place in more marginal areas of the world. Such processes are complex, and this is not the place for a more detailed analysis. What is clear, however, is that at certain times and in certain places we are confronted by a different force from infectious diseases and mortality or the haphazard outcome of wars and rapacity, and that is the systematic "ethnic cleansing" of the aboriginal population — better known as genocide. There is a most urgent need to define the rights of aboriginal peoples and to respect those rights in a manner which makes it possible to live in peace and mutual understanding. To succeed in this, we need people like Rigoberta Menchú Tum. For the Norwegian Nobel Committee it was a happy coincidence that it was precisely in the year of Columbus that she emerged as such a strong candidate for the Nobel Peace Prize.

Rigoberta Menchú Tum chose to dedicate herself to political and social work for her people. In charming and characteristically forthright terms, she tells us in her autobiography what a difficult choice it was not to have a family. She was engaged, she tells us, and felt an obligation to the ancestral principle of seeking happiness not only for oneself but for one's family. A threat of ethnic cleansing of course lends extra weight to such an obligation. But she chose otherwise. "I was very confused," she writes, "Society and so many other things wouldn't leave me alone, I always had a heavy heart." She became an active member of the CUC. Then she participated in the founding of the organization called the Revolutionary Christians. "We understood 'revolutionary' in the real meaning of the word: transformation. If I had chosen the armed struggle, I would be in the mountains now." Owing to her political activity, she has had to spend twelve years in exile in Mexico. She became one of the first Indian delegates to the United Nations, and is a member of the UN group that works for human rights and the cause of the Indian peoples.

In her book *A Strategy for Peace,* the Swedish-American moral philosopher Sissela Bok describes what she calls the "pathology of partisanship", or the brutalising effect of the use of violence. Whoever commits acts of violence will lose his humanity. Thus, violence breeds violence and hate breeds hate. She quotes the English poet Stephen Spender, who experienced this process in himself when he took part in the Spanish Civil War: "It was clear to me that unless I cared about every murdered child impartially, I did not care about children being murdered at all." But how can one break out of the vicious circle of the pathology of partisanship? It is easy enough to keep out and call for non-violence or an end to hatred when one is not oneself confronted with the blind violence of the other side. Nor is it indeed our responsibility to judge or to condemn in such cases. What we can do, however, is to point to the shining individual examples of people who manage to preserve their humanity in brutal and violent surroundings, of persons who for that very reason compel our special respect and admiration. Such people give us a hope that there are ways out of the vicious circle.

I have had occasion to mention Rigoberta Menchú Tum's autobiography a number of times. It is an extraordinary human document. It describes cruelty in sober and matter-of-fact terms. Its driving force is moral indignation. In some connections, she also mentions her hatred of those responsible for the violence and repression. But at the same time, the account reflects a disarming humanity. Almost gaily, she notes funny little concrete details in an otherwise ruthless existence; with love, she describes Indian customs. I know no better example of her disarming attitude than her description here in Oslo last year of her meeting with Colonel Roderigues:

We greeted each other and exchanged a few words. The man who killed my mother congratulated me on my nomination for the Nobel Peace Prize and called it a national honour. I realised then that at bottom we are all human beings. It was like meeting a distant acquaintance. I had a feeling of calm as I spoke to him.

It is stupid to meet the world with too much trust, but even more stupid to meet it with too little. The goal of Rigoberta Menchú Tum's work, as she has said on many occasions, is reconciliation and peace. She knows, better than most, that the foundations for future reconciliation are laid in the manner in which one conducts one's struggle. Even in the most brutal situations, one must retain one's faith that there is a minimum of human feelings in all of us. Rigoberta Menchú Tum has preserved that faith. It is with the deepest respect and in admiration of her efforts that the Norwegian Nobel Committee today awards her the Nobel Peace Prize.

Thank you.

THE NOBEL INSIGNIA AND THE AMOUNT
OF THE PRIZE

In accordance with the statutes of the Nobel Foundation, the Prize-Winners received a diploma, a gold medal and a document indicating the amount of the Prize. The value of each of the Prizes awarded in 1992 was 6,500,000 Swedish kronor.

The sum available for distribution among the Prize-Winners varies according to the annual net revenue of the main fund of the Nobel Foundation. In 1901, the first year in which the Prizes were awarded, each one was worth 150,000 Swedish kronor.

The diplomas presented to the laureate in Physics and in Chemistry have been designed by the artist Philip von Schantz. The diploma presented to the laureate in Literature has been designed by the artist Bo Larsson. The calligraphy was designed by Annika Rücker.

The diplomas presented to the laureates in Physiology or Medicine have only the motif of the Nobel medal. Calligraphy by Susan Duvnäs.

The diploma of the Nobel Prize for Peace, has been designed by the Norwegian artist Håkon Bleken. Calligraphy by Inger Magnus.

Georges Charpak

Rudolph A. Marcus

Edmond H. Fischer

Edwin G. Krebs

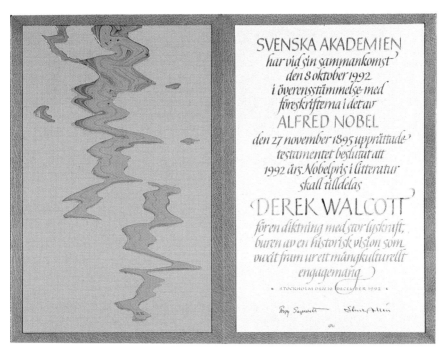

Derek Walcott

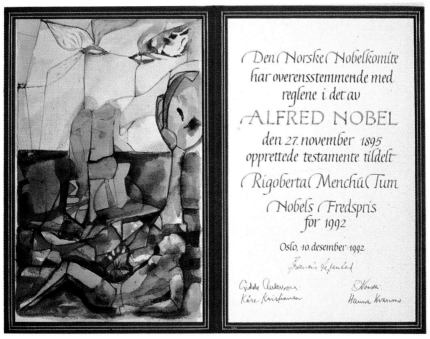

Rigoberta Menchú Tum

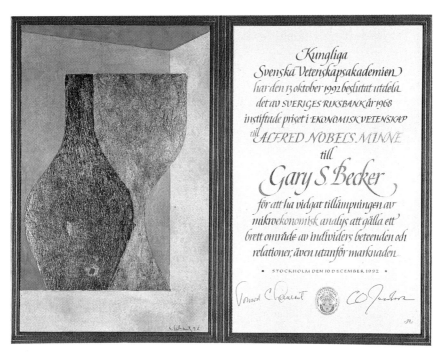

Kungliga
Svenska Vetenskapsakademien
har den 13 oktober 1992 beslutat utdela
det av SVERIGES RIKSBANK år 1968
instiftade priset i EKONOMISK VETENSKAP
till ALFRED NOBELS MINNE
till

Gary S. Becker

för att ha vidgat tillämpningen av
mikroekonomisk analys att gälla ett
brett område av individers beteenden och
relationer, även utanför marknaden.

● STOCKHOLM DEN 10 DECEMBER 1992 ●

Gary S. Becker

THE NOBEL LECTURES

THE PRIZE-WINNERS
BIOGRAPHICAL NOTES

georges Charpak

GEORGES CHARPAK

Né le ler août 1924 à Dabrovica (Pologne)
Naturalisé français en 1946

Etudes

	Lycée Saint-Louis à Paris
	Lycé de Montpellier
1945 — 1947	Ecole des Mines de Paris

Diplômes

1948	Licence des sciences, Ingénieur civil des mines
1954	Docteur en physique, Recherche expérimentale physique nucléaire au Collège de France

Carrière

1948 — 1959	Au Centre National de la Recherche Scientifique (CNRS)
1959 — 1991	Au Centre Européen pour la Recherche Nucléaire (CERN)

Travaux (Extraits)

1960	Participation à la première mesure précise du moment magnétique du muon
1962 — 1967	Invention de divers types de chambres à étincelles sans photographie (division de courant et retard des impulsions)
1962 — 1967	Etudes de structure nucléaire par les réactions (π^+2p)
1968	Introduction des chambres proportionnelles multifils et des chambres à dérive
1974	Introduction de la chambre à dérive sphérique pour l'étude des structures de proteines par diffraction des rayons X (ORSAY)
1979 — 1989	Introduction des chambres à avalanches multiétages et applications aux détecteurs de photons et à l'imagerie de rayonnements ionisants. Participation à des expériences à Fermilab (USA)
1985 — 1991	Introduction des chambres à avalanches lumineuses. Développement d'appareillage pour les recherches en biologie utilisant l'imagerie des rayons β (Centre Médical Universitaire de Genève)

Décorations
Croix de Guerre 39 – 45

Distinction
Prix Ricard de la Société de physique (1980)
Prix du Commissariat à l'énergie atomique de l'Académie des Sciences (1984)
Docteur Honoris Causa de l'Université de Genève (1980)
Académie des Sciences (France) (1985)
Foreign Associate of the National Academy of Sciences of the USA (1986).

ELECTRONIC IMAGING OF IONIZING RADIATION WITH LIMITED AVALANCHES IN GASES

Nobel Lecture, December 8, 1992

GEORGES CHARPAK

CERN, Geneva, Switzerland

Detecting and localizing radiation is the very basis of physicists' work in a variety of fields, especially nuclear or subnuclear physics.

Certain instruments have assumed special importance in the understanding of fundamental phenomena and have been milestones in the building up of modern theories. They make up a long list: the ionization chamber, the cloud chamber, Geiger-Müller counters, proportional counters, scintillation counters, semiconductor detectors, nuclear emulsions, bubble chambers, spark and streamer chambers, multiwire and drift chambers, various calorimeters designed for total absorption and then measurement of particle energy, Cherenkov or transition radiation counters designed to identify or select particles, and many other detectors, some very important examples of which are still being developed. However, some of this equipment has become obsolete as physicists' requirements have changed. Wire and drift-chambers, introduced in 1968, met the then requirements of physicists, whereas the properties of the most productive detectors available at the time, mainly bubble and spark chambers, were no longer capable of meeting those needs.

Multiwire chambers gave rise to further developments in the art of detectors, of which some are highly innovative. Most high-energy physics experiments make use of these methods, but their application has extended to widely differing fields such as biology, medicine, and industrial radiology.

Our study of multiwire proportional chambers, which began in 1967, was triggered by the problems with spark chambers which then faced us. The latter, introduced in 1959 by Fukui and Myamoto, beautifully supplemented the bubble chamber. Whereas the latter was still peerless in the quality of the information which it provided and from which one single exposure could on its own lead to an interesting discovery, the spark chamber gave a repetition rate more than 100 times higher. Moreover, as it had a memory of almost 1 µs, the instrument could be triggered only for events selected by faster auxiliary counters, making it possible to address the study of phenomena which occurred much more rarely in very high-energy interactions. Nevertheless, the need to store the information on photographic films led to a bottleneck: beyond a few million photographs per year or per experiment, the exposure analysis equipment was saturated.

Physicists therefore had to invent methods of reading the sparks which bypassed photographs. We introduced two new methods: one was based on the measurable delay of the signal produced by a spark in reaching the end of an electrode; the second, based on the division of the current produced by a spark in plane or wire electrodes, at the ends of which the current pulses are measured, made it possible to obtain the coordinates of the spark and hence of the particle by purely electronic means. This latter method was developed in several laboratories for the focal planes of spectrometers and we have ourselves thus performed experiments on the nuclear reactions induced by pions.

Other approaches, some of them better than ours, were developed simultaneously: sonic spark chambers and wire spark chambers which gave rise to very important developments. Nevertheless, the fact that it is impossible to trigger spark chambers at rates above about 100 times per second reduced their scope. In the minds of some physicists arose the idea of limiting the discharge produced from electrons released in a gas to a much lower level than that attained by the spark so as not to discharge the capacitance formed by the electrodes; the additional gain thus needed was to be obtained by means of electronic circuits.

In 1967, I undertook this step, armed with some experience acquired at the Collège de France from 1948, some ten years before I joined CERN. I built cylindrical single-wire proportional chambers and also demonstrated the possibility of making use of the light phenomena produced by an avalanche of electrons in a gas. This approach led to no practical method. It was greatly extended later on during work done at the University of Coimbra in Portugal by E. Policarpo. This work, from which I drew a great deal of inspiration, proved very valuable for the experience I gained and, more particularly, the understanding of the principles governing the multiplication of electrons in gases. It led me to an attempt to build chambers with avalanches made visible by short electric pulses. It resulted, in 1956, in the first detector with sparks following the trajectory of particles. It played no role in the introduction of spark chambers in particle physics.

Figure 1 shows the design selected in 1967 to study proportional multiwire structures.

A study of the electric fields shows that, in the region near the wire taken to a positive potential, where a limited-scale avalanche is to be produced, the electric field is the same as that prevailing near a wire tensioned in the axis of a cylindrical tube, as can be seen in figs. 2 and 3. With the parameters we chose, in a gas in common use in proportional counters, the average mean free path of an ionizing collision should, at atmospheric pressure, be about 1 μm (fig. 4). We might therefore expect a gain of about 10^5 for an avalanche extending over a distance close to the diameter of the wire, i.e. 20 μm.

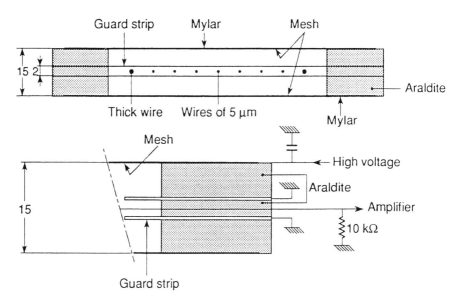

Fig. 1: A few construction details of multiwire chambers. The sensitives anode wires are separated by 2 mm from each other; their diameter is 20 μm. They are stretched between two cathode meshes, in a gas at atmospheric pressure. The edges of the planes are potted in Araldite, allowing only the high voltage to enter and only the pulses to leave to go to a 10 kΩ amplifier.

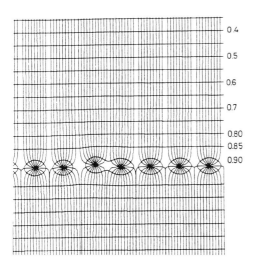

Fig. 2: Equipotentials and electric field lines in a multiwire proportional chamber. The effect of the slight shifting of one of the wires can be seen. It has no effect on the field close to the wire.

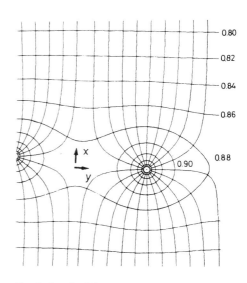

Fig. 3: Detail of fig. 2 showing the electric field around a wire (wire spacing 2 mm, diameter 20 μm).

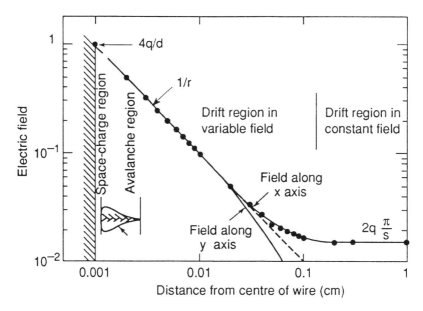

Fig 4: Variation in a proportional chamber of the electric field along the *x* axis perpendicular to the plane of the wires and centred on one of them, and in the *y* direction parallel to this plane. The various regions (electron, avalanche and drift space in a variable and then constant field) are shown.

There still remained one challenging problem, that of the capacitive coupling between the wires. The closer they were, the more likely it was that a pulse induced in one wire would be propagated on its neighbours. This was true for pulses produced by an external electric generator but untrue for the internal generator formed by the positive and negative ions separating under the effect of the electric field. There had, in the past, been examples of wire counters, especially in cosmic-ray experiments, where this fear of coupling led to the insulation of each of the positive amplifying wires by partitions or thick intermediate wires. We merely have to examine the pulse-generation mechanism in a proportional counter to see that, whatever the distance between the wires, the one which is the seat of an avalanche will develop a negative signal, whereas the neighbouring wires and, in general, all the neighbouring electrodes, develop a positive signal which is therefore easy to distinguish from the other.

Most of the electrons produced in the first microns in front of the wire pass through a very small proportion, ΔV, of the potential V applied between the wire and the cathode on their trajectory. The collected charge Q will produce on the wire taken to the potential V only a pulse of charge ΔQ, so that $V \cdot \Delta Q = Q \cdot \Delta V$. With our selected parameters, the time needed to collect the electron charge was a fraction of a nanosecond. However, the positive ions have to pass through the whole of the potential drop V and thus induce almost all of the charge pulse which develops as a function of time according to a law which reflects the considerable field close to the wire and the decreasing field far from it. The initial very fast increase of the pulse gave some people the illusion that the initial pulse observed was caused by the collection of the electrons of the avalanche. For a proportional counter with a radius of 1 cm, and a wire with a diameter of 20 μm, the electron contribution is only 1 %. Figure 5 shows the characteristic shape of the development of a pulse in a proportional chamber owing to the motion of the ions. Although the total time taken for ion collection is close to 500 μs in the example chosen, almost half of the signal develops within a time close to a thousandth of this value, which is very useful for fast detection.

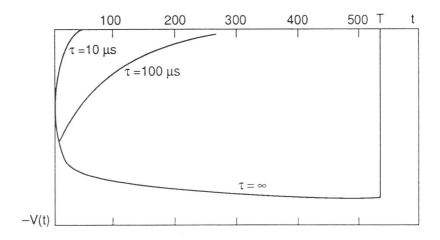

Fig. 5: Development in time *t* of a pulse in a proportional chamber; *T* is the total drift-time of the positive ions between the anode and the cathode. The effect of decreasing differentiation time constants τ is seen. The motion of the positive ions close to the wires produces a very fast-rising pulse .

The key phenomenon is this: whereas the induced signal is negative on the wire from which the positive ions are going away, it is positive on the neighbouring wires or electrodes.

This has two important consequences:
— It is a simple matter to locate the wire which is the seat of the avalanche, whatever the distance between the wires.
— The position of this avalanche along the wire can be obtained if the cathode is made of wires or strips perpendicular to the anode wire.

The distribution of the induced positive signals is then centred on the avalanche. Experience was to show that this observation was of prime importance to the imaging of neutral radiation, photons, or neutrons.

The time resolution of the detector depends on the distance between the wires. Proportional cylindrical chambers had been abandoned in particle-physics experiments as this resolution was poor: the time taken by the electrons released in the gas to reach the multiplication region near the wire is actually variable. It immediately appeared that the delay was easily measured in a multiwire chamber and that it gave precisely the distance of the ionizing particle from the wire.

This cleared the way for a class of detectors derived from wire chambers in which the detecting wires are very far apart and where the coordinate is calculated by measuring the drift-time of the electrons in the gas. From 1968 we showed that it was possible to obtain accuracies of the order of 100 μm with structures such as that of fig. 6, which provide a constant electric field over a long distance. In 1969, a group at Saclay began to build drift chambers with a migration length of 20 cm, while, in Heidelberg, studies were undertaken on chambers constructed, similarly to ordinary wire chambers, with a field wire fitted between the anode wires to repel the electrons. The drift chamber seemed to be the ideal instrument for large detectors; many were the groups which then began to fit considerable areas with these detectors, reaching, for instance, 5 m×5 m, making possible a precision of a few hundred microns, with electronics comprising a limited number of channels.

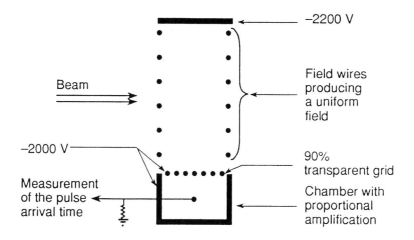

Fig. 6: Operating principle of a detector based on the drift-time of the electrons in a constant electric field (1968).

Starting in 1969, we stressed that the exploitation of electron drift in large volumes, combined with the measurement of the centroid of the avalanches induced in a wire chamber, was the way leading to threedimensional detectors. It was, however, D. Nygren who, by combining the effects of parallel magnetic and electric fields and solving formidable data acquisition problems, succeeded in creating an instrument which provides the finest images of the most complex configurations obtained in colliders; for this purpose the repetition rate must be low enough to accommodate an electron drift over long distances. In fact it was the demands of physics, differing very widely depending on the nature of experiments and accelerators, which dictated the structures of gas detectors, making use of the properties that we demonstrated in 1968.

The development of transistor electronics, however, made it possible to design systems requiring tens of thousands of channels. The advantage of wire over drift chambers was their capacity of accepting very high counting rates. The resolution time, of about 30 ns, and the possible counting rate of 10^5 pulses per second, made it feasible to tackle the study of rare phenomena which were beyond the reach of spark chambers as they needed very high counting rates.

The design study of a giant detector, the Split-Field Magnet (SFM) was launched at CERN in 1970 under the direction of A. Minten for an experiment at the Intersecting Storage Rings (ISR). This detector comprised 70,000 wires, some of them 2 m long. Another group under J. Steinberger undertook the construction of a detector designed to collect a large number of events violating charge parity conjugation in the study of kaon decay. A large number of difficult problems had to be solved to go from the 10 cm $\times$ 10 cm chamber to these large areas. The intensity of the pulses collected on the wires of a chamber was proportional to the energy deposited in the volume defined by the electric field lines ending at a wire. In a cylindrical counter, simple considerations showed that the logarithm of the gain was proportional to a factor of $f = V^{1/2}[(V^{1/2}/V_t^{1/2})\text{-}1]$, where V is the applied voltage and V_t the threshold voltage. The behaviour of the wire chamber is exactly the same as that of a cylindrical counter.

My group was then reinforced by F. Sauli, who, together with collaborators joining the various projects launched by us, contributed greatly to the success of many new detectors. We undertook a systematic study of the factors controlling the accuracy in drift chambers. We investigated the ultimate accuracy which can be reached in multiwire chambers by measuring the signals induced on the cathodes. We showed that the avalanches could extend to only a very limited extent around the wire and that by measuring the centroid of the induced signals it was possible to determine the azimuth of an avalanche. Our results and those of a few others, which started a systematic study of the multiwire structures, led to a generalization of the use of wire chambers and drift chambers with a considerable diversification of the detector's structure best adapted to the variety of situations encountered in particle physics.

Mixtures of up to four gases were found to reduce the cost of the necessary electronics, making it possible to obtain high saturated pulses independent of the energy deposited in the gas, and required less sensitive and expensive electronics than with the proportional system, as well as being sufficiently resistant to ageing effects.

It was demonstrated that these pulses were produced by a series of avalanches which stopped at the uniform low field far from the wire.

A systematic study of chambers filled at very low pressures, conducted in Israel by A. Breskin, was to show that the chambers operated at pressures as low as 1 Torr with astonishing time resolutions: the range of application of wire chambers was widening.

Whereas wire and drift chambers were essential in all the particle physics experiments, rapidly replacing spark chambers and, in some instances, reinforcing bubble chambers with structures outside them, many groups were making use of the new opportunities offered for imaging various types of ionizing radiation. The main applications appeared in the field of X-rays with an energy close to 10 keV. Under the inspiration of V. Perez-Mendez, chambers were built to study the structure of proteins by the imaging of X-rays diffracted by their crystals. Gas detectors had the drawback of being highly transparent to X-rays and the methods used to overcome this required compressed xenon.

We, on our side, tried to solve this problem by building a spherical drift chamber centred on the macromolecule crystal. The radial lines of the electric field eliminate any parallax and the electrons drifting over 15 cm are transferred into a 50 cm$\times$50 cm multiwire chamber in which the avalanches are measured to a precision of 0.5 mm. It is also found that the response is continuous in both dimensions, as the diffusion ensures an expansion of the cloud of ionization electrons which always covers two wires, making it possible to interpolate the position of the avalanche between them.

The apparatus has considerable advantages over photography in terms of data-acquisition rate and the signal-to-noise ratio. Used routinely with the X-ray beams produced by the synchrotron radiation from an electron storage ring at Orsay it gives a good crop of important results.

The imagination shown by various groups has made it possible also to extend the field of application of wire chambers for higher X- or γ-ray energies.

Thus, a Novosibirsk group has developed a chamber making it possible to X-ray the human body with a decrease in dosage over the most powerful equipment available on the market of at least a factor of 10.

A group at Schlumberger has produced a system for radiographing giant containers using X-rays of up to 5 MeV. A. Jeavons has constructed positron cameras capable of detecting 0.511 MeV γ-rays with a precision of about 1 mm. These cameras, which are not efficient enough for the method to be applied to nuclear medicine, made possible a remarkable advance in the field of solid-state physics. Finally, a firm is now marketing a camera for γ-rays, competing with the Anger camera, which is specially suitable for use on children. Its principle is based on a wire chamber filled with compressed xenon. It gives a considerable reduction in the doses administered and also increased precision.

These few examples are enough to show that we may be on the threshold of the general use of radiation detectors originally invented for particle physics. It will develop in line with the progress made in particle physics research laboratories.

An important stage in the widening of the field of application of gas detectors was made with the introduction, by J. Séguinot and T. Ypsilantis, of photosensitive vapours. They make it possible to locate photons in the far ultraviolet of an energy above about 5.3 eV with a precision of less than 1 mm. Major instruments designed to identify particles through Cherenkov radiation are now in use in some giant collider detectors. D. Anderson explored the opportunities provided by the detection of the photons emitted by scintillators. Figure 7 shows a 9 GeV photon spectrum obtained with a chamber containing a tetrakis(dimethylamine)ethylene (TMAE) vapour. Subsequent research also shows that it is possible to use condensed photocathodes compatible with gas amplification.

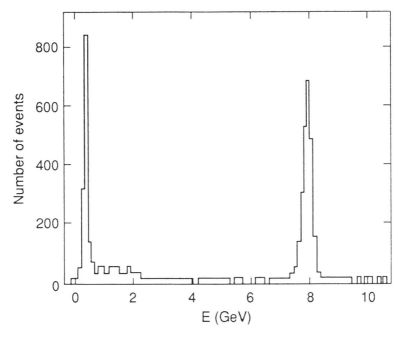

Fig. 7: Energy spectrum of 9 GeV particles (electrons and pions) with BaF_2 crystals coupled to wire chambers filled with a photosensitive gas (TMAE, see text)

As the intensity of accelerators increased, it was found that the wire chambers themselves could not cope with the expected counting rates. Beyond particle fluxes from 10^4 to 10^5 hits per second and per millimetre of wire, the space charge produced by the accumulation of positive ions offset the applied field and annulled the gain.

To overcome this problem I thought, together with F. Sauli, of separating the gas amplification into two stages: a gain in a preamplification structure followed by a partial extraction of the electrons into a drift region fitted with a control grid, and their transfer into a wire chamber which would be required only to amplify the electrons accepted by the grid (fig. 8). It is then possible to accept or reject an event with a time precision of about 30 ns and a delay defined by the electron drift-time. Together with S. Majewski we found a structure reaching this goal. It made it possible easily to amplify single photoelectrons released by an ultraviolet photon in a photosensitive gas. The drift region in fact largely eliminates the effect of the radiations emitted by excited atoms produced in an avalanche, which are responsible for secondary effects by ejecting electrons near the initial position of the photoelectrons. We have built large detectors of this kind in collaboration with Saclay to obtain images of Cherenkov rings in an experiment performed at the Fermi Laboratory Tevatron in the United States. This development proved most fruitful, however, in a special biological field of application. There are several research fields in which it is necessary to obtain the image of the distribution of molecules marked with radioactive elements. Several commercial firms have tried to make use of wire chambers for this imaging purpose. The main difficulty lies in the generally considerable distance which the electrons from the radioactive bodies may have to travel in the gases. We have observed that an amplifying structure based on parallel grids did not suffer from this defect. Multiplying an electron by a Townsend avalanche, in fact, exponentially helps the ionization electrons released in the gas near the cathode, which is the entry window. Precisions of the order of 0.3 mm have thus been obtained for β radiation emitted by phosphorus-32, for instance.

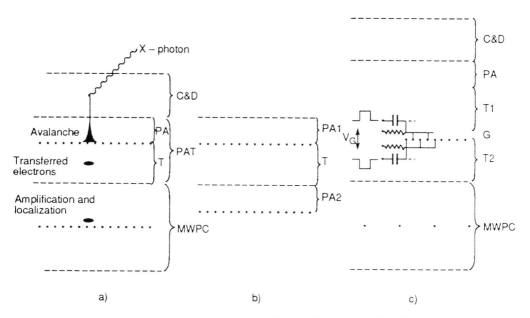

a)   b)   c)

Fig. 8: Various multistage structures. (a) A preamplification (PA) and transfer (T) component is followed by a multiwire proportional chamber (MWPC); the conversion and drift space (C and D) makes it possible to inject a constant charge (X-rays etc.) into the amplification region. (b) Two parallel-plate units with charge transfer from PA1 to PA2. The best time resolutions were obtained with this configuration. (c) A multistage chamber with a gate: the wires of grid G are at alternating potentials of ± 70 V. The electrons are transmitted from component PA + T_1 to MWPC and they are transferred when the wires are brought to the same potential by short pulses of 30 ns, making it possible to select rare events in a high rate environment.

We then took another step by coupling such a multiplication region with a method of reading out the position of the avalanches, making use of the light emitted. We had developed this method in order to study very rare phenomena such as double β decay or collisions between gas atoms and certain types of hidden matter. We thought that only the redundancy provided by photographic methods could characterize a rare event. A British group was also independently tackling this method for imaging Cherenkov photons. They, too, used the multistage chambers which we had introduced and reached the same conclusion: with suitable vapours it was possible to obtain a sufficiently plentiful emission of photons to detect the light emitted by the avalanches with simple optics.

The great advantage of this method lies in the read-out which it permits in the use of hundreds of thousands of channels now making up the CCD (charge-coupling device), which is the basic component of video cameras. Moreover, the fact that the image of a light avalanche covers several pixels makes it possible to interpolate the centre of the avalanche and multiply the number of real channels by almost 10. We were thus able to make an instrument for visualizing the distribution of the electrons emitted by tritium in a slice of rat's kidney, making it possible to observe details of about 100 μm. The fact that the same data (fig. 9) were obtained in a single day instead of the three months previously required by the photographic method aroused immediate interest among certain biologists and gave rise to a development which is still under way.

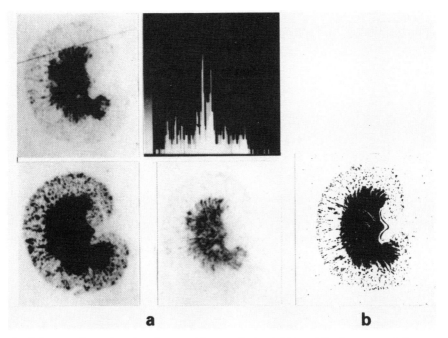

a   b

Fig. 9: Images of samples taken from a tritium-marked rat's kidney. The four parts of diagram (a) were obtained with a gas detector: the window, centred at three different levels, has a grey scale of 256. The intensity spectrum is taken along the oblique line marked on the first view with 40 μm pixels in the sample plane. The gas mixture is xenon with 2.5 % triethylamine. The details of the renal channels, measuring 50 μm, can be seen. This image may be obtained in 20 hours. (b) Autoradiograph showing the adjacent slice of rat's kidney to which a photographic emulsion was applied for 3 months.

Our latest experiment with gas detectors comprising parallel-grid structures helped convince us that the controlled multiplication of avalanches in gases, in structures as diverse as wires or parallel surfaces, by selecting photocathodes compatible with gas amplification is still a source of fruitful developments: in many fields this multiplication may still result in progress in all fields where radiation must be imaged, from ultraviolet photons to γ-rays and the highest-energy particles. At the current stage of high-energy physics, however, simply making use of the location of free electrons near the wires of proportional chambers and the drift-time of the electrons provides an image of configurations rivalling in complexity those provided by bubble chambers. This is shown in fig. 10, the image of an event generated in the ALEPH detector installed at one of the intersections of LEP, the large e^+e^- collider operated at CERN.

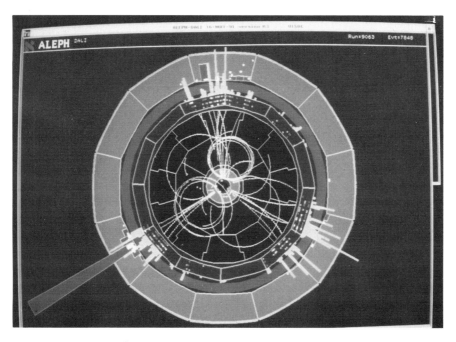

Fig. 10: Image of an e^+e^- collision obtained at the ALEPH experiment at LEP using an instrument making use of the drift-time in a large volume and the read-out of coordinates projected in a wire chamber. Auxiliary outside detectors provide the information on the energy of the particles, the trajectory of which was displayed.

BIBLIOGRAPHY

A very comprehensive historical study with most references corresponding to the period covered by this artide is to be found in

I. Gambaro, The development of electron detectors at CERN (1966—late 1970s), *CERN History Study No. CHS-39,* January 1992.

Our first article that described the properties of multiwire structures is

G. Charpak, R. Bouclier, T. Bressani, J. Favier and C. Zupancic, The use of multiwire proportional chambers to select and localize charged particles, *Nuclear Instruments and Methods* 62 (1968) 202—26.

It was followed by several articles, one of them giving a description of the progress we made during our first year of studies of the wire chambers and the drift chambers:

G. Charpak, D. Rahm and H. Steiner, Some developments in the operation of multiwire proportional chambers, *Nuclear Instruments and Methods* 80 (1970) 13—35.

We refer the reader to highly detailed works such as

F. Sauli, Principles of operation of multiwire proportional and drift chambers, *CERN* 77-09 (1977).

P. Rice-Evans, *Spark, streamer, proportional and drift chambers* (Richelieu, London, 1974),

T. Ferbel, *Techniques and concepts of high-energy physics* (Plenum Press, New York, 1987),

and to a book giving a good analysis of the development of detectors in relation to the evolution of particle physics:

F. Close, M. Marten and C. Sutton, *The particle explosion* (Oxford University Press, 1987).

Rudolph A. Marcus

RUDOLPH A. MARCUS

My first encounters with McGill University came when I was still in a baby carriage. My mother used to wheel me about the campus when we lived in that neighborhood and, as she recounted years later, she would tell me that I would go to McGill. There was some precedent for my going there, since two of my father's brothers received their M.D.'s at McGill.

I have always loved going to school. Since neither of my parents had a higher education, my academic "idols" were these two paternal uncles and one of their uncles, my great-uncle, Henrik Steen (né Markus). My admiration for him, living in faraway Sweden, was not because of a teol.dr. (which he received from the University of Uppsala in 1915) nor because of the many books he wrote — I knew nothing of that — but rather because he was reputed to speak 13 languages. I learned decades later that the number was only 9! Growing up, mostly in Montreal, I was an only child of loving parents. I admired my father's athletic prowess — he excelled in several sports — and my mother's expressive singing and piano playing.

My interest in the sciences started with mathematics in the very beginning, and later with chemistry in early high school and the proverbial home chemistry set. My education at Baron Byng High School was excellent, with dedicated masters (boys and girls were separate). I spent the next years at McGill University, for both undergraduate and, as was the custom of the time, graduate study. Our graduate supervisor, Carl A. Winkler, specialized in rates of chemical reactions. He himself had received his Ph.D. as a student of Cyril Hinshelwood at Oxford. Hinshelwood was later the recipient of the Nobel Prize for his work on chemical kinetics. Winkler brought to his laboratory an enthusiastic joyousness in research and was much loved by his students.

During my McGill years, I took a number of math courses, more than other students in chemistry. Upon receiving a Ph.D. from McGill University in 1946, I joined the new post-doctoral program at the National Research Council of Canada in Ottawa. This program at NRC later became famous, but at the time it was still in its infancy and our titles were Junior Research Officers. The photochemistry group was headed by E.W.R. Steacie, an international figure in the study of free-radical reactions and a major force in the development of the basic research program at NRC. I benefitted from the quality of his research on gas phase reaction rates. Like my research on chemical reaction rates in solution at McGill (kinetics of nitration), it was experimental in nature. There were no theoretical chemists in Canada at the time, and as students I don't think we ever considered how or where theories were conceived.

About 1948 a fellow post-doctoral at NRC, Walter Trost, and I formed a two-man seminar to study theoretical papers related to our experimental work. This adventure led me to explore the possibility of going on a second post-doctoral, but in theoretical work, which seemed like a radical step at the time. I had a tendency to break the glass vacuum apparatus, due to a still present impetuous haste, with time-consuming consequences. Nevertheless, the realization that breaking a pencil point would have far less disastrous consequences played little or no role, I believe, in this decision to explore theory!

I applied in 1948 to six well-known theoreticians in the U.S. for a postdoctoral research fellowship. The possibility that one of them might take on an untested applicant, an applicant hardly qualified for theoretical research, was probably too much to hope for. Oscar K. Rice at the University of North Carolina alone responded favorably, subject to the success of an application he would make to the Office of Naval Research for this purpose. It was, and in February 1949 I took the train south, heading for the University of North Carolina in Chapel Hill. I was impressed on arrival there by the red clay, the sandy walks, and the graciousness of the people.

After that, I never looked back. Being exposed to theory, stimulated by a basic love of concepts and mathematics, was a marvelous experience. During the first three months I read everything I could lay my hands on regarding reaction rate theory, including Marcelin's classic 1915 theory which came within one small step of the Transition State Theory of 1935. I read numerous theoretical papers in German, a primary language for the "chemical dynamics" field in the 1920s and 1930s, attended my first formal course in quantum mechanics, given by Nathan Rosen in the Physics Department, and was guided by Oscar in a two-man weekly seminar in which I described a paper I had read and he pointed out assumptions in it that I had overlooked. My life as a working theorist began three months after this preliminary study and background reading, when Oscar gently nudged me toward working on a particular problem.

Fortunately for me, Oscar's gamble paid off. Some three months later, I had formulated a particular case of what was later entitled by B. Seymour Rabinovitch, RRKM theory ("Rice-Ramsperger-Kassel-Marcus"). In it, I blended statistical ideas from the RRK theory of the 1920s with those of the transition state theory of the mid-1930s. The work was published in 1951. In 1952 I wrote the generalization of it for other reactions. In addition, six months after arrival in Chapel Hill, I was also blessed by marriage to Laura Hearne, an attractive graduate student in sociology at UNC. She is here with me at this ceremony. Our three sons, Alan, Kenneth and Raymond, and two daughters-in-law are also present today.

In 1951, I attempted to secure a faculty position. This effort met with little success (35 letters did not yield 35 no's, since not everyone replied!). Very fortunately, that spring I met Dean Raymond Kirk of the Polytechnic Institute of Brooklyn at an American Chemical Society meeting in Cleveland, which I was attending primarily to seek a faculty position. This meeting with Dean Kirk, so vital for my subsequent career, was arranged by Seymour Yolles, a graduate student at UNC in a course I taught during Rice's illness. Seymour had been a student at Brooklyn Poly and learned, upon accidentally encountering Dr. Kirk, that Kirk was seeking new faculty. After a subsequent interview at Brooklyn Poly, I was hired, and life as a fully independent researcher began.

I undertook an experimental research program on both gas phase and solution reaction rates, wrote the 1952 RRKM papers, and wondered what to do next in theoretical research. I felt at the time that it was pointless to continue with RRKM since few experimental data were available. Some of our experiments were intended to produce more.

After some minor pieces of theoretical study that I worked on, a student in my statistical mechanics class brought to my attention a problem in polyelectrolytes. Reading everything I could about electrostatics, I wrote two papers on that topic in 1954/55. This electrostatics background made me fully ready in 1955 to treat a problem I had just read about on electron transfers. I comment on this next period on electron transfer research in my Nobel Lecture. About 1960, it became clear that it was best for me to bring the experimental part of my research program to a close—there was too much to do on the theoretical aspects—and I began the process of winding down the experiments. I spent a year and a half during 1960−61 at the Courant Mathematical Institute at New York University, auditing many courses which were, in part, beyond me, but which were, nevertheless, highly instructive.

In 1964, I joined the faculty of the University of Illinois in Urbana-Champaign and I never undertook any further experiments there. At Illinois, my interests in electron transfer continued, together with interests in other aspects of reaction dynamics, including designing "natural collision coordinates", learning about action-angle variables, introducing the latter into molecular collisions, reaction dynamics, and later into semiclassical theories of collisions and of bound states, and spending much of my free time in the astronomy library learning more about classical mechanics, celestial mechanics, quasiperiodic motion, and chaos. I spent the academic year of 1975−76 in Europe, first as Visiting Professor at the University of Oxford and later as a Humboldt Awardee at the Technical University of Munich, where I was first exposed to the problem of electron transfer in photosynthesis.

In 1978, I accepted an offer from the California Institute of Technology to come there as the Arthur Amos Noyes Professor of Chemistry. My semiclassical interlude of 1970−80 was intellectually a very stimulating one, but it involved for me less interaction with experiments than had my earlier work on unimolecular reaction rates or on electron transfers. Accordingly, prompted by the extensive experimental work of my colleagues at Caltech in these fields of unimolecular reactions, intramolecular dynamics and of electron transfer processes, as well as by the rapidly growing experimental work in both broad areas world-wide, I turned once again to those particular topics and to the many new types of studies that were being made. Their scope and challenge continues to grow to this day in both fields. Life would be indeed easier if the experimentalists would only pause for a little while!

There was a time when I had wondered about how much time and energy had been lost doing experiments during most of my stay at Brooklyn Poly — experiments on gas phase reactions, flash photolysis, isotopic exchange electron transfer, bipolar electrolytes, nitration, and photoelectrochemistry, among others — and during all of my stay at NRC and at McGill. In retrospect, I realized that this experimental background heavily flavored my attitude and interests in theoretical research. In the latter I drew, in most but not all cases, upon experimental findings or puzzles for theoretical problems to study. The growth of experiments in these fields has served as a continually rejuvenating influence. This interaction of experiment and theory, each stimulating the other, has been and continues to be one of the joys of my experience.

Honors received for the theoretical work include the Irving Langmuir and the Peter Debye Awards of the American Chemical Society (1978, 1988), the Willard Gibbs, Theodore William Richards, and Pauling Medals, and the Remsen and Edgar Fahs Smith Awards, from various sections of the ACS, (1988, 1990, 1991, 1991, 1991), the Robinson and the Centenary Medals of the Faraday Division of the Royal Society of Chemistry (1982, 1988), Columbia University's Chandler Medal (1983) and Ohio State's William Lloyd Evans Award (1990), a Professorial Fellowship at University College, Oxford (1975 to 1976) and a Visiting Professorship in Theoretical Chemistry at Oxford during that period, the Wolf Prize in Chemistry (1985), the National Medal of Science (1989), the Hirschfelder Prize in Chemistry (1993), election to the National Academy of Sciences (1970), the American Academy of Arts and Sciences (1973), the American Philosophical Society (1990), honorary membership in the Royal Society of Chemistry (1991), and foreign membership in the Royal Society (London) (1987) and in the Royal Society of Canada (1993). Honorary degrees were conferred by the University of Chicago and by Goteborg, Polytechnic, McGill, and Queen's Universities and by the University of New Brunswick (1983, 1986, 1987, 1988, 1993, 1993). A commemorative issue of the Journal of Physical Chemistry was published in 1986.

ELECTRON TRANSFER REACTIONS IN CHEMISTRY: THEORY AND EXPERIMENT

Nobel Lecture, December 8, 1992

by

RUDOLPH A. MARCUS

Noyes Laboratory of Chemical Physics, California Institute of Technology, MS 127-72, Pasadena, CA 91125, USA

ELECTRON TRANSFER EXPERIMENTS SINCE THE LATE 1940s

Since the late 1940s, the field of electron transfer processes has grown enormously, both in chemistry and biology. The development of the field, experimentally and theoretically, as well as its relation to the study of other kinds of chemical reactions, represents to us an intriguing history, one in which many threads have been brought together. In this lecture, some history, recent trends, and my own involvement in this research are described.

The early experiments in the electron transfer field were on "isotopic exchange reactions" (self-exchange reactions) and, later, "cross reactions." These experiments reflected two principal influences. One of these was the availability after the Second World War of many radioactive isotopes, which permitted the study of a large number of isotopic exchange electron transfer reactions, such as

$$Fe^{2+} + Fe^{*3+} \rightarrow Fe^{3+} + Fe^{*2+}, \tag{1}$$

and

$$Ce^{3+} + Ce^{*4+} \rightarrow Ce^{4+} + Ce^{*3+}, \tag{2}$$

in aqueous solution, where the asterisk denotes a radioactive isotope.

There is a two-fold simplicity in typical self-exchange electron transfer reactions (so-called since other methods beside isotopic exchange were later used to study some of them): (1) the reaction products are identical with the reactants, thus eliminating one factor which usually influences the rate of a chemical reaction in a major way, namely the relative thermodynamic stability of the reactants and products; and (2) no chemical bonds are broken or formed in *simple* electron transfer reactions. Indeed, these self-exchange reactions represent, for these combined reasons, the simplest class of reactions in chemistry. Observations stemming directly from this simplicity were to have major consequences, not only for the electron transfer field but also, to a lesser extent, for the study of other kinds of chemical reactions as well (cf Shaik *et al*, ref. 2).

A second factor in the growth of the electron transfer field was the introduction of new instrumentation, which permitted the study of the rates of rapid chemical reactions. Electron transfers are frequently rather fast, compared with many reactions which undergo, instead, a breaking of chemical bonds and a forming of new ones. Accordingly, the study of a large body of fast electron transfer reactions became accessible with the introduction of this instrumentation. One example of the latter was the stopped-flow apparatus, pioneered for inorganic electron transfer reactions by N. Sutin. It permitted the study of bimolecular reactions in solution in the millisecond time scale (a fast time scale at the time). Such studies led to the investigation of what has been termed electron transfer "cross reactions," i.e., electron transfer reactions between two different redox systems, as in

$$Fe^{2+} + Ce^{4+} \rightarrow Fe^{3+} + Ce^{3+}, \tag{3}$$

which supplemented the earlier studies of the self-exchange electron transfer reactions. A comparative study of these two types of reaction, self-exchange and cross-reactions, stimulated by theory, was also later to have major consequences for the field and, indeed, for other areas.

Again, in the field of electrochemistry, the new post-war instrumentation in chemical laboratories led to methods which permitted the study of fast electron transfer reactions at metal electrodes. Prior to the late 1940s only relatively slow electrochemical reactions, such as the discharge of an H_3O^+ ion at an electrode to form H_2, had been investigated extensively. They involved the breaking of chemical bonds and the forming of new ones.

Numerous electron transfer studies have now also been made in other areas, some depicted in Figure 1. Some of these investigations were made possible by a newer technology, lasers particularly, and now include studies in the picosecond and subpicosecond time regimes. Just recently, (non-laser) nanometer-sized electrodes have been introduced to study electro-chemical processes that are still faster than those hitherto investigated. Still other recent investigations, important for testing aspects of the electron transfer theory at electrodes, involve the new use of an intervening ordered adsorbed monolayer of long chain organic compounds on the electrode to facilitate the study of various effects, such as varying the metal-solution potential difference on the electrochemical electron transfer rate.

In some studies of electron transfer reactions in solution there has also been a skillful blending of these measurements of chemical reaction rates with various organic or inorganic synthetic methods, as well as with site-directed mutagenesis, to obtain still further hitherto unavailable information. The use of chemically modified proteins to study the distance dependence of electron transfer, notably by Gray and coworkers, has opened a whole new field of activity.

The interaction of theory and experiment in these many electron transfer fields has been particularly extensive and exciting, and each has stimulated

Developments in Electron Transfer Reactions

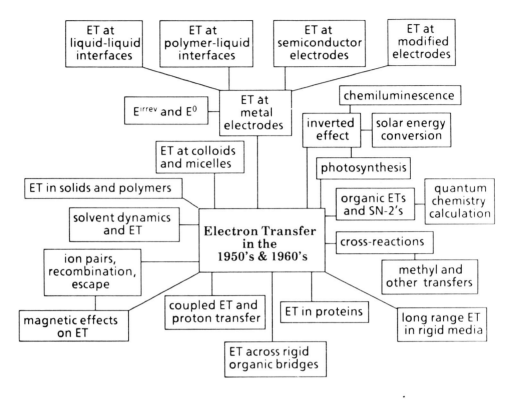

Figure 1. Examples of topics in the electron transfer field (Marcus and Siddarth, ref. 2).

the other. The present lecture addresses the underlying theory and this interaction.

THE EARLY EXPERIENCE

My own involvement in the electron transfer field began in a rather circuitous way. In an accompanying biographical note I have commented on my earlier background, which was in experimental measurements of reaction rates as a chemistry graduate student at McGill University (1943 — 46) and as a post-doctoral associate at the National Research Council of Canada (1946 — 49). A subsequent post-doctoral study at the University of North Carolina (1949 — 51) on the theory of reaction rates resulted in what is now known in the literature as RRKM theory (Rice, Ramsperger, Kassel, Marcus).

This unimolecular reaction field reflects another long and extensive interaction between theory and experiment. RRKM theory enjoys widespread use and is now usually referred to in the literature only by its acronym (or by the texts written about it, ref. 4), instead of by citation of the original articles.

After the theoretical post-doctoral, I joined the faculty of the Polytechnic Institute of Brooklyn in 1951 and wondered what theoretical research to do next after writing the RRKM papers (1951—52). I remember vividly how a friend of mine, a colleague at Brooklyn Poly, Frank Collins, came down to my office every day with a new idea on the liquid state transport theory which he was developing, while I, for theoretical research, had none. Perhaps this gap in not doing anything immediately in the field of theory was, in retrospect, fortunate: In not continuing with the study of the theory of unimolecular reactions, for which there were too few legitimate experimental data at the time to make the subject one of continued interest, I was open for investigating quite different problems in other areas. I did, however, begin a program of experimental studies in gas phase reactions, prompted by my earlier studies at NRC and by the RRKM work.

In the biographical note I have also recalled how a student in my statistical mechanics class in this period (Abe Kotliar) asked me about a particular problem in polyelectrolytes. It led to my writing two papers on the subject (1954—55), one of which required a considerable expansion in my background in electrostatics, so as to analyze different methods for calculating the free energy of these systems: In polyelectrolyte molecules, it may be recalled, the ionic charges along the organic or inorganic molecular backbone interact with each other and with the solvent. In the process, I read the relevant parts of the texts that were readily available to me on electrostatics (Caltech's Mason and Weaver's was later to be particularly helpful!). When shortly thereafter I encountered some papers on electron transfer, a field entirely new to me, I was reasonably well prepared for treating the problems which lay ahead.

DEVELOPING AN ELECTRON TRANSFER THEORY

Introduction

My first contact with electron transfers came in 1955 as a result of chancing upon a 1952 symposium issue on the subject in the Journal of Physical Chemistry. An article by Bill Libby caught my eye—a use of the Franck-Condon principle to explain some experimental results, namely, why some isotopic exchange reactions which involve electron transfer between pairs of small cations in aqueous solution, such as reaction (1), are relatively slow, whereas electron transfers involving larger ions, such as $Fe(CN)_6^{3-}$ — $Fe(CN)_6^{4-}$ and MnO_4^{-} — MnO_4^{2-}, are relatively fast.

Libby explained this observation in terms of the Franck-Condon principle, as discussed below. The principle was used extensively in the field of spectroscopy for interpreting spectra for the excitation of the molecular electronic-vibrational quantum states. An application of that principle to chemical reaction rates was novel and caught my attention. In that paper Libby gave a "back-of-the-envelope" calculation of the resulting solvation energy barrier which slowed the reaction. However, I felt instinctively that even though the idea—that somehow the Franck—Condon principle was involved—seemed strikingly right, the calculation itself was incorrect. The next month of study of the problem was, for me, an especially busy one. To place the topic in some perspective I first digress and describe the type of theory that was used for other types of chemical reaction rates at the time and continues to be useful today.

Reaction rate theory
Chemical reactions are often described in terms of the motion of the atoms of the reactants on a potential energy surface. This potential energy surface is really the electronic energy of the entire system, plotted versus the positions of all the atoms. A very common example is the transfer of an atom or a group B from AB to form BC

$$AB + C \rightarrow A + BC. \tag{4}$$

An example of reaction (4) is the transfer of an H, such as in $IH + Br \rightarrow I + HBr$, or the transfer of a CH_3 group from one aromatic sulfonate to another. To aid in visualizing the motion of the atoms in this reaction, this potential energy function is frequently plotted as constant energy contours in a space whose axes are chosen to be two important relative coordinates such as, in reaction (4), a scaled AB bond length and a scaled distance from the center of mass of AB to C, as in Figure 2.

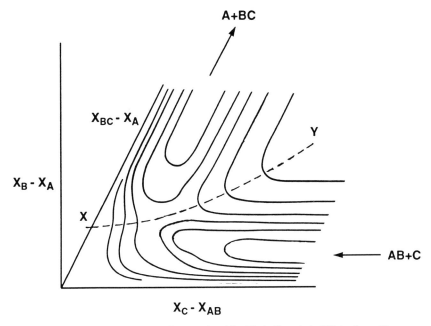

Potential Energy Contours for an Atom or Group Transfer

Figure 2. Potential energy contours for reaction (4), $AB + C \rightarrow A + BC$, in the collinear case.

A point representing this reacting system begins its trajectory in the lower right region of the figure in a valley in this plot of contours, the "valley of the reactants." When the system has enough energy, appropriately distributed between the various motions, it can cross the "mountain pass" (saddle-point region) separating the initial valley from the products' valley in the upper left, and so form the reaction products. There is a line in the figure, XY, analogous to the "continental divide" in the Rocky Mountains in the U.S., which separates systems which could spontaneously flow into the reactants' valley from those which could flow into the products' one. In chemists' terminology this line represents the "transition state" of the reaction.

In transition state theory a quasi-equilibrium between the transition state and the reactants is frequently postulated, and the reaction rate is then calculated using equilibrium statistical mechanics. A fundamental dynamical basis, which replaces this apparently *ad hoc* but common assumption of transition state theory and which is perhaps not as well known in the chemical literature as it deserves to be, was given many years ago by the physicist and one-time chemical engineer, Eugene Wigner (1938). He used a classical mechanical description of the reacting system in the many-dimensional space (of coordinates and momenta). Wigner pointed out that the quasi-equilibrium would follow as a dynamical consequence if each trajectory of a moving point representing the reacting system in this many-dimensional space did not recross the transition state (and if the distribution of the reactants in the reactants' region were a Boltzmann one). In recent times, the examination of this recrossing has been a common one in classical mechanical trajectory studies of chemical reactions. Usually, recrossings are relatively minor, except in nonadiabatic reactions, where they are readily treated (cf discussion, later).

In practice, transition state theory is generalized so as to include as many coordinates as are needed to describe the reacting system. Further, when the system can "tunnel" quantum mechanically through the potential energy barrier (the "pass") separating the two valleys, as for example frequently happens at low energies in H-transfer reactions, the method of treating the passage across the transition state region needs, and has received, refinement. (The principal problem encountered here has been the lack of "dynamical separability" of the various motions in the transition state region.)

Electron transfer theory. Formulation
In contrast to the above picture, we have already noted that in simple electron transfer reactions no chemical bonds are broken or formed and so a somewhat different picture of the reaction is needed for the electron transfer reaction.

In his 1952 symposium paper, Libby noted that when an electron is transferred from one reacting ion or molecule to another, the two new molecules or ions formed are in the wrong environment of the solvent molecules, since the nuclei do not have time to move during the rapid electron jump: in reaction (1) a Fe^{2+} ion would be formed in some configuration of the many nearby dipolar solvent molecules that was appropriate to the original Fe^{3+} ion. Analogous remarks apply to the newly formed Fe^{3+} ion in the reaction. On the other hand, in reactions of "complex ions," such as those in the $Fe(CN)_6^{-3} - Fe(CN)_6^{-4}$ and $MnO_4^{-} - MnO_4^{2-}$ self-exchange reactions, the two reactants are larger, and so the change of electric field in the vicinity of each ion, upon electron transfer, would be smaller. The original solvent environment would therefore be less foreign to the newly formed charges, and so the energy barrier to reaction would be less. In this way Libby explained the faster self-exchange electron transfer rate for these complex ions. Further confirmation was noted in the ensuing discussion in the symposium: the self-exchange $Co(NH_3)_6^{3+} - Co(NH_3)_6^{2+}$ reaction is very slow, and it was pointed out that there was a large difference in the equilibrium Co-N bond lengths in the $3+$ and the $2+$ ions, and so each ion would be formed in a very "foreign" configuration of the vibrational coordinates, even though the ions are "complex ions."

After studying Libby's paper and the symposium discussion, I realized that what troubled me in this picture for reactions occurring in the dark was that energy was not conserved: the ions would be formed in the wrong high-energy environment, but the only way such a non-energy conserving event could happen would be by the absorption of light (a "vertical transition"), and not in the dark. Libby had perceptively introduced the Franck-Condon principle to chemical reactions, but something was missing.

In the present discussion, as well as in Libby's treatment, it was supposed that the electronic interaction of the reactants which causes the electron transfer is relatively weak. That view is still the one that seems appropriate today for most of these reactions. In this case of weak-electronic interaction, the question becomes: how does the reacting system behave in the dark so as to satisfy both the Franck-Condon principle and energy conservation? I realized that fluctuations had to occur in the various nuclear coordinates, such as in the orientation coordinates of the individual solvent molecules and indeed in any other coordinates whose most probable distribution for the products differs from that of the reactants. With such fluctuations, values of the coordinates could be reached which satisfy both the Franck-Condon and energy conservation conditions and so permit the electron transfer to occur in the dark.

For a reaction such as reaction (1), an example of an initial and final configuration of the solvent molecules is depicted in Figure 3. Fluctuations from the original equilibrium ensemble of configurations were ultimately needed, prior to the electron transfer, and were followed by a relaxation to the equilibrium ensemble for the products, after electron transfer.

The theory then proceeded as follows. The potential energy U_r of the entire system, reactants plus solvent, is a function of the many hundreds of relevant coordinates of the system, coordinates which include, among others, the position and orientation of the individual solvent molecules (and

Electron Transfer in Solution

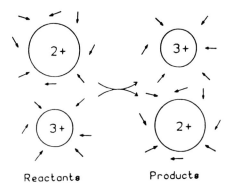

Figure 3. Typical nuclear configurations for reactants, products, and surrounding solvent molecules in reaction (1). The longer M-OH$_2$ bond length in the +2 state is indicated schematically by the larger ionic radius. (Sutin, ref. 2)

hence of their dipole moments, for example), and the vibrational coordinates of the reactants, particularly those in any inner coordination shell of the reacting ions. (E.g., the inner coordination shell of an ion such as Fe^{2+} or Fe^{3+} in water is known from EXAFS experiments to contain six water molecules.) No longer were there just the two or so important coordinates that were dominant in reaction (4).

Similarly, after the electron transfer, the reacting molecules have the ionic charges appropriate to the reaction products, and so the relevant potential energy function U_p is that for the products plus solvent. These two potential energy surfaces will intersect if the electronic coupling which leads to electron transfer is neglected. For a system with N coordinates this intersection occurs on an (N-1) dimensional surface, which then constitutes in our approximation the transition state of the reaction. The neglected electronic coupling causes a well-known splitting of the two surfaces in the vicinity of their intersection. A schematic profile of the two potential energy surfaces in the N-dimensional space is given in Figure 4. (The splitting is not shown.)

Due to the effect of the previously neglected electronic coupling and the coupling between the electronic motion and the nuclear motion near the intersection surface S, an electron transfer can occur at S. In classical terms, the transfer at S occurs at fixed positions and momenta of the atoms, and so the Franck-Condon principle is satisfied. Since U_r equals U_p at S, energy is also conserved. The details of the electron transfer depend on the extent of electronic coupling and how rapidly the point representing the system in this N-dimensional space crosses S. (It has been treated, for example, using as approximation the well-known one-dimensional Landau-Zener expression for the transition probability at the near-intersection of two potential energy curves.)

74

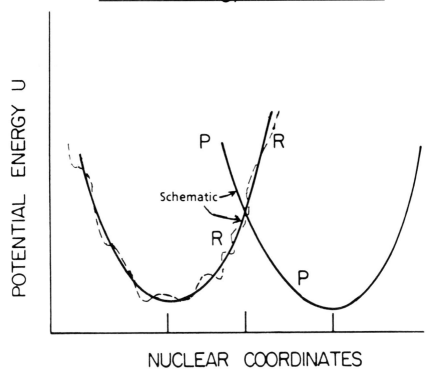

POTENTIAL ENERGY U

NUCLEAR COORDINATES

Figure 4. Profile of potential energy surfaces for reactants plus environment, R, and for products plus environment, P. Solid curves: schematic. Dashed curves: schematic but slightly more realistic. The typical splitting at the intersection of U_r and U_p is not shown in the Figure (Marcus and Siddarth, ref. 2).

When the splitting caused by the electronic coupling between the electron donor and acceptor is large enough at the intersection, a system crossing S from the lower surface on the reactants' side of S continues onto the lower surface on the products' side, and so an electron transfer in the dark has then occurred. When the coupling is, instead, very weak, ("non-adiabatic reactions") the probability of successfully reaching the lower surface on the products' side is small and can be calculated using quantum mechanical perturbation theory, for example, using Fermi's "Golden Rule," an improvement over the 1-dimensional Landau-Zener treatment.

Thus, there is some difference and some similarity with a more conventional type of reaction such as reaction (4), whose potential energy contour plots were depicted in Figure 2. In both cases, fluctuations of coordinates are needed to reach the transition state, but since so many coordinates can now play a significant role in the electron transfer reaction, because of the major and relatively abrupt change in charge distribution on passing through the transition state region, a rather different approach from the conventional one was needed to formulate the details of the theory.

Electron transfer theory. Treatment

In the initial paper (1956) I formulated the above picture of the mechanism of electron transfer and, to make the calculation of the reaction rate tractable, treated the solvent as a dielectric continuum. In the transition state the position-dependent dielectric polarization $\mathbf{P}_u(\mathbf{r})$ of the solvent, due to the orientation and vibrations of the solvent molecules, was not the one in equilibrium with the reactants' or the products' ionic charges. It represented instead, some macroscopic fluctuation from them. The electronic polarization for the solvent molecules, on the other hand, can rapidly respond to any such fluctuations and so is that which is dictated by the reactants' charges and by the instantaneous $\mathbf{P}_u(\mathbf{r})$.

With these ideas as a basis, what was then needed was a method of calculating the electrostatic free energy G of this system with its still unknown polarization function $\mathbf{P}_u(\mathbf{r})$. I obtained this free energy G by finding a reversible path for reaching this state of the system. Upon then minimizing G, subject to the constraint imposed by the Franck-Condon principle (reflected in the electron transfer occurring at the intersection of the two potential energy surfaces), I was able to find the unknown $\mathbf{P}_u(\mathbf{r})$ and, hence, to find the G for the transition state. That G was then introduced into transition state theory and the reaction rate calculated.

In this research I also read and was influenced by a lovely paper by Platzmann and Franck (1952) on the optical absorption spectra of halide ions in water and later by work of physicists such as Pekar and Frohlich (1954) on the closely related topic of polaron theory. As best as I can recall now, my first expressions for G during this month of intense activity seemed rather clumsy, but then with some rearrangement a simple expression emerged that had the right "feel" to it and that I was also able to obtain by a somewhat independent argument. The expression also reduced reassuringly to the usual one, when the constraint of arbitrary $\mathbf{P}_u(\mathbf{r})$ was removed. Obtaining the result for the mechanism and rate of electron transfer was indeed one of the most thrilling moments of my scientific life.

The expression for the rate constant k of the reaction is given by

$$k = A\exp\left(\frac{-\Delta G^*}{k_B T} \right), \tag{5a}$$

where ΔG^*, in turn, is given by

$$\Delta G^* = \frac{\lambda}{4}\left(1 + \frac{\Delta G^0}{\lambda} \right)^2. \tag{5b}$$

The A in Eq. (5a) is a term depending on the nature of the electron transfer reaction (e.g., bimolecular or intramolecular), ΔG^0 is the standard free energy of reaction (and equals zero for a self-exchange reaction), λ is a "reorganization term," composed of solvational (λ_o) and vibrational (λ_i) components.

$$\lambda = \lambda_o + \lambda_i \tag{6}$$

In a two-sphere model of the reactants, λ_o was expressed in terms of the two ionic radii a_1 and a_2 (including in the radius any inner coordination shell), the center-to-center separation distance R of the reactants, the optical (D_{op}) and static (D_s) dielectric constants of the solvent, and the charge transferred Δe from one reactant to the other:

$$\lambda_o = (\Delta e)^2 \left(\frac{1}{2a_1} + \frac{1}{2a_2} - \frac{1}{R} \right) \left(\frac{1}{D_{op}} - \frac{1}{D_s} \right) \tag{7}$$

For a bimolecular reaction, work terms, principally electrostatic, are involved in bringing the reactants together and in separating the reaction products, but are omitted from Eq. (5) for notational brevity. The expression for the vibrational term λ_i is given by

$$\lambda_i = \frac{1}{2} \sum_j k_j (Q_j^r - Q_j^p)^2 \tag{8}$$

where Q_j^r and Q_j^p are equilibrium values for the jth normal mode coordinate Q, and k_j is a reduced force constant $2k_j^r k_j^p /(k_j^r + k_j^p)$ k_j^r being the force constant for the reactants and k_j^p being that for the products. (I introduced a "symmetrization" approximation for the vibrational part of the potential energy surface, to obtain this simple form of Eqs. (5) to (8), and tested it numerically.)

In 1957 I published the results of a calculation of the λ_i arising from a stretching vibration in the innermost coordination shell of each reactant, (the equation used for λ_i was given in the 1960 paper). An early paper on the purely vibrational contribution using chemical bond length coordinates and neglecting bond-bond correlation had already been published for self-exchange reactions by George and Griffiths in 1956.

I also extended the theory to treat electron transfers at electrodes, and distributed it as an Office of Naval Research Report in 1957, the equations being published later in a journal paper in 1959. I had little prior knowledge of the subject, and my work on electrochemical electron transfers was facilitated considerably by reading a beautiful and logically written survey article of Roger Parsons on the equilibrium electrostatic properties of electrified metal-solution interfaces.

In the 1957 and 1965 work I showed that the electrochemical rate constant was again given by Eqs. (5)−(8), but with A now having a value appropriate to the different "geometry" of the encounter of the participants in the reaction. The $1/2a_2$ in Eq. (7) was now absent (there is only one reacting ion) and R now denotes twice the distance from the center of the reactant's charge to the electrode (it equals the ion-image distance). A term $e\eta$ replaced the ΔG^o in Eq.(5b), where e is the charge transferred between the ion and the electrode, and η is the activation overpotential, namely the metal-solution potential difference, relative to the value it would have if the rate constants for the forward and reverse reactions were equal. These rate constants are equal when the minima of the two G curves in Figure 5 have the same height.

77

Free Energy Curves

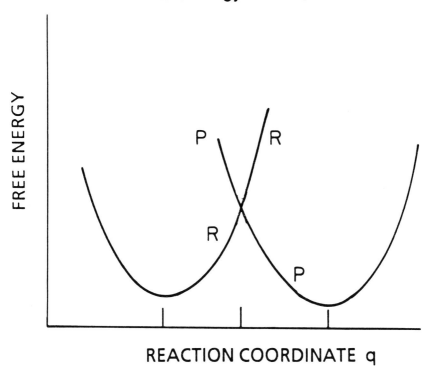

Figure 5. Free energy of reactants plus environment vs. the reaction coordinate q (R curve), and free energy of products plus environment vs. reaction coordinate q (P curve). The three vertical lines on the abscissa denote, from left to right, the value for the reactants, for the transition state, and for the products. (Marcus and Siddarth, ref. 2).

When $|e\eta| < \lambda$, most electrons go into or out of quantum states in the metal that are near the Fermi level. However, because of the continuum of states in the metal, the inverted effect (described below) was now predicted to be absent for this process, i.e., the counterpart of Eq. (5b) is applicable only in the region $|e\eta| < \lambda$: In the case of an intrinsically highly exothermic electron transfer reaction at an electrode, the electron can remove the immediate "exothermicity" by (if entering) going into a high unoccupied quantum state of the metal, or (if leaving) departing from a low occupied quantum state, each far removed from the Fermi level. (The inverted region effect should, however, occur for the electron transfer when the electrode is a narrow band semiconductor.)

After these initial electron transfer studies, which were based on a dielectric continuum approximation for the solvent outside the first coordination shell of each reactant, I introduced a purely molecular treatment of the reacting system. Using statistical mechanics, the solvent was treated as a collection of dipoles in the 1960 paper, and later in 1965 a general charge distribution was used for the solvent molecules and for the reactants. At the same time I found a way in this 1960 paper of introducing rigorously a global reaction coordinate in this many-dimensional (N) coordinate space of the reacting system. The globally defined coordinate so introduced was equivalent to using $U_p - U_r$, the potential energy difference between the products plus solvent (U_p) and the reactants plus solvent (U_r) (cf A. Warshel, 1987). It was, thereby, a coordinate defined everywhere in this N-dimensional space.

The free energy G_r of a system containing the solvent and the reactants, and that of the corresponding system for the products, G_p, could now be defined along this globally defined reaction coordinate. (In contrast, in reactions such as that depicted by Figure 2, it is customary, instead, to define a reaction coordinate locally, namely, in the vicinity of a path leading from the valley of the reactants through the saddle point region and into the valley of the products.)

The potential energies U_r and U_p in the many-dimensional coordinate space are simple functions of the vibrational coordinates but are complicated functions of the hundreds of relevant solvent coordinates: there are many local minima corresponding to locally stable arrangements of the solvent molecules. However, I introduced a "linear response approximation," in which any hypothetical change in charge of the reactants produces a proportional change in the dielectric polarization of the solvent. (Recently, I utilized a central limit theorem to understand this approximation better — beyond simple perturbation theory, and plan to submit the results for publication shortly.) With this linear approximation the free energies G_r and G_p became simple quadratic functions of the reaction coordinate.

Such an approach had major consequences. This picture permitted a depiction of the reaction in terms of parabolic free energy plots in simple and readily visualized terms, as in Figure 5. With them the trends predicted from the equations were readily understood. It was also important to use the free energy curves, instead of oversimplified potential energy profiles, because of the large entropy changes which occur in many electron transfer cross-reactions, due to changes in strong ion-polar solvent interactions. (The free energy plot is legitimately a one-coordinate plot while the potential energy plot is at most a profile of the complicated U_r and U_p in N-dimensional space.)

With the new statistical mechanical treatment of 1960 and 1965 one could also see how certain relations between rate constants initially derivable from the dielectric continuum-based equations in the 1956 paper could also be valid more generally. The relations were based, in part, on Equations (5) and (initially via (7) and (8)) on the approximate relation

$$\lambda_{12} \cong \frac{1}{2} (\lambda_{11} + \lambda_{22}) \qquad (9)$$

where λ_{12} is the λ for the cross-reaction and the λ_{11} and λ_{22} are those of the self-exchange reactions.

Predictions

In the 1960 paper I had listed a number of theoretical predictions resulting from these equations, in part to stimulate discussion with experimentalists in the field at a Faraday Society meeting on oxidation-reduction reactions, where this paper was to be presented. At the time I certainly did not anticipate the subsequent involvement of the many experimentalists in testing these predictions. Among the latter was one which became one of the most widely tested aspects of the theory, namely, the "cross-relation." This expression, which follows from Eqs. (5) and (9), relates the rate constant k_{12} of a cross-reaction to the two self-exchange rate constants, k_{11} and k_{22}, and to the equilibrium constant K_{12} of the reaction.

$$k_{12} \cong (k_{11}k_{22}K_{12}f_{12})^{1/2}, \tag{10}$$

where f_{12} is a known function of k_{11}, k_{22} and K_{12} and is usually close to unity.

Another prediction in the 1960 paper concerned what I termed there the inverted region: In a series of related reactions, similar in λ but differing in ΔG^{o}, a plot of the activation free energy ΔG^{*} vs. ΔG^{o} is seen from Eq. (5b) to first decrease as ΔG^{o} is varied from 0 to some negative value, vanish at $\Delta G^{o} = -\lambda$, and then increase when ΔG^{o} is made still more negative. This initial decrease of ΔG^{*} with increasingly negative ΔG^{o} is the expected trend in chemical reactions and is similar to the usual trend in "Bronsted plots" of acid or base catalyzed reactions and in "Tafel plots" of electrochemical reactions. I termed that region of ΔG^{o} the "normal" region. However, the prediction for the region where $-\Delta G^{o} > \lambda$, the "inverted region," was the unexpected behavior, or at least unexpected until the present theory was introduced.

This inverted region is also easily visualized using Figures 6 and 7: Successively making ΔG^{o} more negative, by lowering the products' G curve vertically relative to the reactant curve, decreases the free energy barrier ΔG^{*} (given by the intersection of the reactants' and products' curves): that barrier is seen in Figure 6 to vanish at some ΔG^{o} and then to increase again.

Other predictions dealt with the relation between the electrochemical and the corresponding self-exchange electron transfer rates, the numerical estimate of the reaction rate constant k and, in the case of non-specific solvent effects, the dependence of the reaction rate on solvent dielectric properties. The testing of some of the predictions was delayed by an extended sabbatical in $1960-61$, which I spent auditing courses and attending seminars at the nearby Courant Mathematical Institute.

Comparisons of Experiment and Theory

Around 1962, during one of my visits to Brookhaven National Laboratory, I showed Norman Sutin the 1960 predictions. Norman had either measured via his stopped-flow apparatus or otherwise knew rate constants and equilibrium constants which permitted the cross-relation Eq. (10) to be tested. There were about six such sets of data which he had available. I remember vividly the growing sense of excitement we both felt as, one by one, the

The Inverted Region Effect

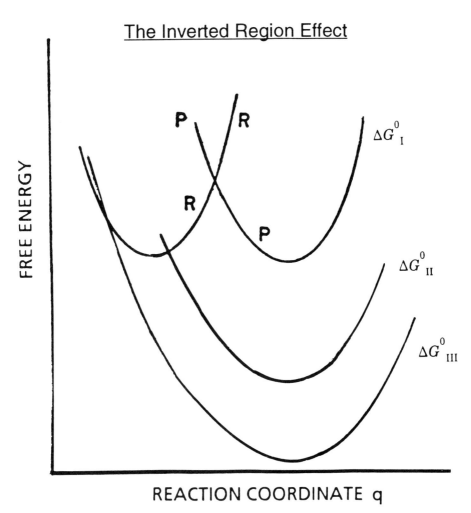

Figure 6. Plot of the free energy G versus the reaction coordinate q, for reactants' (R) and products' (P), for three different values of ΔG^0, the cases I to III indicated in Figure 7 (Marcus and Siddarth, ref. 2).

The Inverted Region Effect

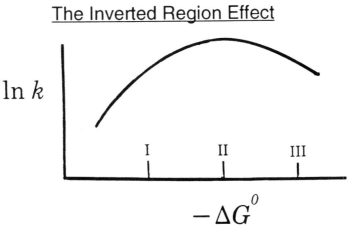

Figure 7. Plot of ln k_r vs $-\Delta G^0$. Points I and III are in the normal and inverted regions, respectively, while point II, where ln k_r is a maximum, occurs at $-\Delta G^0 = \lambda$ (Marcus and Siddarth, ref. 2).

81

observed k_{12}'s more or less agreed with the predictions of the relation. I later collected the results of this and of various other tests of the 1960 predictions and published them in 1963. Perhaps by showing that the previously published expressions were not mere abstract formulae, but rather had concrete applications, this 1963 paper, and many tests by Sutin and others, appear to have stimulated numerous subsequent tests of the cross-relation and of the other predictions. A few examples of the cross-relation test are given in Table 1.

The encouraging success of the experimental tests given in the 1963 paper suggested that the theory itself was more general than the approximations (e.g., solvent dipoles, unchanged force constants) used in 1960 and stimulated me to give a more general formulation (1965). The latter paper also contains a unified treatment of electron transfers in solution and at metal electrodes, and served, thereby, to generalize my earlier (1957) treatment of the electrochemical electron transfers.

The best experimental evidence for the inverted region was provided in 1984 by Miller, Calcaterra and Closs, almost 25 years after it was predicted.

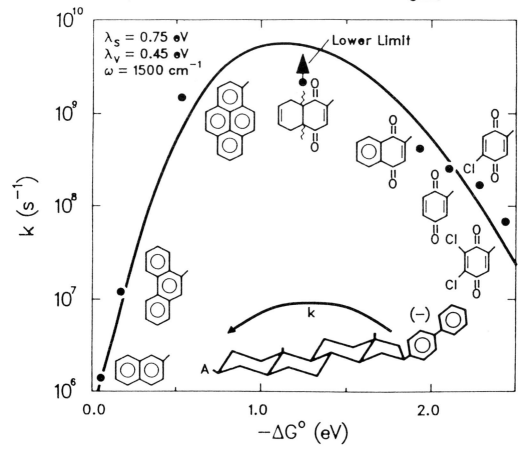

Figure 8. Inverted region effect in chemical electron transfer reactions. (Miller, et al, ref. 3).

This successful experimental test, which was later obtained for other electron transfer reactions in other laboratories, is reproduced in Figure 8. Possible reasons for not observing it in the earlier tests are several-fold and have been discussed elsewhere.

Previously, indirect evidence for the inverted region had been obtained by observing that electron transfer reactions with a very negative ΔG^* may result in chemiluminescence: when the G_r and G_p curves intersect at a high ΔG^* because of the inverted region effect, there may be an electron transfer to a more easily accessible G_p curve, one in which one of the products is electronically excited and which intersects the G_r curve in the normal region at a low ΔG^*, as in Figure 9. Indeed, experimentally in some reactions 100% formation of an electronically excited state of a reaction product has been observed by Bard and coworkers, and results in chemiluminescence.

Another consequence of Eq. (5) is the linear dependence of $k_B T \ln k$ on $-\Delta G^o$ with a slope of $1/2$, when $|\Delta G^o/\lambda|$ is small, and a similar behavior at electrodes, with ΔG^o replaced by $e\eta$ the product of the charge transferred

Formation of Electronically Excited Products

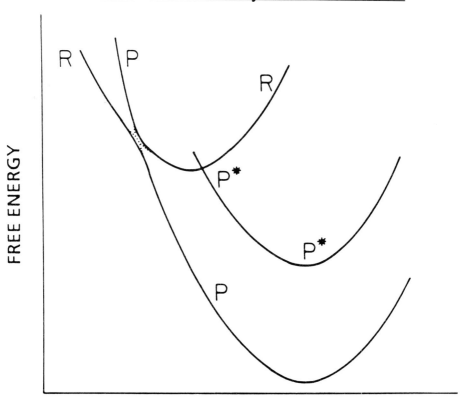

Figure 9. A favored formation of an electronically excited state of the products (Marcus and Siddarth, ref. 2).

and the activation overpotential. Extensive verification of both these results has been obtained. More recently, the curvature of plots of ln k vs. $e\eta$, expected from these equations, has been demonstrated in several experiments. The very recent use of ordered organic molecular monolayers on electrodes, either to slow down the electron transfer rate or to bind a redox-active agent to the electrode, but in either case to avoid or minimize diffusion control of the fast electron transfer processes, has considerably facilitated this study of the curvature in the ln k vs. $e\eta$ plot.

Comparison of experiment and theory has also included that of the absolute reaction rates of the self-exchange reactions, the effect on the rate of varying the solvent, an effect sometimes complicated by ion pairing in the low dielectric constant media involved, and studies of the related problem of charge transfer spectra, such as

$$DA + h\upsilon \rightarrow D^+A^- \tag{11}$$

Here, the frequency of the spectral absorption maximum υ_{max} is given

$$h\upsilon_{max} = \lambda + \Delta G^o. \tag{12}$$

Comparisons with Eq. (12), using Eq.(7) for λ, have included those of the effects of separation distance and of the solvent dielectric constant.

Comparisons have also been made of the self-exchange reaction rates in solution with the rates of the corresponding electron transfer reactions at

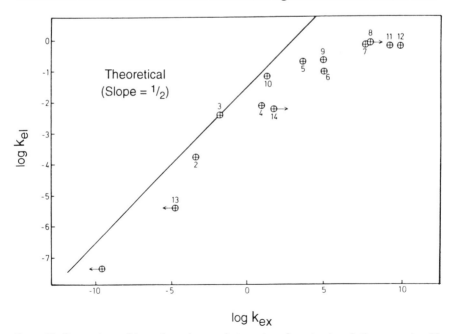

Figure 10. Comparison of isotopic exchange electron transfer rates in solution, covering 20 orders of magnitude, with rates of corresponding electron transfers at metal electrodes. (Cannon, ref. 2).

electrodes. An example of the latter is the plot given in Figure 10, where the self-exchange rates are seen to vary by some twenty orders of magnitude. The discrepancy at high k's is currently the subject of some reinvestigation of the fast electrode reaction rates, using the new nanotechnology. Most recently, a new type of interfacial electron transfer rate has also been measured, electron transfer at liquid-liquid interfaces. In treating the latter, I extended the "cross relation" to this two-phase system. It is clear that much is to be learned from this new area of investigation. (The study of the transfer of ions across such an interface, on the other hand, goes back to the time of Nernst and of Planck, around the turn of the century.)

Other Applications and Extensions

As noted in Figure 1, one aspect of the electron transfer field has been its continued and, indeed, ever-expanding growth in so many directions. One of these is in the biological field, where there are now detailed experimental and theoretical studies in photosynthetic and other protein systems. The three-dimensional structure of a photosynthetic reaction center, the first membrane protein to be so characterized, was obtained by Deisenhofer, Michel and Huber, who received the Nobel Prize in Chemistry in 1988 for this work. A bacterial photosynthetic system is depicted in Figure 11, where the protein framework holding fast the constituents in this reaction center is not shown.

The Reaction Center

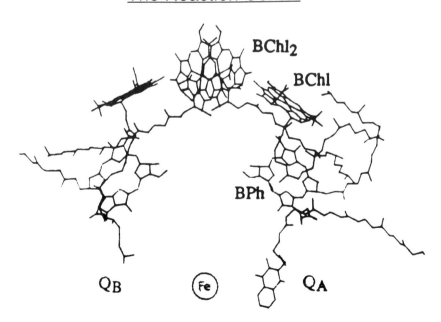

Figure 11. Redox-active species involved in the initial charge separation for a photosynthetic bacterium (cf Deisenhofer *et al*, ref. 3, and Yeates *et al*, ref. 3), with labels added, to conform to the present text; they include a missing Q_B.

In the photosynthetic system there is a transfer of electronic excitation from "antenna" chlorophylls (not shown in Figure 11) to a special pair $BChl_2$. The latter then transfers an electron to a pheophytin BPh within a very short time (~ 3 picoseconds) and from it to a quinone Q_A in 200 psec and thence to the other quinone Q_B. (Other chemical reactions then occur with these separated charges at each side of the membrane, bridged by this photosynthetic reaction center.)

To avoid wasting the excitation energy of the $BChl_2$* unduly it is necessary that the $-\Delta G^o$ of this first electron transfer to BPh be small. (It is only about 0.25 eV out of an overall excitation energy of $BChl_2$* of 1.38 eV.) In order that this electron transfer also be successful in competing with two wasteful processes, the fluorescence and the radiationless transition of $BChl_2$*, it is also necessary that ΔG^* for that first electron transfer step be small and hence, by Eq. (5b), that the λ be small. The size of the reactants is large, and the immediate protein environment is largely nonpolar, so leading to a small λ (cf Eq.(7)). Nature appears, indeed, to have constructed a system with this desirable property.

Furthermore, to avoid another form of wasting the energy, it is also important that an unwanted back electron transfer reaction from the BPh^- to the $BChl_2^+$ not compete successfully with a second forward electron transfer step from BPh^- to Q_A. That is, it is necessary that the back transfer, a "hole-electron recombination" step, be slow, even though it is a very highly exothermic process ($\sim 1.1eV$). It has been suggested that the small λ ($\sim 0.25eV$) and the resulting inverted region effect play a significant role in providing this essential condition for the effectiveness of the photosynthetic reaction center.

There is now a widespread interest in synthesizing systems which can mimic the behavior of nature's photosynthetic systems, and so offer other routes for the harnessing of solar energy. The current understanding of how nature works has served to provide some guidelines. In this context, as well as that of electron transfer in other proteins, there are also relevant experiments in long range electron transfer. Originally the studies were of electron transfer in rigid glasses and were due to Miller and coworkers. More recently the studies have involved a donor and receptor held together by synthetically made rigid molecular bridges. The effect of varying the bridge length has been studied in the various systems. A theoretical estimate of the distance dependence of electron transfers in a photosynthetic system was first made by Hopfield, who used a square barrier model and an approximate molecular estimate of the barrier height.

Recently, in their studies of long range electron transfer in chemically modified proteins, Gray and coworkers have studied systematically the distance or site dependence of the electronic factor, by attaching an appropriate electron donor or acceptor to a desired site. For each such site the reactant chosen should be such that $-\Delta G^o \approx \lambda$, i.e., which has a k at the maximum of the $\ln k$ vs. $-\Delta G^o$ curve (cf Eq. (5)). The value of k then no longer depends on a ΔG^*. Since ΔG^* is distance-dependent (cf Eq.(7)), it is particularly desirable to make $\Delta G^* \approx 0$, so that the relative k's at the various sites now reflect only the electronic factor. Dutton and coworkers have treated data similarly for a number of reactions by using, where possible, the k at the maximum of each $\ln k$ vs. ΔG^o curve. Of particular interest in such studies is whether there is a simple exponential decrease of the electronic factor on the separation distance between donor and acceptor, or whether there are deviations from this monotonic behavior, due to local structural factors.

In a different development, the mechanism of various organic reactions has been explored by several investigators, notably by Eberson (ref. 2), in the light of current electron transfer theory. Other organic reactions have been explored by Shaik and Pross, in their analysis of a possible electron transfer mechanism vs. a conventional mechanism, and by Shaik *et al* (ref.2).

Theoretical calculations of the donor-acceptor electronic interactions, initially by McConnell and by Larsson, and later by others, our group among them, have been used to treat long-range electron transfer. The methods have recently been adapted to large protein systems. In our studies with Siddarth we used an "artificial intelligence" searching technique to limit the number of amino acids used in the latter type of study.

Another area of much current activity in electron transfers is that of solvent dynamics, following the pioneering treatment for general reactions by Kramers (1940). Important later developments for electron transfer were made by many contributors. Solvent dynamics affects the electron transfer reaction rate when the solvent is sufficiently sluggish. As we showed recently with Sumi and Nadler, the solvent dynamics effect can also be modified significantly, when there are vibrational (λ_i) contribution to λ.

Computational studies, such as the insightful one of David Chandler and coworkers on the $Fe^{2+} + Fe^{3+}$ self-exchange reaction, have also been employed recently. Using computer simulations they obtained a verification of the parabolic G curves, even for surprisingly high values of the fluctuation in G. They also extended their studies to dynamical and quantum mechanical effects of the nuclear motion. Studies of the quantum mechanical effects on the nuclear motion on electron transfer reactions were initiated in 1959 by Levich and Dogonadze, who assumed a harmonic oscillator model for the polar solvent medium and employed perturbation theory. Their method was related to that used for other problems by Huang and Rhys (1951) and Kubo and Toyozawa (1954).

There were important subsequent developments by various authors on these quantum effects, including the first discussion of quantum effects for the vibrations of the reactants by Sutin in 1962 and the important work of Jortner and coworkers in 1974−75, who combined a Levich and Dogonadze type approach to treat the high frequency vibrations of the reactants with the classical expression which I described earlier for the polar medium. These quantum effects have implications for the temperature dependence of k, among other effects. Proceeding in a different (classical) direction Saveant recently showed how to extend Eq. (5b) to reactions which involved the rupture of a chemical bond by electron transfer and which he had previously studied experimentally: $M(e) + RX \rightarrow M + R + X^-$, where R is an alkyl group, X a halide and M a metal electrode.

A particularly important early development was that by Taube in the 1950s; he received the Nobel Prize for his work in 1983. Taube introduced the idea of different mechanisms for electron transfer—outer sphere and inner sphere electron transfers, which he had investigated experimentally. His experimental work on charge transfer spectra of strongly interacting systems ("Creutz-Taube" ion, 1959, 1973) and of weakly interacting ones has been similarly influential. Also notable has been Hush's theoretical work on charge transfer spectra, both of intensities and absorption maxima (1967), which supplemented his earlier theoretical study of electron transfer rates (1961).

There has been a "spin-off" of the original electron transfer theory to other types of chemical reactions as well. In particular, the ΔG^* vs ΔG^o relation and the cross-relation have been extended to these other reactions, such as the transfer of atoms, protons, or methyl groups. (Even an analog of Eqs. (5b) and (9), but for binding energies instead of energy barriers has been introduced to relate the stability of isolated protonbound dimers AHB^+ to those of AHA^+ and BHB^+!)

Since the transfer of these nuclei involves strong electronic interactions, it is not well represented by intersecting parabolic free energy curves, and so a different theoretical approach was needed. For this purpose I adapted (1968) a "bond-energy-bond-order" model of H. Johnston, in order to treat the problem for a reaction of the type given by Eq.(4). The resulting simple expression for ΔG^* is similar to Eq.(5), when $|\Delta G^o/\lambda|$ is not large ($< 1/2$), but differs from it in not having any inverted region. It has the same λ property as that given by Eq.(9), and has resulted in a cross-relation analogous to Eq. (10). The cross-relation has been tested experimentally for the transfer of methyl groups by E. Lewis, and the ΔG^* vs ΔG^o relation has been used or tested for other transfers by Albery and by Kreevoy and their coworkers, among others.

It is naturally gratifying to see one's theories used. A recent article, which showed the considerable growth in the use of papers such as the 1956 and 1964 articles (ref. 5), points up the impressive and continued vitality of the field itself. The remarks above on many areas of electron transfer and on the spin-off of such work on the study of other types of reactions represent a necessarily brief picture of these broad-based investigations.

ACKNOWLEDGMENTS

My acknowledgments are to my many fellow researchers in the electron transfer field, notably Norman Sutin, with whom I have discussed so many of these matters for the past thirty or more years. I also thank my students and post-doctorals, whose presence was a constant source of stimulation to me, both in the electron transfer field and in the other fields of research

Table I. Comparison of Calculated and Experimental k_{12} Values[a]

Reaction	k_{12}, M^{-1} sec^{-1}	
	Observed	Calculated
$IrCl_6^{2-} + W(CN)_8^{4-}$	6.1×10^7	6.1×10^7
$IrCl_6^{2-} + Fe(CN)_6^{4-}$	3.8×10^5	7×10^5
$IrCl_6^{2-} + Mo(CN)_8^{4-}$	1.9×10^6	9×10^5
$Mo(CN)_8^{3-} + W(CN)_8^{4-}$	5.0×10^6	4.8×10^6
$Mo(CN)_8^{3-} + Fe(CN)_6^{4-}$	3.0×10^4	2.9×10^4
$Fe(CN)_6^{3-} + W(CN)_8^{4-}$	4.3×10^4	6.3×10^4
$Ce^{IV} + W(CN)_8^{4-}$	$>10^8$	4×10^8
$Ce^{IV} + Fe(CN)_6^{4-}$	1.9×10^6	8×10^6
$Ce^{IV} + Mo(CN)_8^{4-}$	1.4×10^7	1.3×10^7
L-$Co[(-)PDTA]^{2-} + Fe(bipy)_3^{3+}$	8.1×10^4	$\geq 10^5$
L-$Fe[(-)PDTA]^{2-} + Co(EDTA)^-$	1.3×10^1	1.3×10^1
L-$Fe[(-)PDTA]^{2-} + Co(ox)_3^{3-}$	2.2×10^2	1.0×10^3
$Cr(EDTA)^{2-} + Fe(EDTA)^-$	$\geq 10^6$	10^9
$Cr(EDTA)^{2-} + Co(EDTA)^-$	$\simeq 3 \times 10^5$	4×10^7
$Fe(EDTA)^{2-} + Mn(CyDTA)^-$	$\simeq 4 \times 10^5$	6×10^6
$Co(EDTA)^{2-} + Mn(CyDTA)$	9×10^{-1}	2.1
$Fe(PDTA)^{2-} + Co(CyDTA)^-$	1.2×10^1	1.8×10^1
$Co(terpy)_2^{2+} + Co(bipy)_3^{3+}$	6.4×10	3.2×10
$Co(terpy)_2^{2+} + Co(phen)_3^{3+}$	2.8×10^2	1.1×10^2
$Co(terpy)_2^{2+} + Co(bipy)(H_2O)_4^{3+}$	6.8×10^2	6.4×10^4
$Co(terpy)_2^{2+} + Co(phen)(H_2O)_4^{3+}$	1.4×10^3	6.4×10^4
$Co(terpy)_2^{2+} + Co(H_2O)_6^{3+}$	7.4×10^4	2×10^{10}
$Fe(phen)_3^{2+} + MnO_4^-$	6×10^3	4×10^3
$Fe(CN)_6^{4-} + MnO_4^-$	1.3×10^4	5×10^3
$V(H_2O)_6^{2+} + Ru(NH_3)_6^{3+}$	1.5×10^3 [a]	4.2×10^3
$Ru(en)_3^{2+} + Fe(H_2O)_6^{3+}$	8.4×10^4	4.2×10^5
$Ru(NH_3)_6^{2+} + Fe(H_2O)_6^{3+}$	3.4×10^5	7.5×10^6
$Fe(H_2O)_6^{2+} + Mn(H_2O)_6^{3+}$	1.5×10^4	3×10^4

[a] Bennett, ref. 3.

which we have explored. In its earliest stage and for much of this period this research was supported by the Office of Naval Research and also later by the National Science Foundation. The support of both agencies continues to this day and I am very pleased to acknowledge its value and timeliness here.

In my Nobel lecture, I concluded on a personal note with a slide of my great uncle, Henrik Steen (né Markus), who came to Sweden in 1892. He received his doctorate in theology from the University of Uppsala in 1915, and was an educator and a prolific writer of pedagogic books. As I noted in the biographical sketch in *Les Prix Nobel,* he was one of my childhood idols. Coming here, visiting with my Swedish relatives—some thirty or so descendants—has been an especially heartwarming experience for me and for my family. In a sense I feel that I owed him a debt, and that it is most fitting to acknowledge that debt here.

REFERENCES

Some of my relevant articles, largely from the 1956−65 period, are listed in ref.1 below, and some general references which review the overall literature are listed in ref. 2. Several additional references for the Table and for the Figures are given in ref. 3. Classic texts on unimolecular reactions are given in ref. 4.

1. R. A. Marcus, J. Chem. Phys. **24**, 966 (1956); *ibid.*, **24**, 979 (1956); *ibid.*, **26**, 867 (1957); *ibid,* **26**, 872 (1957); Trans. N. Y. Acad. Sci. **19**, 423 (1957); ONR Technical Report No. 12, Project NR 051-331 (1957), reproduced in *Special Topics in Electrochemistry,* P. A. Rock, ed., Elsevier, New York, 1977, p. 181; Can. J. Chem. **37**, 155 (1959); Discussions Faraday Soc. **29**, 21 (1960); J. Phys. Chem. **67**, 853, 2889 (1963); J. Chem. Phys. **38**, 1858 (1963); ibid., **39**, 1734 (1963); Ann. Rev. Phys. Chem. **15**, 155 (1964); J.Chem.Phys. **43**, 679 (1965); ibid., **43**, 1261 (1965); ibid., **43**, 2654 (1965), (corr.) **52**, 2803 (1970); J. Phys. Chem. **72**, 891 (1968)

2 R. A. Marcus and N. Sutin, Biochim. Biophys. Acta, **811**, 265 (1985); J.R. Bolton, N. Mataga and G. McLendon (eds.) Adv. Chem.Ser., **228**, (1991), assorted articles; M.D. Newton and N. Sutin, Ann.Rev.Phys.Chem., **35**, 437 (1984); N. Sutin, Prog. Inorg. Chem., **30**, 441 (1983); M.D. Newton, Chem.Rev., **91**, 767 (1991); R.D. Cannon, *Electron Transfer Reactions*, Butterworths, London, 1980; L. Eberson, *Electron Transfer Reactions in Organic Chemistry,* Springer, New York, 1987; M.A. Fox and M. Chanon (eds.), *Photoinduced Electron Transfer,* Elsevier, New York, 1988, 4 vols.; M.V. Twigg (ed.), *Mechanisms of Inorganic and Organometallic Reactions,* vol. 7, 1991, Chaps. 1 and 2, and earlier volumes; R. A. Marcus and P. Siddarth, in *Photoprocesses in Transition Metal Complexes, Biosystems and Other Molecules: Experiment and Theory,* E. Kochanski, ed., Kluwer, Norwall, Massachusetts,1992, p. 49; S.S. Shaik, H.B. Schlegel and S. Wolfe, *Theoretical Aspects of Physical Organic Chemistry, J.* Wiley, New York, 1992; N. Sutin, Pure & Applied Chem. **60**, 1817 (1988); Assorted articles in Chem.Revs. **92**, No. 3 (1992); R.A. Marcus Commemorative Issue, J.Phys.Chem. **90**, (1986).

3. L. E. Bennett, Prog.Inorg.Chem. **18**, 1 (1973); J.R. Miller, L.T. Calcaterra and G.L. Closs, J.Am.Chem.Soc. **106**, 3047 (1984); J. Deisenhofer, O. Epp, K. Miki, R. Huber and H. Michel, J.Mol.Biol. **180**, 385 (1984); J. Deisenhofer and H. Michel, Angew.Chem.Int.Ed.Engl. **28**, 829 (1989); T.G. Yeates, H. Komiya, D.C. Rees, J.P. Allen and G. Feher, Proc.Nat.Acad.Sci. **84**, 6438 (1987).

4. P. J. Robinson and H.A. Holbrook, *Unimolecular Reactions,* J.Wiley, New York 1972; W. Forst, *Theory of Unimolecular Reactions,* Academic Press, New York, 1973; cf also the very recent text, R.G. Gilbert and S.C. Smith, *Theory of Unimolecular and Recombination Reactions,* Blackwells, Oxford, 1990.

5. Science Watch, **3**, No.9, November,1992, p.8.

EDWIN G. KREBS

I was born in Lansing, Iowa on June 6, 1918, the third of the four children of William Carl Krebs and Louise Helen (Stegeman) Krebs. My maternal grandmother, Bertha Stegeman, lived with us for most of her life. My father was a Presbyterian minister, who had started his ministry in the Moravian Church in Wisconsin. My mother taught school until she was married. (She must have been an excellent student because she could still help me with problems during my second course of algebra.) As was common in ministers' families, we moved several times, first to Newton, Illinois and later, when I was age 6, to Greenville, Illinois. The family stayed in Greenville, which I always think of as my "home town", until I was fifteen. Greenville is a small college town, has good schools, and is surrounded by pleasant countryside where I loved to go on walks with my older brothers — as soon as I became old enough that they didn't mind having me tag along. In addition to hiking, other recreational pursuits included sand-lot sports, fishing, stamp collecting, and eventually ham radio. The last hobby was picked up not so much because of any strong scientific interests on my part in radio theory but rather from a desire to be able to talk to a grade school playmate who had moved to Chicago. I loved to read — mostly historical novels about the Civil War, the settling of the West, and related adventure stories. I worked hard at school in order to succeed, but I cannot claim to have been a highly intellectual child. I liked to make gun powder using materials purchased from the local drug store or taken from my older brother's chemistry set, but I had no childhood aspirations of becoming a chemist. The closest that I came to expressing an interest in biology was the maintaining of a balanced aquarium.

At the end of my first year in high school my father died suddenly. I was fifteen and was strongly influenced by this unexpected event. Although I had never aspired to follow in his footsteps and become a minister, I had great affection for him and admired the skill that he had in some of his avocations such as carpentry and gardening. My mother was deeply affected by Dad's death, but after recovering from the initial shock began making major decisions mostly centered around providing advanced educational opportunities for her children. It was determined that the family, which had very limited income (It was 1933.), would move to Urbana, Illinois, where my two older brothers were already enrolled at the University of Illinois. There we rented a large enough house so that we could rent out a room to help with expenses. Everyone got some kind of part-time job. The planning for these changes involved the entire family and without doubt had a maturing influence on both of my brothers and certainly had one on me.

In the period from 1933 to 1940 in Urbana I completed the last three years of high school and carried out undergraduate work at the University of Illinois. Urbana High School was an excellent institution with highly dedicated teachers and a broad range of extracurricular activities that were useful in helping me make up my mind as to what I wanted to do in life. This problem was one that was occupying my mind increasingly at this time. Because these were depression years, my thinking about various professions was colored by the question of whether or not a given choice of work was one in which I could earn a livelihood. I gravitated toward a scientific career, not because of deep interest in the challenges of the unknown, but because I felt that there was security in becoming a scientist. Science courses, more than the others, provided subject matter that I felt could actually be used. These feelings were strongly reinforced by the success of my older brother in obtaining an excellent position after obtaining a Ph.D. in chemical engineering in the mid 1930s. Medicine, as an applied science, was also appealing and offered the advantage of being directly concerned with people.

In 1936, I entered the University of Illinois with the idea of majoring in some branch of science related to chemistry, but I did not have a very clear idea of where I was headed. Taking advantage of an "individual curriculum" program that was available to those with reasonably good scholastic records—and for this reason presumably knew where they were going—I was relieved of the necessity of meeting many specific requirements and could pick and choose courses that I wanted. In this way I was able to take enough biology to meet premedical requirements but could also take the math, chemistry, and physics courses designed for professionals in these fields. By the beginning of my fourth year in college, I had narrowed my choices either to getting an advanced degree in organic chemistry or going to medical school. For the latter financial help would be required. This became available in the form of a scholarship to attend Washington University School of Medicine in St. Louis. At this point I assumed that the agony of indecision was over and my future was now defined. I would become a physician.

During my fourth year at the University of Illinois I carried out undergraduate research in organic chemistry and found it to be a fascinating experience. This was probably the first time that I had ever taken a "course" that seemed like fun. Because I was ahead in my credits, I was able to spend virtually unlimited time in the laboratory. My mentors were Harold Snyder and Charles Price, and to them I will always be grateful for having introduced me to research. Another influential teacher during this period was Carl S. Marvel. Had this research experience come earlier in my college career, I might well have opted for a Ph.D. in organic chemistry rather than going to medical school. But as it turned out, this introduction to research influenced my medical training and without doubt was a strong factor in my eventually becoming a research biochemist rather than a clinician.

94

Washington University School of Medicine proved to be an excellent choice as a place where I could receive classical medical training but at the same time learn to appreciate "medical research." The basic science courses were the equivalent of graduate courses and there was no attempt to water down the curriculum based on the idea that physicians only need "core" knowledge in the various sciences In addition to basic course work that took us to the fringes of knowledge in the various disciplines, students were encouraged to participate in laboratory projects. I personally undertook several projects, first under Dean Philip A. Schafer, who was also chairman of the Department of Biochemistry, and later under Arda A. Green, a faculty member associated with Dr. Carl and Gerty Cori. Ethel Ronzoni also offered me help and advice in some of the work that I carried out. During this period I first heard about the enzyme, phosphorylase, which was crystallized by Arda Green and the Coris and was found to exist in two interconvertible forms that they referred to as phosphorylase b and phosphorylase a. Phosphorylase b required 5'-AMP for enzymic activity whereas phosphorylase a was active without this nucleotide. This enzyme was later to play an important part in my life.

The medical school years, 1940–1943, were war years, and although I did some research as a medical student, my main preoccupation was with becoming a physician who could serve in the armed forces. Nobody knew how long the war would last and our immediate concerns were with being a part of the war effort. After graduation from medical school I had eighteen months of residency training in internal medicine at Barnes Hospital in St. Louis, and then went on active duty as a medical office in the navy. The war ended and so did the period of my life in which I actively used my medical training in any practical sense. I believe I would have been happy practicing medicine but this was not to be.

After being discharged from the Navy in 1946, I returned to St. Louis with the idea of continuing residency and becoming an academic internist. However, it immediately became apparent that I would have to wait my turn to get back into hospital work, and I was advised by my professor of medicine, Dr. W. B. Wood, to study in a basic science department during the interim. Because of my background in chemistry, I chose biochemistry for this and was fortunate in being accepted by Dr. Carl and Gerty Cori as a postdoctoral fellow. After two years in their laboratory, during which time I studied the interaction of protamine with rabbit muscle phosphorylase, I became so enamored with biochemistry that I decided to remain in that field rather than returning to internal medicine. Again, I had found laboratory experience to be very satisfying just as it had been when I was a senior in college.

While I was on active duty in the navy, my ship had put into Seattle, and I had been impressed by the beauty of the city. So in 1948, when I had an opportunity to go there as an assistant professor of biochemistry, I jumped at the chance. Because I was quite uncertain of my ability to succeed in biochemistry, however, I made certain that I was duly licensed and registered in the State of Washington, so that if worse came to worse I could always "hang out my shingle." Happily, things seemed to go along reasonably well, and I did not find it necessary to use this insurance policy.

In 1950, Hans Neurath became the first permanent chairman of the Department of Biochemistry at the University of Washington and began to build what was to become one of the major departments in the country. The emphasis in the department was on protein chemistry and enzymology, and this provided an excellent environment in which to develop and pursue a research field. I had been in Seattle for five years when Ed Fischer joined the Department. Ed had had experience with potato phosphorylase during his graduate student days and, as indicated earlier, I had become acquainted with mammalian skeletal muscle phosphorylase in St. Louis. Together we decided to see whether or not we could determine the mechanism by which 5'-AMP served as an activator of phosphorylase b. We didn't solve that problem, but in the course of trying we discovered the molecular mechanism by which interconversion of the two forms of phosphorylase takes place; namely, reversible protein phosphorylation. Similar work was being carried out on liver phosphorylase at approximately the same time in the laboratory of Earl Sutherland who discovered cyclic AMP, the second messenger of hormone action, which he showed was involved in phosphorylase a formation. A number of years were to elapse before it became apparent that reversible protein phosphorylation is a general process affecting countless cellular proteins.

During the early years of our work on protein phosphorylation, Ed Fischer and I worked together very closely even to the point that if one had to leave to give a lecture the other could carry on the experiment of the day. Later, as the field developed we each concentrated on our own specific areas related to the central problem. One of my own projects was concerned with the molecular mechanism of action of cyclic AMP in promoting the phosphorylase b to a reaction. This was eventually solved with the finding of the cyclic AMP-dependent protein kinase by one of my postdoctoral fellows, Donal A. Walsh. This discovery occurred just prior to my leaving the University of Washington in 1968.

In addition to the motivation provided by my research, I was also motivated by interests in teaching and various aspects of administration. These interests led to a desire on my part to become a departmental chairman, and I was attracted by the opportunity that presented itself at the University of California in Davis where a new medical school was taking shape in the late 1960's. I went there in 1968 as the founding chairman of the Department of Biological Chemistry and stayed for a period of eight years. In 1977, however, I returned to the University of Washington as Chairman of the Department of Pharmacology. In each place, I viewed the principal role of the chairman to be the selection of good faculty members, and I feel proud of the results of my efforts in each place. Other aspects of these chairmanships were also rewarding, particularly the opportunity to interact with colleagues in the development of the respective institutions.

96

An important part of this autobiographical sketch, which I have saved for the end, concerns my family. During my residency years at Barnes Hospital I met my wife, Deedy, who was a student nurse at Washington University. We were married in 1945 shortly before I left to serve in the Navy. We had three children, Sally, Robert, and Martha and now have five grandchildren. After completing her degree in nursing my wife gave up her own career, but she has been a constant and important source of support for me in my own. We shared in the major decisions of our lives, and I feel that I owe her very much, not only for her constant help in my career but also in keeping me aware that there are other important aspects of life.

PROTEIN PHOSPHORYLATION AND CELLULAR REGULATION, I

Nobel Lecture, December 8, 1992

by

Edwin G. Krebs

Departments of Pharmacology and Biochemistry, School of Medicine, SL-15, University of Washington, Seattle, WA 98195, USA.

INTRODUCTION

This presentation and the one to be given immediately thereafter will be concerned with the reversible phosphorylation of proteins and the role of this process in biological regulation. In addition to discussing our own early contributions to this field, Ed Fischer and I will describe some of the developments that have occurred subsequently. These developments have led to the realization that protein phosphorylation constitutes a major mechanism by which cellular processes are controlled. My own remarks will review the historical background that provided the setting in which our joint work was carried out in the 1950s and early 1960s. Then I'll turn to a discussion of this work itself, to be followed by comments on the cyclic AMP-dependent protein kinase. Finally I will talk about the intracellular transmission of hormone and growth factor signals through protein kinase cascades.

BACKGROUND

By 1940, which is the year in which I entered medical school at Washington University in St Louis, it was well established that the breakdown of glycogen in skeletal muscle and other types of cells occurs by the process of phosphorolysis, catalyzed by the enzyme phosphorylase (for review, see ref. 1). Carl Cori was Professor and Chairman of the Department of Pharmacology at Washington University, when I started my training there, but he was soon to take over the Department of Biological Chemistry. I gradually came to know him, at first distantly, the way medical students usually know their professors, but later on somewhat better after I had become a teaching assistant in biochemistry. In this latter role I also became acquainted with Arda Green, who, together with Carl and Gerty Cori, was purifying rabbit muscle phosphorylase. It was not long until I began to hear about the unusual properties of this remarkable enzyme, which they had found existed in skeletal muscle in two different forms that they designated as phosphorylase *b* and phosphorylase *a* (2,3). The *a* form was purified and obtained as a crystalline enzyme. Kinetically, it was shown that phosphorylase *b* required high concentrations of 5'-AMP for activity whereas phosphorylase *a* was active in the absence of this nucleotide. Since the concentration of 5'-AMP required for the activity of phosphorylase *b* was considerably higher than that found in muscle, this form was considered to be physiologically inactive. Phosphorylase *a* was thought of as the physiologically active species. Evidence was obtained that the two forms are interconvertible within the cell, and it was postulated by the Coris that interconversion of the forms of phosphorylase constitutes a physiologically significant regulatory mechanism. Resting muscle was reported to contain phosphorylase predominantly in the *a* form, whereas electrically stimulated muscle contained the *b* form (4). As will be discussed later (see below) the reverse is actually true. Regardless of this latter point, however, the finding that an enzyme might shuttle back and forth between two forms within the cell was a remarkable advance, which set the stage for important later developments.

The Coris were unaware of the chemical nature of the interconversion reactions of phosphorylase, but they did discover an enzyme that would convert phosphorylase *a* to phosphorylase *b in vitro*. This enzyme was called the "PR enzyme" based on the assumption that it acted by removing a prosthetic group from phosphorylase *a*, which was thought of as a holoenzyme form (2); phosphorylase *b*, lacking the putative group, was considered to be the apoenzyme form. Based on the fact that phosphorylase *b* could be activated by 5'-AMP, this nucleotide bound to the enzyme was thought of as the likely candidate for the prosthetic group of phosphorylase *a*. However, all attempts to identify 5'-AMP as a product formed when phosphorylase *a* was converted to phosphorylase *b* by the PR enzyme were unsuccessful (2,3). Because trypsin treatment of phosphorylase *a* led to the formation of a phosphorylase *b*-like form, i.e. an enzyme that could be activated by 5'-AMP (3), it was believed that the PR enzyme might be a protease. No enzyme that could convert phosphorylase *b* to *a in vitro* in the presence of 5'AMP, or under any other condition that these workers tried, could be demonstrated. This did not seem unreasonable, however, if it were supposed that such a conversion might require peptide bond biosynthesis, because at that time the likelihood that such a reaction could be shown to occur *in vitro* was considered unlikely. These early concepts with respect to the interconversion reactions of phosphorylase are illustrated in Fig. 1.

Although as a medical student I heard about the research on phosphorylase, particularly as a result of my friendship with Arda Green, my first "hands on" experience with this enzyme came after World War II had ended, when I started postdoctoral work in the Coris' laboratory (My residency training in internal medicine had been interrupted by the war, and, although at that time I expected to return to clinical medicine in due course, I had decided to work in a basic science department for a year or two before resuming hospital-based training.) The problem that was given

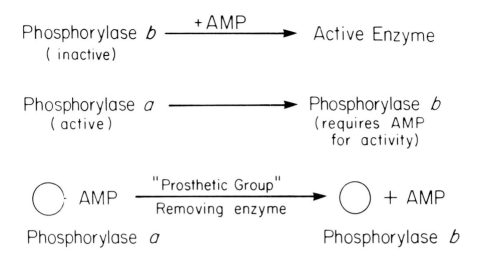

Fig. 1. *Early concepts of the interconversion reactions of muscle phosphorylase.* Inactive phosphorylase *b* becomes an active enzyme in the presence of 5'-AMP. Phosphorylase *a*, the physiologically active form of the enzyme, is inactivated by the prosthetic group removing (PR) enzyme. It was thought likely that 5'-AMP would be product of this reaction, but this could not be demonstrated.

to me by the Coris involved solubility measurements on phosphorylase, and I also studied the effect of protamine and polylysine on the two forms of the enzyme. It was of interest that in the presence of these polyanionic substances, inosinic acid, as well on 5'-AMP, was very effective as an activator of phosphorylase *b*. All of these studies on the effects of nucleotides on phosphorylase were carried out before the revelations of Jacob and Monod concerning allosterism and protein conformation and at that time were viewed simply as unexplained phenomenology. Indeed for several years Carl Cori advised against my publishing these findings unless I could explain them. Eventually, after Neil Madsen found that protamine could physically bind to phosphorylase, which was at least a step in the direction of how it might affect the activity of the enzyme, Cori let me send in my paper.

Although, as I have pointed out, knowledge with respect to the properties of phosphorylase as an enzyme increased significantly during the 1940s, it was often difficult to explain their physiological importance. This can be understood if one considers what was known about glycogen metabolism at that time. The epochal work of Leloir on the mechanism of glycogen synthesis was still to come, i.e. the role of UDG in polysaccharide synthesis and the existence of the enzyme, glycogen synthase, were completely unknown. Hence, it was believed that phosphorylase was involved in glycogen synthesis as well as in glycogenolysis (Fig. 2). It was assumed that the direction of the phosphorylase reaction would be determined by the concentrations of the components of the reaction, particularly by the concentration of inorganic phosphate. This situation obviously made it difficult to interpret findings relating to the interconversion reactions of phosphory-

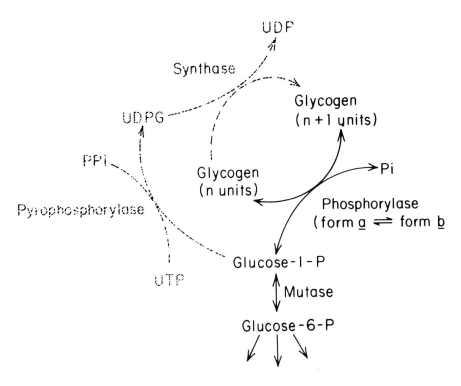

UDP

Synthase

Glycogen
(n + 1 units)

UDPG

PPi

Glycogen
(n units)

Pi

Phosphorylase
(form $\underline{a}$ ⇌ form $\underline{b}$

Pyrophosphorylase

Glucose-1-P

UTP

Mutase

Glucose-6-P

Fig. 2.Glycogen metabolism as depicted circa 1945. The stippled portion of the metabolic scheme was unknown. It was assumed that glycogen synthesis and degradation were catalyzed by phosphorylase, the direction of the reaction being determined the concentration of reaction components Within the cell phosphorylase was believed to shuttle back and forth between forms *a* and *b*, but the chemical nature of the interconversion reaction was unknown. Conversion of phosphorylase *a* to *b* had been demonstrated *in vitro*.

lase *b* and *a*. Nonetheless, in the late 1940s and the early 1950's a clear story was beginning to emerge with respect to the action of the glycogenolytic hormones, glucagon, and epinephrine and their effects on interconversion of the forms phosphorylase as studied in liver cells. Earl Sutherland, working initially in the Coris' laboratory and later independently at Western Reserve University, found that epinephrine and glucagon caused the rapid conversion of liver phosphorylase *a* to phosphorylase *b* (5), and it was also shown that epinephrine caused the same change in the muscle diaphragm (6). Inasmuch as epinephrine and glucagon were known to be glycogenolytic hormones, Sutherland's findings clearly supported the concept that the activation of phosphorylase is associated with glycogen degradation. Why then, should electrical stimulation and muscle contraction, which were also known to result in glycogenolysis, be associated with the conversion of phosphorylase *a* to the inactive form, phosphorylase *b* (4).

CONVERSION OF RABBIT SKELETAL MUSCLE PHOSPHORYLASE *b* TO PHOSPHORYLASE *a* *IN VITRO*

In Fall 1953, Ed Fischer joined the Department of Biochemistry at the University of Washington, where I was already a faculty member. As a graduate student in Geneva, Ed had worked on potato phosphorylase, and we thus shared a common interest in this particular enzyme. We discussed some of the puzzling features of phosphorylase and were particularly intrigued by the still unsolved nature of the 5'-AMP effect, i.e. how 5'AMP activates phosphorylase *b* but is seemingly unnecessary for phosphorylase *a*. It seemed worthwhile, purely as a secondary undertaking for each of us, since we both had problems that we considered as our major areas of concentration, to pool our efforts to see whether or not we could obtain information on this point. The initial experiment that we undertook together was simply to prepare pure crystalline phosphorylase *a* by the Coris' procedure (7). However, our initial attempts to do this were woefully unsuccessful. The enzyme would not crystallize, a step that was essential in order to obtain pure protein. More puzzling was the fact that the partially pure enzyme, which we did obtain, was always in the *b* form rather than the *a* form. Insofar as we could determine we had followed the Coris' procedure exactly except that we had clarified the original muscle extract by centrifugation rather than by filtration through paper. Although this seemed like a trivial change, we nonetheless included the filtration step in our next preparation. To our surprise, this time we obtained phosphorylase *a*, which crystallized readily as it was supposed to do. Two conclusions could be drawn that would explain these results. First, "resting" rabbit muscle extracts must contain phosphorylase predominantly in the *b* form rather than the *a* form as had been postulated by the Coris (4,8), and second, filtration of muscle extracts through paper must trigger conversion of phosphorylase *b* to *a* *in vitro* (9). Subsequently we found that thorough washing of the filter paper before use eliminated conversion of *b* to *a*, implying that some component in the paper must have been extracted to account for the effect. It was also found that this conversion failed to occur if the muscle extract were aged prior to filtration. The critical component from the filter paper that was required in the *b* to *a* step was shown to be calcium, and the essential component in the extract that was lost on aging was found to be ATP.

Armed with the knowledge that there is an ATP requirement for conversion of phosphorylase *b* to phosphorylase *a*, we thought it likely that we were dealing with a phosphotransferase reaction in which the terminal phosphoryl group of ATP was being transferred either to the protein itself or possibly to a nonprotein component bound to the enzyme. It soon became apparent that a "converting enzyme", which could be separated from phosphorylase *b*, was required in the reaction (10). After it had been determined that ADP, as well as phosphorylase *a* were products of the reaction (11), we spoke of this enzyme as phosphorylase *b* kinase, or simply

102

phosphorylase kinase, rather than converting enzyme (11). The nature of the Ca^{2+} requirement for the b to a reaction was not apparent immediately, but eventually it was determined by one of our graduate students, William L. Meyer, that the effect of this metal was two-fold. On the one hand Ca^{2+} was needed for the activation of a kinase activating factor, (KAF), but in addition it was. also required for the activity of phosphorylase kinase itself (12). KAF was later shown to be a Ca^{2+}-dependent protease by another student, R. Bruce Huston (13). (The current name for this protease is calpain.) We determined the stoichiometry of the phosphorylase b to phosphorylase a reaction (11) and also obtained the amino acid sequence surrounding the phosphorylated serine in phosphorylase a (14). It was demonstrated that inorganic phosphate is released in the muscle phosphorylase a to b reaction catalyzed by the PR enzyme, which could now be termed phosphorylase phosphatase. Thus, by the late 1950's, it was possible to write specific equations for the interconversion reactions of muscle phosphorylase as follows:

$$
\begin{array}{lll}
& \text{phosphorylase} & \\
& \text{kinase} & \\
\text{phosphorylase } b + 2\text{ATP} & \longrightarrow & \text{phosphorylase } a + 2\text{ADP} \\
\text{(dimer)} & & \text{(dimer)} \\
& \text{phosphorylase} & \\
& \text{phosphatase} & \\
\text{phosphorylase } a + 2\text{H}_2\text{O} & \longrightarrow & \text{phosphorylase } b + 2\text{Pi} \\
\text{(dimer)} & & \text{(dimer)}
\end{array}
$$

During the same period that our work on the muscle phosphorylase system was being carried out, very similar studies relating to liver phosphorylase were being conducted independently in the laboratory of Earl Sutherland at Western Reserve University. Sutherland's major coworkers in this effort were Walter D. Wosilait and Theodore W. Rall. In an early study (15) these investigators obtained evidence that inorganic phosphate was released when partially purified active liver phosphorylase was incubated with what they referred to as inactivating enzyme, and they also determined that phosphate was incorporated into phosphorylase when liver slices were incubated in the presence of ^{32}p phosphate. Later they showed that both of the interconversion reactions of liver phosphorylase could be demonstrated in cell free systems (16,17). A monumental "ancillary finding" that grew out of the work on liver phosphorylase by the Sutherland laboratory was, of course, the discovery of cyclic AMP, the first identified "second messenger" of hormone action (18).

It is of interest to consider whether there had been any indications that the phosphorylation and dephosphorylation of proteins might be of regulatory significance prior to elucidation of the muscle and liver phosphorylase systems. The existence of phosphoproteins had, of course, been known for many years before 1950. Phosphoproteins were classified as "conjugated proteins" and for the most part consisted of proteins of nutritional significance associated with the feeding of the young, e.g. casein of milk and several phosphoproteins found in egg yolk. Interestingly, it was also appreciated that pepsinogen contained one mole of firmly bound phosphate per mole of enzyme, but the significance of this wasn't (and still isn't) known. It was also known that nonspecific phosphatases could catalyze the release of phosphate from phosphoproteins. In an important study that was carried out at about the same time as the work on phosphorylase was underway, Burnett and Kennedy described an enzyme that catalyzed the phosphorylation of casein (19). These workers were aware of the high rate of turnover of phosphate in proteins and were the first to describe a protein kinase. In general, however, a realization that protein phosphorylation-dephosphorylation is a dynamic process affecting enzymes and important in the control of metabolism had not been forseen.

PROTEIN PHOSPHORYLATION AND THE TRANSMISSION OF EXTRACELLULAR SIGNALS

As we have seen, an interest in the mechanisms of action of epinephrine and glucagon had an important part in work on the interconversion reactions of phosphorylase (5,6), which in turn led to discovery of the dynamic phosphorylation and dephosphorylation of proteins. Going back even further, however, it can be noted that the original studies of the Coris, which led to the finding of phosphorylase itself, grew out of the longstanding interest of these investigators on the role of epinephrine in the regulation of glycogen metabolism (20). That an interest in hormone action would contribute importantly to the development of the field of protein phosphorylation-dephosphorylation was no accident, since we now know that one of the major functions of protein phosphorylation as a regulatory process is in the transmission of signals that impinge on cells. This is true not only with respect to the transduction of hormone and growth factor signals but for other types of stimuli as well. For example, as mentioned earlier, electrical stimulation of muscle leads to changes in protein phosphorylation within the cell. It is probably more than coincidental that the extent of protein phosphorylation is much greater in eukaryotic cells than it is prokaryotes, particularly in eukaryotic cells of higher animals that are subject to complex forms of external regulation.

It was apparent very early that the relative amounts of phosphorylase *b* and *a* that would be present within the cell at any particularly time would depend on the relative rates of the phosphorylase kinase and phosphatase reactions, and it was anticipated that one or both of these enzymes must be subject to regulation. Furthermore, two factors capable of influencing the balance between the two forms of phosphorylase had been found. As noted, these were calcium ions, identified as the metal ion that caused phosphorylase *a* formation in muscle extracts (9) and cyclic AMP, which promoted phosphorylase *a* formation in liver cells and homogenates (reviewed in ref. 21). We subsequently showed that cyclic AMP would also cause phosphorylase *a* formation in muscle extracts (22). In the muscle system it was determined that the effects of Ca^{2+} and cyclic AMP in stimulating phosphorylase activation *in vitro* were a result of phosphorylase kinase activation rather than phosphorylase phosphatase inhibition (11).

The coupling of muscle contraction to glycogenolysis: The finding that the major form of phosphorylase present in resting muscle is phosphorylase *b* *(8)* rather than phosphorylase *a* (4,7), together with a realization that phosphorylase *b* can be converted to phosphorylase *a* if Ca^{2+} is introduced into muscle extracts containing ATP (9), made it possible to arrive at a rational position with respect to the effect of electrical stimulation on phosphorylase. In 1956 (23) Cori was able to demonstrate that muscle contraction causes conversion of phosphorylase *b* to *a*, rather than the other way around; this was in keeping with the known effect of contraction on glycogen breakdown. The effect of Ca^{2+} on the activation of phosphorylase kinase now fits well into a scheme (Fig. 3) whereby this metal, acting as a messenger substance associated with muscle contraction, could be responsible for the coupling of glycogenolysis (an energy-yielding process) to contraction (an energy-utilizing process). Of the two different mechanisms by which Ca^{2+} could regulate phosphorylase kinase, i.e. through limited proteolysis involving KAF, or as a result of the requirement of phosphorylase kinase for Ca^{2+} per se (12), only the latter was considered to be physiologically significant. The work of Ozawa *et al.* (24), who quantified the effect of Ca^{2+} on the phosphorylase kinase reaction, was critical with respect to our understanding of this process. Many years later the actual mechanism by

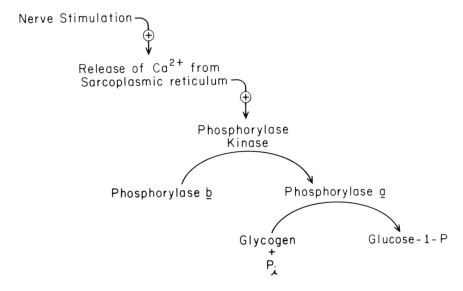

Fig. 3 The role of calcium ions in regulating glycogenolysis (circa 1962).

105

which Ca^{2+} stimulates phosphorylase kinases became apparent when it was found that calmodulin is a subunit of phosphorylase kinase (25).

The mechanism of action of cyclic AMP and the cyclic AMP-dependent protein kinase: The mechanism by which cyclic AMP causes an increase in phosphorylase kinase activity turned out to be more complex than that of Ca^{2+}. Whereas Ca^{2+} is an essential activating component in the phosphorylase *b* to *a* reaction itself, cyclic AMP causes activation of phosphorylase kinase by promoting its phosphorylation. The first clue that phosphorylation might be involved in the activation of the kinase came with the finding that ATP is required in order to observe the activation reaction and the cyclic AMP effect in rabbit skeletal muscle extracts (22). A key coworker who carried out the initial experiment that revealed this requirement was a graduate student, Donald A. Graves. Activation of muscle phosphorylase kinase was characterized by marked enhancement of its activity as measured at pH 7 or below, and only moderate increases in activity were seen when the *b* to *a* reaction was carried out at higher pH values. The ratio of activity at pH 6.8 to activity at pH 8.2 was found to serve as a useful index of the state of phosphorylase kinase activation (26). Significantly, once phosphorylase kinase had been activated by preincubation with ATP, the presence of cyclic AMP was no longer essential — as might be anticipated if the kinase were being modified covalently in an activation process stimulated by cyclic AMP (22).

Phosphorylase kinase was purified extensively and obtained as a nearly homogeneous high molecular weight protein, (Mr = 1.2 X 10^6), which still retained the ability to be activated by preincubation with MgATP in a reaction that was strongly stimulated by cyclic AMP. Although there were indications that a second protein kinase might be involved in the activation process (27), the kinetics of the reaction were complex and the work of DeLange *et al.* (28) suggested instead that an autocatalytic reaction was occurring. However, the existence of a separate "cyclic AMP-dependent phosphorylase kinase kinase", which accompanied phosphorylase kinase kinase during its purification, was eventually established by Donal A. Walsh and John P. Perkins, postdoctoral fellows in my laboratory (29). They succeeded in purifying the new kinase about 200-fold from rabbit muscle extract and separated it completely from phosphorylase kinase. The kinase was referred to as the "cyclic AMP-dependent protein kinase" rather than phosphorylase kinase kinase, because it was found (29) to have a broader specificity than would have been implied by use of the more restrictive name. In retrospect, the cyclic AMP-dependent protein kinase probably represents the same activity reported by Huijing and Larner (30) to be involved in cyclic AMP-stimulated glycogen synthase phosphorylation. The finding of a cyclic AMP-dependent protein kinase separable from phosphorylase kinase made it possible to construct a complete cascade mechanism showing the effect of epinephrine on glycogenolysis (Fig. 4). This represented the first example of a protein kinase cascade in which one protein kinase is phosphorylated and activated by another. Despite the

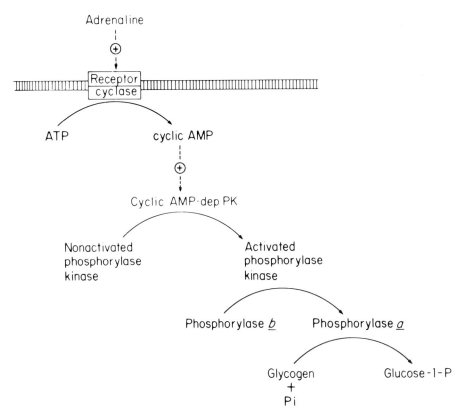

Fig. 4 The regulation of glycogenolysis by epinephrine (adrenaline).

potential usefulness of a cascade device (amplification of the signal, provision of branch points etc.) very few other examples have been reported. Recently, however, a complicated multi-step protein kinase cascade related to the action of numerous growth factors has been detected; this will be discussed at the end of this lecture.

The cyclic AMP-dependent protein kinase has served as a prototype for studies on protein kinases in general. This kinase is made up of regulatory (R) and catalytic (C) subunits and has the general structure, R_2C_2. In the next lecture Ed Fischer will speak about the mechanism by which cyclic AMP regulates the activity of the kinase. The catalytic subunit of this enzyme was the first protein kinase for which the complete amino acid sequence was determined (31), and it was also the first protein kinase to have had its X-ray crystallographic structure elucidated (32). The cyclic AMP-dependent protein kinase also played a very significant part in our understanding of protein kinase specificity, which has become increasingly important as the number of known kinases has sky rocketed. Although it will not be possible to do more than touch on this latter topic here, it can be noted that the cyclic AMP-dependent protein kinase was the first kinase for which a "consensus" phosphorylation site sequence was clearly recognized (33-37). This sequence, Arg-Arg-X-Ser-X, is found in many, but not all,

107

substrates for the cyclic AMP-dependent protein kinase. In connection with the specificty studies that were carried out within my own laboratory, I would like to call particular attention to the work of David B. Bylund and Bruce E. Kemp.

A protein serine/threonine kinase cascade activated in response to insulin and related growth factors: One of the enduring problems in endocrinology has been the question of the mechanism of action of insulin. Indeed, investigators have been interested in this area for decades, and over the years information on this subject gradually accumulated through the application of whatever tools became available. At first, experiments were carried out with intact animals, later with perfused organs, eventually with isolated tissues such as the muscle diaphragm, and finally with cells in culture. Until comparatively recently it had not been possible, however, to demonstrate a meaningful insulin response in homogenates or other types of cell-free system. Approximately ten years ago, however, it was found that the EGF receptor is a protein tyrosine kinase, and shortly after that it was determined that this is also true for the insulin receptor (38,39). Now it is known that eight or nine different growth factor receptors are protein tyrosine kinases. These findings ushered in a new era of research with respect to insulin and related hormones or growth factors. However, although most workers in the field felt that it would now be a simple matter to identify meaningful substrates for these receptor/kinases, and to elucidate the complete intracellular signal transduction pathway involved, this did not occur. Several tyrosine-phosphorylated proteins were found in cells treated with insulin or the other growth factors, but none of these proteins could at first be readily connected with the known cellular actions of the growth factors involved. Nonetheless, it was clearly demonstrated that the protein tyrosine kinase activity of these receptors was essential for their action, and there was little if any doubt that initiation of their signals must involve ligand-stimulated tyrosine phosphorylation.

An investigator who is interested in determining the steps of a signal transduction pathway can either work "downstream" from a receptor in order to identify components of the pathway, or he can work "upstream" toward the receptor starting with a well established cellular effect of the growth factor in question. A number of laboratories, including my own, which are interested in signaling from the insulin or related receptors, have used the latter strategy in their approach. The particular cellular effect that these groups have chosen as their starting point has been the activation of protein serine and threonine kinases, which results from the simulation of tyrosine kinases. It has long been known that the stimulation of protein tyrosine kinases in cells results in changes in serine/threonine phosphorylation as well as in changes in tyrosine phosphorylation, but the mechanism involved in the coupling of the two types of protein phosphorylation has been unknown (40).

One of the cellular proteins that is readily phosphorylated on serine residues in response to the stimulation of receptors having protein tyrosine kinase activity is ribosomal protein S6, although the role of this phosphory-lation insofar as the regulation of protein synthesis is not clear. This phenomenon had been discovered a number of years ago, prior to the involvement of my own laboratory in the problem, and a good start had already been made in identifying components involved in regulating S6 phosphorylation. For example, it had been shown that in adipocytes or Swiss 3T3 cells stimulated by insulin an S6 kinase becomes activated (41,42) and there was good evidence that the activation was due to covalent modifi-cation, i.e. phosphorylation. It was determined that the protein serine/threonine phosphatases would inactivate the activated (43,44). Maller and coworkers had shown that an S6 Kinase (S6 Kinase II), purified to homo-geneity from *Xenopus laevis* eggs, could also be inactivated by protein phosphatases (45). Importantly, this latter S6 kinase could be reactivated by a different protein serine/threonine kinase, microtubule-associated protein 2 kinase (MAP kinase), which was known to be stimulated by insulin treat-ment of 3T3 Ll cells (46). These results strongly suggested the existence of a protein serine/threonine kinase cascade in which one growth factor-activat-ed protein kinase phosphorylated and activated a second protein kinase. Gregory *el al.* (47) confirmed these findings using a phosphatase-treated S6 kinase from rabbit liver and MAP kinase from insulin-stimulated Rat 1 HIRc B cells. Then in this laboratory we showed that an EGF or insulin-stimulated MAP kinase from Swiss 3T3 cells could phosphorylate and activate an S6 kinase obtained from this same cell type (48). MAP kinase, in its active form, appeared to have been activated as a result of serine/threo-nine phosphorylation, since it could be inactivated by protein phosphatase 2A. This suggested the existence of even a third protein serine/threonine kinase in this growth factor-stimulated process.

A finding of major significance from Sturgill's laboratory was the fact that MAP kinase in its active form contains phosphotyrosine as well as phos-phothreonine, and that in addition to being inactivated by protein phospha-tase 2A, it can also be inactivated by CD45, a protein tyrosine phosphatase (49). These investigators went on to show that phosphorylation of MAP kinase on tyrosine and threonine is essential for its activity, and it seemed likely that two different types of protein kinase, i.e. a protein serine/threo-nine kinase and a protein tyrosine kinase, would be involved as upstream components involved in its activation. There was no evidence, however, that a receptor-type protein tyrosine kinase could serve as either one of these kinases. It was thus of great interest to search for an enzyme or enzymes, MAP kinase kinases, that would catalyze MAP kinase phosphorylation and activation.

In this laboratory Natalie Ahn *et al.* (50) discovered two separable activa-ting factors from Swiss 3T3 cells that catalyzed the activation of an inactive form of MAP kinase *in vitro*. Each of these factors required the presence of MgATP in order to bring about activation of MAP kinase, and it did not matter whether the latter had first been inactivated by a protein serine/threonine phosphatase or by a protein tyrosine phosphatase. This made it appear probable that the factors were "dual specificity" kinases capable of phosphorylating proteins or serine and threonine residues as well as tyrosine residues. The existence of dual specificity had, in fact, been found in yeast. At first we hesitated to call the activating factors "MAP kinase kinases", because in work carried out by Rony Seger et al. (51) we had determined that MAP kinase can undergo a slow but distinct autophosphorylation reaction, i.e. that it can catalyze its own phosphorylation, and that in this reaction threonine and tyrosine residues are phosphorylated. Moreover, autophosphorylation resulted in activation of the kinase. This result made it appear possible that a MAP kinase kinase as such might be unnecessary and that the next upstream component could be a protein factor that simulated autophosphorylation. Eventually it was shown, however, that the MAP kinase activating factors were, in fact, protein kinases capable of phosphorylating a mutant form of MAP kinase that lacked enzymic activity (52,53). Moreover, amino acid sequence data obtained in our laboratory and elsewhere, showed that the activating factors contain protein kinase amino acid sequence motifs. Later, similar "activators", i.e. MAP kinase kinases, were found in PC12 cell stimulated by nerve growth factor or bradykinin (54,55). Gomez and Cohen showed that activated MAP kinase kinase could be inactivated by a protein serine/threonine phospha-

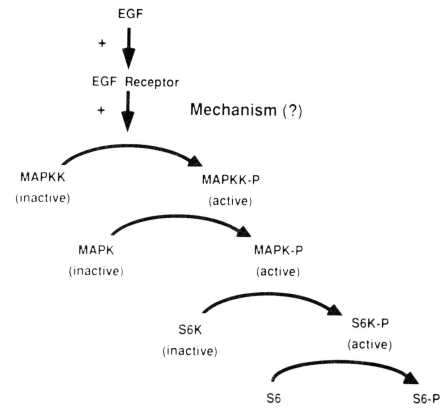

Fig. 5 The MAP kinase cascade.

tase but was not affected by protein tyrosine phosphatases (54). This latter result indicated that an additional upstream protein serine/threonine kinase, i.e. a MAP kinase kinase kinase, was probably a component of the pathway. The present status of the MAP kinase cascade, without the putative MAP kinase kinase kinase, is shown in Fig. 5.

Intense effort on the part of many different laboratories is currently centered on the question of the identity of MAP kinase kinase kinase and the mechanism by which such an enzyme might be regulated. It was reported by Kyriakis *et al.* that Raf-1 activates MAP kinase kinase and thus might itself be a candidate for the kinase kinase kinase (56). This result was confirmed by Dent *et al.* (57). Other studies have implicated the possibility that cdc2 might be an upstream component of the MAP kinase cascade but not an immediate kinase kinase kinase itself (58). Finally, there is considerable evidence that p21 ras is a component acting at some site between the receptor and the components of the cascade as currently identified (59 – 62). A somewhat neglected area of study with respect to the MAP kinase cascade relates to the question of its precise function and the reasons for the existence of such a complicated scheme. It is probable that numerous substrates may exist for each of the protein kinases in the cascade, and in this connection it is noteworthy that a number of transcription factors appear to be targeted by MAP kinase and by the S6 kinase. The different kinases may also have specific metabolic enzyme targets that have not as yet been identified. Finally, some of the kinases may branch off and regulate still other kinases (63).

CONCLUSION

In this talk I have reviewed the early work on the interconversion reactions of the two forms of glycogen phosphorylase and phosphorylase kinase. A third enzyme that played an important part in early work on protein phosphorylation-dephosphorylation was glycogen synthase. Much of the original research on that enzyme was carried out by Joseph Larner and his associates during the early 1960s. These investigators found that, in contrast to the effect of phosphorylation on phosphorylase and phosphorylase kinase, phosphorylation caused a decrease in the activity of the synthase. Because the "field" of protein phosphorylation during the first ten years was dominated by those interested in glycogen metabolism, some even expressed the idea that perhaps regulation of enzymes by phosphorylation-dephosphorylation might be restricted to this area. However, the finding of a multifunctional cyclic AMP-dependent protein kinase, which was almost immediately shown by Kuo and Greengard (64) to be very widespread in nature, served to change this concept. Another important finding that dispelled the idea that protein phosphorylation was very limited in scope was the report that pyruvate dehydrogenase is regulated by phosphorylation (65). As can be noted in Fig. 6, the number of enzymes reported to undergo regulation as a result of this being phosphorylated started growing precipi-

Enzymes Reported to Undergo Phosphorylation – Dephosphorylation

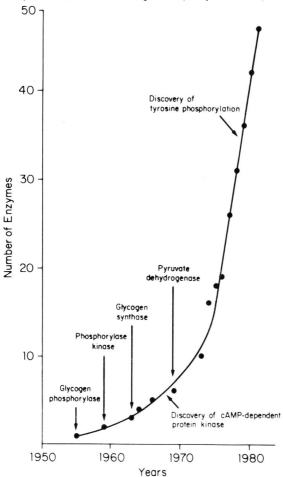

Fig. 6 *Growth in an awareness of protein phosphorylation as a mechanism for regulating enzymes.* The total number of enzymes reported to undergo phosphorylation dephosphorylation as a function of time is plotted against years.

tously in 1970. If reports on protein phosphorylation involving nonenzymic proteins were included, the growth curve in Fig. 6 would be even steeper. In the next talk Ed Fischer will trace some of the developments that have contributed to this explosion. I anticipate that he may also "correct" some of the errors that I may have made in my historical account of our work together.

ACKNOWLEDGMENTS

I would like to dedicate this lecture to my parents who had the education of their children as a major goal in their lives and to my wife, Deedy, who has always been extremely supportive of my work. In addition, I recognize the very important contributions made by numerous talented unnamed students and postdoctoral fellows, some but not all of whom I have mentioned in this article, who carried out the actual experiments reported here and in addition helped to provide direction for many of the studies that are reported.

REFERENCES

1. Cori, C.(1939) *Cold Spring Harbor Symposia on Quantitative Biology,* Vol. VII, p. 260 – 268.
2. Cori, G. T. and Green, A. A. (1945) *J. Biol. Chem.* **158,** 321 – 332.
3. Cori, G. T. and Cori, C F. (1943) *J. Biol. Chem.,* **151,** 31 – 38.
4. Cori, G. T. (1945) *J. Biol. Chem.,* **158,** 333 – 339.
5. Sutherland, E. W. and Cori, C. F. (1951) *J. Biol. Chem.,* **188,** 531 – 543.
6. Sutherland, F. W.(1950) Recent Progress in Hormone Research, Proceedings of the Laurentian Hormone Conference, Vol. 5, Academic Press, New York, p. 441463.
7. Green, A. A. and Cori, G. T. (1943) *J. Biol. Chem.,* **151,** 21 – 29.
8. Krebs, E. G. and Fischer, E. H. (1955) *J. Biol. Chem.,* **216,** 113 – 120.
9. Fischer, F. H. and Krebs, E. G. (1955) *J. Biol. Chem.,* 216, 121 – 132.
10. Krebs, E. G. and Fischer, E. H. (1956) *Biochim. Biophys. Acta,* **20,** 150 – 157.
11. Krebs, E. G., Kent, A. B. and Fischer, E. H. (1958) *J. Biol. Chem.,* **231,** 78 – 83.
12. Meyer, W. L., Fischer, E. H. and Krebs, F. G. (1964) *Biochemistry,* **3,** 1033 – 1039.
13. Huston, R. B. and Krebs, E. G. (1968) *Biochemistry,* **7,** 2116 – 2122.
14. Fischer, E. H., Graves, D. J., Crittenden, E. R. S. and Krebs, E. G. (1959) *J. Biol. Chem.,* **234,** 1698 – 1704.
15. Sutherland, E. W. and Wosilait, W. D. (1955) *Nature,* **175,** 169.
16. Rall, T. W., Sutherland, E. W. and Wosilait, W. D. (1956) *J. Biol. Chem.,* 218,
17. Wosilait, W. D. (1958) *J. Biol. Chem.* **233,** 597.
18. Sutherland, E. W. and Rall, T. W. (1958) *J. Biol. Chem.,* **233,** 1077 – 1091.
19. Burnett, G. and Kennedy, E. P. (1954) *J. Biol. Chem.,* **211,** 969 – 988.
20. Cori, C. F. and Cori, G. T. (1928) *J. Biol. Chem.,* **79,** 309 – 355.
21. Sutherland, E. W. (1962) *The Harvey Lectures, Series 57,* Academic Press, New York, p. 17 – 33.
22. Krebs, E. G., Graves, D. J. and Fischer, E. H. (1959) *J. Biol. Chem.* 234:2867 – 2873.
23. Cori, C. F. in O. H. Gaebler, ed., Enzymes: *Units of Biological Structure and Function,* Academic Press, New York, 1956, p. 573.
24. Ozawa, E., Hosoi, K., and Ebashi, S. (1967) *J. Biochem.* **61,** 531 – 533.
25. Grand, R. J. A., Shenolikar, S. and Cohen, P. (1981) *Eur. J. Biochem.* **113,** 359 – 367.
26. Posner, J. B., Stern, R. and Krebs, E. G. (1965) *J. Biol. Chem.,* **240,** 982 – 985.
27. Krebs, E. G., DeLange, R. J., Kemp, R. G. and Riley, W. D. (1966) *Pharmacol. Rev.,* **18,** 163 – 171.
28. DeLange, R. J., Kemp, R. G., Riley, W. D., Cooper, R. A. and Krebs, E. G. (1968) *J. Biol. Chem.,* **243,** 2200 – 2208.
29. Walsh, D. A., Perkins, J. P. and Krebs, E. G. (1968) *J. Biol. Chem.,* **243,** 3763 – 3765.
30. Huijing, F. and Larner, J. (1966) *Biochem. and Biophs. Res. Commun.,* **23,** 259 – 263.

31. Shoji, S., Parmelee, D. C., Wade, R. D., Kumar, S., Ericsson, L H., Walsh, K. A., Neurath, H., Long, G. L., DeMaille, J. G., Fischer, E. H. and Titani, K. (1981) Proc. Natl. Acad. Sci. USA, **78**, 848−851.

32. Knighton, D. R., Zheng, J., Eyck, L. F. T., Ashford, V. A., Xuong, N.-H., Taylor, S. S. and Sowadski, J. M. (1991) *Science*, **253**, 407−414.

33. Kemp, B. E., Bylund, D. B., Huang, T. S. and Krebs, E. G. (1975) *Proc. Natl. Acad. Sci. USA*, **72**, 3448−3452.

34. Humble, E., Berglund, L., Titanji, V., Ljunstrom, O., Edlund, B., Zetterquist, O. and Engstrom, L. (1975) *Biochem. Biophys. Res. Commun.* **66**, 614−621.

35. Daile, P., Carnegie, P. R. and Young, J. D. (1975) Nature, 257, 416−418.

36. Zetterquist, O., Ragnarsson, U., Humble, E., Berglund, L. and Engstrom, L. (1976) *Biochem. Biophys. Res. Commun.* **70**, 696−703.

37. Kemp, B. E., Graves, D. J., Benjamini, E. and Krebs, E. G. (1977) *J. Biol. Chem.*, **252**, 4888−4894.

38. Cohen, S., Carpenter, G. and King, L. E., Jr. (1980) *J. Biol. Chem.*, **255**, 4834−4842.

39. Kasuga, M., Zick, Y., Blithe, D. L.., Karlsson, F. A., Haring, H. U., and Kahn, C. R. (1982) J. Biol. Chem., 257, 9891−9894.

40. Denton, R. M. (1986) *Advances in Cyclic Nucleotide and Protein Phosphorylation Research* (P. Greengard and G. A. Robinson, Eds.) Raven Press, New York, p. 293−341.

41. Cobb, M. H. and Rosen, O. M. (1982) *J. Biol. Chem.*, **258**, 12472−12481.

42. Novak-Hofer, I., and Thomas, G. (1984) *J. Biol. Chem.*, **259**, 5995−6000.

43. Ballou, L. M., Jeno, P. and Thomas, G. (1988) *J. Biol. Chem.*, **263**, 1188−1194.

44. Ballou, L. M., Siegmann, M. and Thomas, G. (1988) *Proc. Natl. Acad. Sci. USA*, **85**, 7154−7158.

45. Andres, J. L. and Maller, J. L. (1989) *J. Biol. Chem.*, **264**, 151−156.

46. Sturgill, T. W., Ray, L. B., Erickson, E. and Maller, J. L. (1988) *Nature*, **334**, 715−718.

47. Gregory, J. S., Boulton, T. G., Sang, B.-C., and Cobb, M. H. (1989) *J. Biol. Chem.*, **264**, 18, 397−18, 401.

48. Ahn, N. G. and Krebs, E. G. (1990) *J. Biol. Chem.*, **265**, 11495−11501.

49. Anderson, N. G., Maller, J. L., Tonks, N. K., and Sturgill, T. W. (1990) *Nature*, **343**, 651−653.

50. Ahn, N. G., Seger, R., Bratlien, R. L., Diltz, C. D., Tonks, N.K. and Krebs, E. G. (1991) *J. Biol. Chem.*, **266**, 4220−4227.

51. Seger, R., Ahn, N. G., Boulton, T. G., Yancopoulos, G. D., Panayotatos, N., Radziejewska, E., Ericsson, L., Bratlien, R. L., Cobb, M. H. and Krebs, E. G. (1991) *Proc. Natl. Acad. Sci. USA*, **88**, 6142−6146,

52. Posada, J. and Cooper, J. A. (1992), *Science*, **255**, 212−215.

53. Seger, R., Ahn, N. G., Posada, J., Munar, E. S., Jensen, A. M., Cooper, J. A., Cobb, M. H., and Krebs, E. G. (1992) *J. Biol. Chem.*, **267**, 14373−14381.

54. Gomez, N. and Cohen, P. (1991) *Nature*, **351**, 69−72.

55. Ahn, N. G., Robbins, D. J., Haycock, J. W., Seger, R., Cobb, M. H., and Krebs, E. G. (1992) *J. Neurochemistry*, 147−156.

56. Kyriakis, J. M., App, H., Zhang, X., Banerjee, P., Brautigan, D. L., Rapp, U. R., Avruch, J. (1992) *Nature*, **358**, 417−421.

57. Dent, P., Haser, W., Haystead, T. A. J., Vincent, L. A., Roberts, T. M., Sturgill, T. W. (1992) *Science*, **257**, 1404−1406.

58. Matsuda, S., Kosako, H., Takenaka, K., Moriyama, K., Sakai, H., Akiyama, T., Gotoh, Y., Nishida, E. (1992) *EMBO J.*, **11**, 973−982.

59. Thomas, S. M., DeMarco, M., D'Arcangelo, G., Halegoua, S., Brugge, J. S. (1992) *Cell*, **68**, 1031−1040.

60. Wood, K. W., Sarnecki, C., Roberts, T. M., Blenis, J. (1992) *Cell*, **68**, 1041−1050.

61. deVries-Smits, A. M. M., Burgering, B. M. T., Leevers, S. J., Marshall, C. J., Bos, J. L. (1992) *Nature,* **357,** 602−604.
62. Robbins, D. J., Cheng, M., Zhen, E., Vanderbilt, C. A., Feig, L. A., Cobb, M. H. (1992) *Proc. Natl. Acad. Sci. USA,* **89,** 6924−6928.
63. Stokoe, D., Campbell, D. G., Nakielny, S., Hidaka, H., Leevers, S. J., Marshall, C. and Cohen, P. (1992) *EMBO J.,* **11,** 3985−3994.
64. Kuo, J. F. and Greengard, P. (1969) *J. Biol. Chem.,* **244,** 3417−3419.
65. Linn, T. C., Pettit, F. H., Hucho, F. and Reed, L. J. (1969a) *Proc. Natl. Acad. Sci. USA,* **64,** 227−234.

EDMOND H. FISCHER

Memories of my early childhood are clouded with uncertainties because I was essentially separated from my parents since the early age of seven. I was born in Shanghai, China on April 6, 1920. My father had come there from Vienna, Austria after earning doctorates in law and business. My mother, born Renée Tapernoux, had arrived from France with her parents via Hanoi. Her father had left Switzerland as a young man to become a journalist for L'Aurore. This journal published the letter by Emile Zola entitled "J'accuse" in which he denounced the government cover-up during the Affaire Dreyfus which tore France apart at the turn of the century. When the case against Dreyfus collapsed in the early 1900s my grandfather left for French Indochina, then called le Tonkin. He later went to Shanghai where he founded the "Courrier de Chine", the first French newspaper published in China. He also helped to establish "l'Ecole Municipale Française" where I first went to school.

At age 7, my parents sent my two older brothers and me to La Châtaigneraie, a large Swiss boarding school overlooking Lake Geneva. My oldest brother, Raoul, was the first to leave to attend the ETH, the Swiss Federal Polytechnical Institute in Zürich where he was awarded a degree in engineering. My brother Georges went to Oxford and read law.

In 1935, I entered Geneva's all boys Collège de Calvin from which I obtained my Maturité Fédérale four years later, even as the specter of World War II loomed evermore menacing. While in school, I formed a lifelong friendship with my classmate Wilfried Haudenschild who dazzled me with his tinkering abilities, off-the-wall ideas and mechanical inventiveness. Together we decided that one of us should go into the Sciences and the other into Medicine so that we could cure all the ills of the world.

Another important event marked my High School days: I was admitted to the Geneva Conservatory of Music. I had heard Johnny Aubert give an unforgettable rendition of Beethoven's 5th Piano Concerto. I decided on the spot that I wanted to study with him. After an audition in which I nervously presented Mendelssohn's Rondo Capriccioso and Chopin's A-maj. Polonaise, he took me on, and that spelled the beginning of many enthralling years. Music had always played an important part in my life, to such an extent that I even wondered whether I should not make a career of it. But finally I thought it better to keep music purely for pleasure.

It was my goal to become a microbiologist but Fernand Chodat, the Professeur of Bacteriology, argued that there was little future in that field, which was probably the case in Switzerland at that time. He advised me to get a diploma in Chemistry saying that, in any case, test tubes were of more use than a microscope to modern microbiologists.

I therefore entered the School of Chemistry just at the start of World War II. Two years of quantitative inorganic analyses seemed endless. Organic chemistry finally arrived like a breath of fresh air, if not a reprieve on life. I earned two Licences ès Sciences, one in Biology, the other in Chemistry and, two years later, the Diploma of "Ingénieur Chimiste". For my thesis, I elected to work with Prof. Kurt H. Meyer, Head of the Department of Organic Chemistry. "Le Patron" as we affectionately called him, was a most impressive person. At the time when most scientists showed little understanding of natural high polymers, Kurt Meyer had already authored several books on the subject, starting with the epochal "Meyer-Mark: Der Aufbau der hochpolymeren organischen Naturstoffe" and "Makromolekulare Chemie". His main interest lay in the structure of polysaccharides, particularly starch and glycogen. To unravel the structure of these molecules, enzymes were needed: α- and β-amylases, phosphorylase, etc. Therefore, the lab was divided into two groups: the enzymologists under the guidance of Peter Bernfeld and carbohydrate chemists under Roger Jeanloz. I decided to work on the purification of hog pancreas amylase. Within a couple of years, we succeeded in crystallizing α-amylase from pork pancreas and soon after that, from a variety of other sources including human pancreas and saliva, two strains of *A. oryzae*, *B. subtilis* and *P. saccharophila*. It is at that time that Eric A. Stein joined the laboratory, beginning a marvelous 15-year collaboration and a lifelong friendship.

It had always been my intention to go to the United States to pursue my studies in Biochemistry. In those days, that field was in its infancy in most European universities to such an extent that I was asked to present the very first course in Enzymology as a Privat Docent at the University of Geneva in 1950. Two events hastened my departure for the USA: the untimely death of Kurt Meyer following an asthma attack and my being abruptly issued a US immigration visa. Apparently, the US consulates abroad were clearing their files before the complicated McCarran Act would come into effect. I had decided to go to CalTech on a Swiss Post-doctoral Fellowship that Professor Paul Karrer succeeded in securing for me on a moment's notice. Some friends who knew of my arrival in New York had arranged for me to give some seminars on my way to Pasadena: Maria Fuld at Pittsburgh and Henry Lardy at Madison. To my utter surprise, I was offered a job in both places. Then, upon my arrival at CalTech I found a letter from Hans Neurath, Chairman of the Department of Biochemistry at the University of Washington, inviting me to come to Seattle, apparently for the same purpose. I thought that the Americans had to be crazy since at that time, academic positions in Europe were one-in-a-million. I visited Seattle with my wife and thought that the surrounding mountains, forests and lakes were beautiful, reminiscent of Switzerland. The Medical School was brand-new and when I was offered an Assistant Professorship, I accepted and have never regretted that decision.

There were only seven of us on the faculty and we quickly became close friends. I remember the amused expressions of my colleagues seated in the back row of the class listening to my fractured English when lecturing the medical students. I also remember Ed Krebs' broad smile whenever I lapsed into French. What Ed didn't realize, though, is that within two years, while my English didn't improve very much, his deteriorated completely!

Within six months of my arrival, Ed Krebs and I started to work together on glycogen phosphorylase. He had been a student of the Cori's in St. Louis. They believed that AMP had to serve some kind of co-factor function for that enzyme. In Geneva, on the other hand, we had purified potato phosphorylase for which there was no AMP requirement. Even though essentially no information existed at that time on the evolutionary relationship of proteins, we knew that enzymes, whatever their origin, used the same co-enzymes to catalyze identical reactions. It seemed unlikely, therefore, that muscle phosphorylase would require AMP as a co-factor but not potato phosphorylase. We decided to try to elucidate the role of this nucleotide in the phosphorylase reaction. Of course, we never found out what AMP was doing: that problem was solved 6-7 years later when Jacques Monod proposed his allosteric model for the regulation of enzymes. But what we stumbled on was another quite unexpected reaction: i.e. that muscle phosphorylase was regulated by phosphorylation-dephosphorylation. This is yet another example of what makes fundamental research so attractive: one knows where one takes off but one never knows where one will end up.

These were very exciting years when just about every experiment revealed something new and unexpected. At first we worked alone in a small, single laboratory with stone sinks. Experiments were planned the night before and carried out the next day. We worked so closely together that whenever one of us had to leave the laboratory in the middle of an experiment, the other would carry on without a word of explanation. Ed Krebs had a small group that continued his original work, determining the structure and function of DPNH-X, a derivative of NADH. I was still studying the α-amylases with Eric Stein. In collaboration with Bert Vallee, we were able to demonstrate that these enzymes were in reality calcium-containing metalloproteins.

In those days, we waited all year for the next Federation Meeting or Gordon Conference. It was an occasion for me to get together with my friends on the East Coast: Herb and Eva Sober and Chris and Flossie Anfinsen from NIH, Bill and Inge Harrington from Johns Hopkins, Bert and Kuggie Vallee from the Brigham and Al and Lee Meister, then at Tufts and later at Cornell, and many others. I have forgotten much about the meetings themselves. There was the excitement of hearing about the latest breakthroughs, the frantic preparations for talks that had to be given, and the numerous notebooks filled with information, questions and problems that had to be solved. I will never forget, though, the marvelous time we had together speaking far into the night about anything and everything. Some of these friends are gone today but their memory is still vivid.

I have two sons, François and Henri, from my first wife Nelly Gagnaux, a Swiss National who died in 1961. I married my present wife Beverley née Bullock from Eureka, California, in 1963. She has a daughter Paula from a first marriage. All three of our children are now married and my two sons each has a son.

I received the Werner Medal from the Swiss Chemical Society, the Lederle Medical Faculty Award; the Prix Jaubert from the University of Geneva and, jointly with Ed Krebs, the Senior Passano Award and the Steven C. Beering Award from Indiana University. I received Doctorates Honoris Causa from the University of Montpellier, France and the University of Basel, Switzerland and was elected to the American Academy of Arts and Sciences in 1972 and to the National Academy of Sciences in 1973.

PROTEIN PHOSPHORYLATION AND CELLULAR REGULATION, II

Nobel Lecture, December 8, 1992

by

EDMOND H. FISCHER

Department of Biochemistry, SJ-70, University of Washington, Seattle, WA 98195, USA.

In the talk he just gave, Ed Krebs retraced for you the early history of glycogen phosphorylase and its regulation by reversible phosphorylation. In retrospect, we were extraordinarily lucky in more ways than one to have selected this particular enzyme to work on. First, it is extremely abundant in skeletal muscle so that material was never limiting. In fact, when 20 years later, we undertook its total amino acid sequence with Ko Titani and Ken Walsh (1), we used no less than 10 grams of the crystalline enzyme to complete the analysis. Second, the phosphorylation reaction was unambiguous, converting a totally inactive enzyme into a fully active species. Third, the phosphorylation ran to completion, introducing 1 mole of phosphate per mole of enzyme subunit. Fourth, only one site became phosphorylated; and fifth, this site occurred within a loose N-terminal arm of the molecule that could be easily cleaved by limited proteolysis, leaving behind the bulk of the enzyme intact. This made it easy to separate the phosphopeptide and determine its structure (2), though it took a long time since in the mid fifties sequences had to be carried out by paper chromatography. We could show that a single seryl residue had been phosphorylated (Fig. 1). Incidentally, it took another five years to extend this sequence by 9 residues (3). The longer structure showed the presence of several positive charges, mainly upstream, and forming those recognition motifs whose significance became apparent only later (4,5).

Fig. 1: Sequence of the site phosphorylated during the phosphorylase b to a reaction.

The phosphorylation reaction was so straightforward and simple that there was no doubt in our minds that it would represent the prototype for such kinds of interconversions. As it turned out, it was really the exception. Six years went by before Joe Larner identified the next enzyme to be regulated by phosphorylation-dephosphorylation, namely, glycogen synthase (6). He found that this enzyme was inactivated rather than activated by phosphorylation (7), which made sense: closing off the backward reaction when the forward one is turned on guarantees that there would be no recycling of the system that would inevitably result in a useless expenditure of energy. Joe Larner rapidly found, however, that far more than one phosphate was introduced during the interconversion (8); about six per mole of synthase. At that time, the idea that a single phosphorylation event was all that was needed to alter the state of activity of an enzyme was so ingrained that I remember that we thought: "How can this be possible? It would imply that glycogen synthase is made up of 6 identical subunits, each of approximately 15,000 MW." And Joe Larner himself thought along these lines (8,9). Of course, we know today from his work as well as that of Phil Cohen (10), Peter Roach (11) and others, that the enzyme is phosphorylated on no less than seven sites by seven different protein kinases, all totally unknown at that time (Fig. 2). Furthermore, some of these phosphorylation events follow a most complicated program of successive reactions that have to proceed in a strictly prescribed order. The enzyme is inhibited by phosphorylation by glycogen synthase kinase 3 (or GSK-3) but not until a first phosphate is introduced by casein kinase 2 (CK-2). This then allows phosphorylation of the next residue, then the next and the next after that until all sites are finally occupied (12). Imagine the incredible difficulties we would have encountered had we decided to study this enzyme rather than phosphorylase.

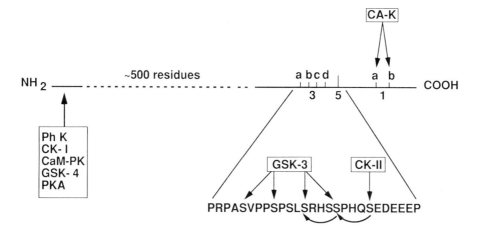

Fig. 2: Major phosphorylation sites in glycogen synthase. PhK, phosphorylase kinase; CK casein kinase; CaM-PK, multifunctional calcium/calmodulin-dependent kinase; GSK, glycogen synthase kinase; PKA or CA-K, cAMP-dependent protein kinase (from P. Roach).

We did not know at that time whether the phosphorylation reaction was a unique occurrence, a rare event restricted to the control of these two enzymes or perhaps to carbohydrate metabolism. It was well known, for example, that during glycogenolysis, inorganic phosphate was picked up from the medium and used for the production of many sugar phosphate intermediates. Could nitrogen metabolism be regulated by another type of covalent modification, for instance, amidation/deamidation, or lipid metabolism by acetylation/deacetylation? Or had we discovered a more general type of reaction that would apply widely to many different systems. Once again, as luck would have it, reversible protein phosphorylation turned out to be one of the most widespread mechanisms by which cellular processes can be regulated (13,14).

Allosteric and Covalent Regulation
Here, a question should be raised. Ed Krebs already told you that phosphorylase could also be activated by AMP. Why are two mechanisms required to control the activity of an enzyme when, in both cases, they lead to an active conformation (Fig. 3)? According to the allosteric model proposed by Jacques Monod in the early 1960s, the enzyme responds to effectors that are generated during the normal maintenance of the cell and reflect its overall internal condition: whether it is proliferating or quiescent, actively metabolizing or not, its energy balance, i.e., its ratio of AMP to ATP, etc. According to the rule that enzymes are subjected to end-product or feedback inhibition, phosphorylase would be expected to be inhibited by G6P that accumulates during its reaction, and by ATP, the ultimate end product of carbohydrate metabolism. By the same token, it would be activated by AMP as indeed it is. But then, many enzymes of carbohydrate metabolism would be similarly affected by the same effectors; in proceeding down the metabolic path, all these "doors" would become open at the same time. By contrast, the kinase reaction is highly specific: it allows the activation of phosphorylase only without affecting the activity of any other enzyme.

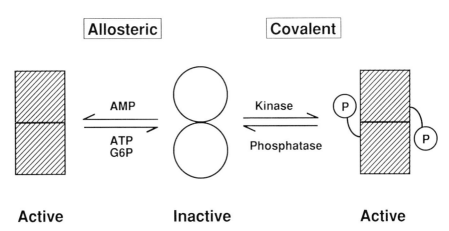

Fig. 3: Allosteric and covalent regulation of phosphorylase.

Furthermore, and this is perhaps one of the major lessons we have learned over the last 30 years, covalent regulation responds mainly to extracellular signals (Fig. 4). These external signals come in the form of hormones, or neurotransmitters, growth factors and other stimuli such as drugs, light, odorants, and perhaps touch in plants. Each will act on its own membrane receptor and either cause the release of second messengers (cA, cG, Ca2+, DAG, IP3, etc.) in reactions regulated by G-proteins, or induce the intrinsic tyrosine kinase activity of the receptors themselves. These second messengers or internal signals will act on kinases or phosphatases, then on target enzymes to finally elicit a physiological response. One finds here all the elements of a cascade system such as those described by Ed Krebs earlier: enzymes acting on enzymes, resulting in the enormous amplification of an external signal. In addition, it allows the coordinate regulation of different physiological events through the pleiotropic action of some of the enzymes involved.

The Protein Kinases

Today, one knows several hundred protein kinases that can be classified according to their mode of regulation or substrate specificity (15) (Table I). Among the large family of Ser/Thr kinases, some are dependent on the second messengers mentioned above, others on specific components of the system that they are called upon to regulate. Such is the case of the heme-regulated kinase that blocks the initiation of globin synthesis when heme or iron comes to be missing, or the double-stranded RNA-dependent kinase that is induced by interferon in cells under viral attack. There are the so-called "independent kinases" such as the casein kinases for which no precise mode of control has been elucidated as yet.

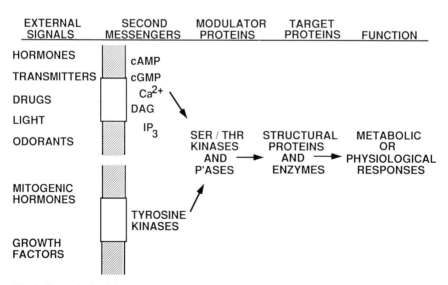

Fig. 4: Control of cellular processes by protein phosphorylation. Cascade systems triggered by extracellular stimuli.

Next come the mixed function kinases that can phosphorylate their substrates on both tyrosine or serine/threonine, or that can be regulated by tyrosine and serine/threonine phosphorylation. This is the case for the enzymes that Ed Krebs has just described (16): MAP kinase, the MAP kinase kinase, perhaps Raf, or the cell cycle kinases such as p34cdc2 (17). They stand guard at crucial crossroads of signal transduction. They form the link between a signaling system that originates at the membrane level and relies on tyrosine phosphorylation, and the more widespread serine/threonine phosphorylation reactions that occur downstream. Their dual control and specificity would ensure that no accidental initiation of important cellular events occurs at inappropriate times, just as one would need two keys to get access to a safety deposit box.

Finally, there is the large class of tyrosine kinases which will be discussed later. Not listed are the less common histidine kinases such as those involved in bacterial chemotaxis (18) and the double-headed kinase/phosphatase that regulates bacterial isocitrate dehydrogenase (19).

Regulation of Protein Kinases

All these enzymes have homologous catalytic domains but vary greatly in the structure of their regulatory segments. They have consensus sequences,

I. Second Messenger-dependent Ser / Thr Kinases

    A. Cyclic Nucleotides: cAMP, cGMP PKs
    B. Ca^{2+}/ CaM : Phos. Kinase, MLCK, CaM Kinase II
    C. DAG / Ca^{2+}: PKC

II. Second Messenger-independent Ser / Thr PKs

    A. Heme-, ds RNA-, (INF) - dep. eIF2 Kinases
    B. CK-I, CK-II, GSK-3, S6 Kinases

III. Dual Specifity (Ser / Thr and Tyr) PKs

    MAPK, MAPKK, Raf (?)
    $P34^{cdc2}$

IV. Protein Tyrosine Kinases (PTK's)

    A. Cellular or viral (oncogenic) PTK's
    B. Receptor- linked PTK's

Table I. Classification of protein kinases.

such as the motifs that are involved in the binding of ATP, by which they can be identified by searching the database (20,21). Most are regulated by segments that block their activity, often by virtue of the fact that they contain pseudo-substrate motifs that interact with, and shield, their catalytic sites. These autoinhibitory domains can exist on separate subunits as in the cAMP-dependent protein kinase (cA PK) first characterized by Ed Krebs and Don Walsh (22), or within the same peptide chain, as in the cG PK, where the two segments have become fused in the course of evolution. Initially, for the cA PK, the reaction seemed simple enough: the enzyme exists as an inactive complex between catalytic and regulatory subunits; cAMP induces a change in conformation in the regulatory subunits resulting in the dissociation of the enzyme and the liberation of active catalytic subunits. It soon became apparent, however, that the inactive complex had a more substantial purpose, namely, to prevent the translocation of the free catalytic subunits to other compartments of the cell, particularly the nucleus (23). But we know today that the regulation of this enzyme is even more sophisticated: the regulatory subunits themselves contain structural determinants that allow them to recognize and bind with high affinity to anchoring proteins distributed at specific locations within the cell (24-27). More than two dozen of these have been identified; they are particularly abundant in brain and the thyroid. Conceivably, some of these could co-localize with particular cAMP-generating receptor. This would confer a certain degree of selectivity to the hormonal response by targeting the kinase toward a given set of substrates (27) (Fig. 5).

Enzyme translocation may also play an important role in the regulation of protein kinase C first described by Nishizuka (28, 29). Depending on which subspecies of PKC is involved, the enzyme contains up to three regulatory

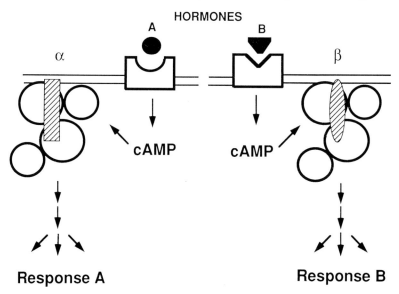

Fig. 5: Hypothetical selectivity in hormonal response by juxtaposition of cAMP-dependent protein kinase anchoring proteins with specific adenylate cyclase receptors.

126

domains responsible for the binding of Ca^{2+}, diacylglycerol and phospholipids. Binding of these allosteric effectors can promote the translocation of the enzyme to the plasma membrane where it could bind to specific anchoring proteins (30). Once again, this could determine which particular signal pathway would become affected.

Enzyme translocation might also be one of the functions of the cyclins, those regulatory subunits that are transiently expressed during various phases of the cell cycle. They associate strongly with the cell cycle-dependent kinases and operate particularly at the G1/S and G2/M transitions (31-33). But in *S. cerevisiae*, for instance, between 4 and 5 dozen cyclins have been identified (34). While their multiciplicity would provide the cell with the redundancy it needs to protect itself from accidental failures, it would seem unlikely that their sole purpose would be to modulate the activity of the kinases. Some of these complexes must become operative at other set points along the cell cycle. More importantly, perhaps, they could be essential to target the enzymes toward those elements that become operative during the profound cytoskeletal reorganizations that accompany cell division.

Targeting of Serine/Threonine Phosphatases
Targeting subunits are particularly crucial for serine/threonine phosphatases because these enzymes are not geared to recognize specific sequences, or structural determinants within their substrates. Furthermore, unlike the kinases, they consist of just a few types of enzymes that have broad and overlapping specificities (35-37). Thus they have to depend on regulatory subunits or binding proteins to direct them toward particular compartments of the cell where they will encounter particular substrates. That is the case, for instance, of the type 1 phosphatase whose catalytic subunit can bind to a glycogen-recognizing subunit, a myosin-recognizing subunit or an inhibitory molecule called Inhibitor 2. In each of these forms, the enzyme recognizes a particular set of substrates. Formation or dissociation of these complexes is under hormonal control (38-41). This is the theme that I propose to develop in the second part of this talk devoted to the role of regulatory/localization domains in the function of tyrosine phosphatases.

Protein Tyrosine Phosphorylation
Three remarkable discoveries, 14 years ago, provided considerable excitement to the field of cellular regulation by protein phosphorylation. First, the finding by the groups of Ray Erickson (42,43) and Varmus-Bishop (44) that the product of the src gene responsible for the oncogenicity of Rous sarcoma virus was a protein kinase they designated as pp60[src]. Second, the unexpected report by Tony Hunter and Bart Sefton that this kinase, unlike all previously known enzymes, phosphorylated its protein substrates exclusively on tyrosyl residues (45). Third, the identification of the non-transforming homolog of v-src (46-50), i.e., the cellular c-src. c-src encodes a product, (pp60[c-src]) which differs from its oncogenic viral counterpart by

127

having, among other discrete mutations, a short extension at the C-terminus. This extension carries a phosphotyrosyl residue that keeps the activity of the enzyme under control. Today we know more than a dozen tyrosine kinases of cellular or viral origin and their number continues to grow (15,50).

Finally came the seminal discovery from the laboratory of Stanley Cohen (51,52) that the receptor for epidermal growth factor was itself a tyrosine kinase whose activity was induced by binding of the ligand. Since then, many families of receptors with tyrosine kinase activities have been identified (53). They all have an external, ligand-binding domain, some with cystein rich regions, a single transmembrane segment and a cytoplasmic tyrosine kinase domain (Fig. 6).

Just as mutation of the intracellular tyrosine kinases can lead to cell transformation, mutation of the growth factor receptors can lead to oncogenic products. The first to be identified was the retroviral oncogene v-erb B (54,55) generated by a truncation of the external domain of the EGF receptor, its cellular progenitor. Many others have since been cloned and characterized; they usually result from truncation of the molecule at one end or the other or both, fusion with certain viral elements and other kinds of mutations.

With accumulating evidence implicating tyrosine phosphorylation in cell proliferation and transformation, it is hardly surprising that many groups would become interested in the enzymes that would catalyze the reverse reaction, namely, the protein tyrosine phosphatases.

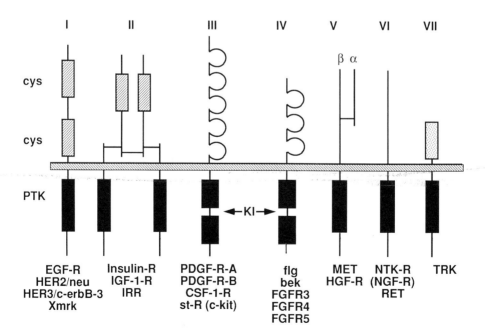

Fig. 6: Growth factor tyrosine kinase receptors.

Protein Tyrosine Phosphatases

First evidence for phosphotyrosine dephosphorylation was obtained by Graham Carpenter and Stanley Cohen (51,56) using A431 cell membranes overexpressing the EGF receptor, allowing these to undergo autophosphorylation, and then monitoring their rate of dephosphorylation. Similar observations were made by Bart Sefton and Tony Hunter using cells transformed with a temperature sensitive mutant of Rous sarcoma virus (57). Then followed a flurry of studies by a number of groups, including our own six years ago (58-60). The work was originated with Nick Tonks, a superb Post Doctoral Fellow and second generation Seattleite since he had just obtained his PhD degree with Phil Cohen at Dundee who himself had been in our laboratory some 20 odd years before. When we started, we also assumed that if transformation could be brought about by overexpression of the tyrosine kinases, or mutations that would render them constitutively active, then overexpression of the phosphatases might block or reverse these reactions. This assumption was too simplistic.

Within a couple of years, a tyrosine phosphatase was isolated in homogeneous form from human placenta (61,62). The enzyme was totally specific for phosphotyrosyl residues and extremely active. It had a specific activity about one order of magnitude higher than most viral tyrosine kinases and up to 3 orders of magnitude higher than certain receptor tyrosine kinases. This high activity suggested that it had to be tightly regulated to allow for those mitogenic signals that are necessary for normal cell development.

The Leukocyte Common Antigen, CD45: a Tyrosine Phosphatase

The surprise came when the amino acid sequence of the enzyme was determined by Ken Walsh and Harry Charbonneau because it showed no homology with any of the other protein phosphatases (63). However, a search of the data base indicated that the enzyme was structurally related to an abundant and already well-known surface antigen, the leukocyte common antigen also designated as CD45 (64) (Fig. 7). The leukocyte common antigen represents a broad family of membrane-spanning molecules found in all hematopoietic cells except mature erythrocytes (65). Their intracellular moiety is highly conserved and contains two internally homologous domains of approximately 30 kDa each. It is those two domains that are structurally related to the placenta phosphatase. CD45 has been implicated in the regulation of lymphocyte function, including cytotoxicity, proliferation and differentiation and in modulating IL2 receptor expression.

Here, I must open a parenthesis with biblical overtone. Had we obtained the sequence of the placenta phosphatase before that of CD45 was determined, nobody would have paid much attention - and we neither - because it would just have been the sequence of another enzyme. And it is those working on CD45 - Ian Trowbridge, Allen Williams, Matt Thomas, etc. who, once they got their sequence and searched it through the data base, would have made the surprising observation that their receptor was, in fact, a tyrosine phosphatase. What this means is that in this business, it really pays

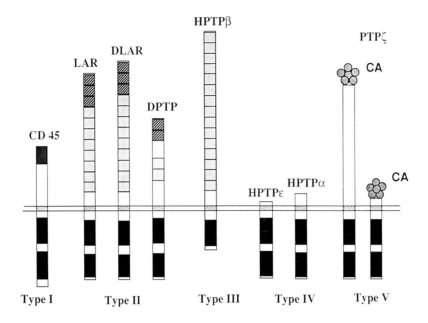

Fig. 7: Tyrosine phosphatase receptors.

to be last, precisely as recorded in the Gospel which states that "The last shall be first and the first last".

Since then, a great variety of receptor forms have been identified (58—60). All but one display the same double catalytic domains in their cytoplasmic portion but considerable diversity in their external segments (Fig. 7). Some have structural characteristics of cell adhesion molecules such as the leukocyte common antigen-related LARs first cloned by Saito and Schlossman. They are related to the N-CAMs (Neural Cell Adhesion Molecules) or fasciclin II suggesting that they might be involved in homophilic cell-cell interactions and perhaps modulate morphogenesis and tissue development. Others contain fibronectin type III repeats and might be involved in cell-cell or cell-matrix signaling. Some have very short external domains. Perhaps the most intriguing receptors are the ones recently cloned independently by Schlessinger (66) and Saito (67). At the end of an external segment, one finds a large globular domain almost identical to carbonic anhydrase except that it contains only one of the 3 histidines involved in the binding of Zn^{2+}. Except for CD45, no ligand has been found for any of these structures.

The Intracellular Tyrosine Phosphatases in cell cycle progression and transformation

Likewise, the low molecular weight, intracellular tyrosine phosphatases display a great diversity of structures, either preceding or following a highly conserved catalytic core. These are undoubtedly involved in the regulation

130

and localization of the enzymes (Fig. 8). Some PTPs have segments homologous to cytoskeletal proteins such as band 4.1, ezrin and talin; others contain two SH2 (src-homology 2) domains which might allow them to interact with phosphotyrosyl residues at sites of autophosphorylation of growth factor receptors. Tyrosine phosphatases are also found as the gene products (YOPs) of virulence plasmids from bacteria of the genus Yersinia (such as *Y. pestis* responsible for the bubonic plague).

I would like to discuss now the role that these regulatory domains might play in enzyme localization and function, focussing on the human T-cell enzyme cloned by Debbie Cool (68) (Fig. 9). The regulatory domain is entirely hydrophilic until one reaches the last 19 residues that are very hydrophobic, reminiscent of a transmembrane domain. There is also a short stretch of 5 basic residues that could serve as a nuclear localization signal (67).

The 11 kDa segment of the enzyme was mutated, as well as other segments of putative physiological importance. As a first step, a premature stop codon was introduced after the catalytic domain to delete the entire C-terminal tail. When this is done, the truncated enzyme becomes soluble whereas the wild-type protein is particulate (69,70), localizing with the endoplasmic reticulum (ER). Expression of the C-terminal tail as a fusion protein with β-galactosidase shows that the soluble β-galactosidase now becomes attached to the ER. Finally, if one deletes just the C-terminal hydrophobic stretch, the enzyme localizes in the nucleus (J. Lorenzen, unpublished data).

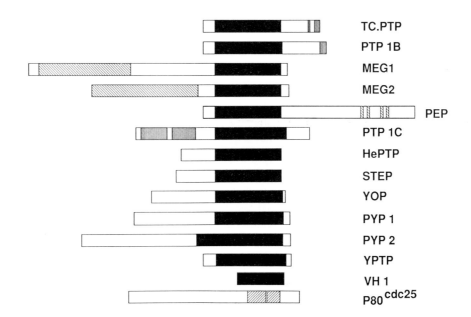

Fig. 8: Intracellular tyrosine phosphatases, aligned on the basis of their conserved, catalytic domains.

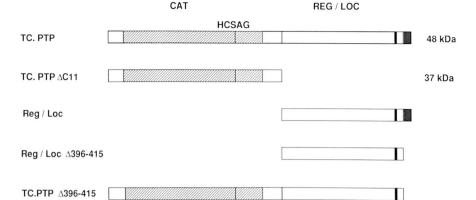

Fig. 9: Schematic representation of the human T-cell tyrosine phosphatase (TC-20) and some of its mutated forms. Illustrated are the full-length, wild-type 48 kDa enzyme, the 37 kDa truncated form containing only the catalytic domain; the 11 kDa regulatory/localization domain; and two mutant forms in which the hydrophobic 19-residue segment at the C-terminus (dark band) has been deleted.

Because of lack of time, I will only discuss the differences one observes in cell cycle progression and transformation when one expresses the wild-type enzyme vs. its truncated form obtained by introducing a premature stop codon after the catalytic domain. In BHK cells in which the wild-type enzyme is overexpressed, there is no obvious change in cell morphology. By contrast, 60-70% of the cells expressing the truncated form become multinucleated (71) due to a failure in cytokinesis.

Multinucleation is not unusual; it can occur by cell fusion, with certain drugs or with antibodies against myosin ATPase since cytokinesis is an actomyosin-dependent process (72,73). But in all these instances, when nuclear division goes on, it goes on synchronously. What is unusual in these BHK cells is that nuclear division is more often than not asynchronous (Fig. 10): that is, one nucleus will divide while the other will not. Therefore, one will see cells with nuclei at all phases of cell cycle. At this time, we don't know which inter nuclei signals have been disrupted.

Differences in cell behavior brought about by expression of the wild-type vs. truncated T-cell enzyme can also be seen in cell transformation, using the same highly tumorigenic BHK cell line. Transformation is the change a cell undergoes when it becomes malignant and no longer abides by the constraints under which a normal cell must operate. A normal cell does not grow on soft agar as it needs a solid support to which it can adhere, whereas a transformed cell will. As expected, the transformed BHK cell line grows readily on soft agar but it grows just as well, if not better, when transfected with the wild-type enzyme. By contrast, overexpression of the truncated form almost abolishes growth under these conditions, as if transformation had been suppressed (D. Cool, unpublished data).

A similar enhancement in tumorigenicity by overexpression of the full-length phosphatase is observed when these cells are injected into athymic

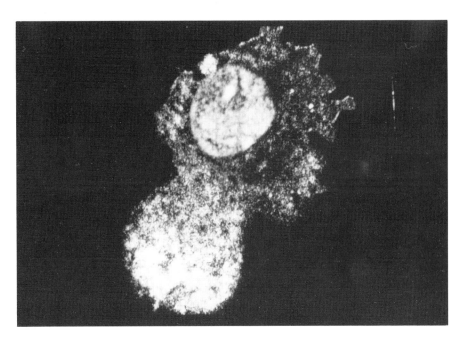

Fig. 10: BHK cells overexpressing the truncated 37 kDa form of the T-cell tyrosine phosphatase showing asynchronous nuclear division. The cell has rounded up around the lower nucleus ready to undergo mitosis. The nucleus on top is in an interphase configuration (71).

nude mice. The tumors produced are highly vascularized, as compared to tumors formed from control BHK cells. On the other hand, tumor formation is greatly reduced if not suppressed with BHK cells containing the truncated form. In several animals, no tumor was detected.

Since the nature of the transforming agent in these BHK cells was not defined, these studies were repeated in embryonic Rat-2 cells transformed with the well-characterized viral oncogene v-fms (74). v-fms was first isolated from a feline sarcoma virus and belongs to the platelet-derived growth factor (PDGF) family of tyrosine kinase receptors (75). Its non-transforming progenitor, the cellular protooncogene c-fms, encodes the receptor for CSF-1, the macrophage colony-stimulating factor. Binding of CSF-1 triggers signaling events that lead to the transcription of CSF-1 genes necessary for mononuclear phagocyte growth, differentiation and survival (76).

Control Rat-2 cells display typical, non-transformed, cobblestone morphology — as opposed to the spindle-shape v-fms transformed cells (74). Cells overexpressing the full-length enzyme have the same stringy transformed appearance, whereas clones containing the truncated form have the Rat-2, non-transformed cobblestone phenotype (Fig. 11). The transformed cells will grow on soft agar, the others will not. To achieve a high level of expression of the tyrosine phosphatase, the enzyme was packaged in retroviruses with which the cells were infected. None of the cells containing the truncated enzyme grew very well on soft agar. That these cells had reverted to a non-transformed state was further demonstrated by the appearance of their cytoskeleton (Fig. 12). Transformed cells exhibit a disruption of actin microfilaments and a loss of focal adhesions; i.e., the structures through which normal cells adhere to their substratum. The actin fibers are restored in cells expressing the truncated enzyme and many more focal adhesions can be seen (D. Cool, unpublished results).

Finally, the same differences were observed in the ability of these two types of cells to form tumors when injected into nude mice. All cells containing the v-fms oncogenes produced large tumors, as those co-expressing the wild-type phosphatase. As observed in BHK cells, tumor formation was abolished in most cells transfected with the truncated enzyme.

Concluding Remarks

The above data, plus others I did not have the time to develop, indicate that phosphatases cannot be viewed simply as providing an "off" switch in an "on/off" kinase/phosphatase system. In certain cases and depending on the form of the enzyme involved, tyrosine phosphatases can clearly act synergistically with the kinases to bring about a particular physiological

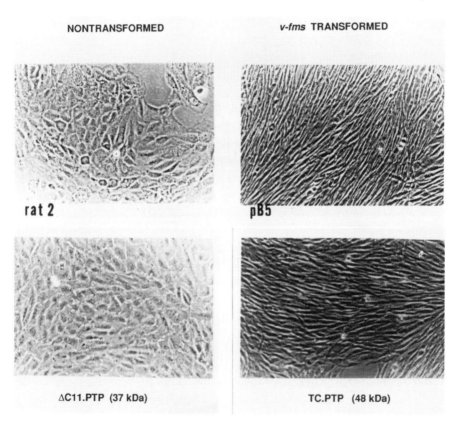

Fig. 11: Morphology of non-transformed Rat-2 cells (upper left) or cells transformed with v-fms (upper right). The v-fms-transformed cell lines were co-transfected with full-length T-cell tyrosine phosphatase (lower right) or its 37 kDa truncated form (lower left). The data indicate that while the full-length enzyme has not altered the transformed (spindle-shape) morphology, cells containing the truncated enzymes display a non-transformed phenotype.

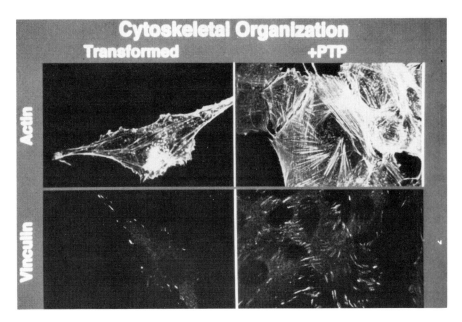

Fig. 12: Cytoskeleton morphology of v-fms transformed Rat-2 cells before (left) and after detransformation by co-expression of the truncated (37 kDa) form of the T-cell enzyme. Upper frames: actin stained with rhodamine-labeled phalloidin; lower frames: stained with anti-vinculin antibodies to mark the focal adhesions (bright spots).

response. An obvious way by which they could do that would be by activating the src family kinases which are repressed by phosphorylation at the C-terminus (Fig. 13). Furthermore, the factors that would determine whether a phosphatase would enhance or oppose a kinase reaction would seem to depend less on its state of activity than on its subcellular localization. An analogous situation is found with pp60[v-src]. Removal of the myristoyl group required for its binding to the plasma membrane does not affect its enzymatic properties but abolishes its transforming abilities (77). Association with the membrane is, therefore, essential for its oncogenicity. The above data would indicate that if one wanted to control transformation through the phosphatases, one should try to manipulate the segments involved in their localization - or whatever anchoring proteins to which they may bind - rather than their catalytic domains. There are, of course, many questions that need to be answered. To mention a few:

a) What controls the activity of phosphatases under normal conditions? It may be easier to achieve high level expression of these enzymes in transformed lines in which the signal pathways are turned on, rather than in normal cells; as if a balance existed between kinases and phosphatases.

b) Do the differences between wild-type and truncated enzymes depend solely on their localization or is enzyme specificity also implicated?

c) Would the same effects be observed with any oncogene, including those that are not tyrosine kinases (such as ras, raf, mos, etc.)?

d) Which are the steps in the signaling pathway that are specifically affected by the enzymes? And finally,

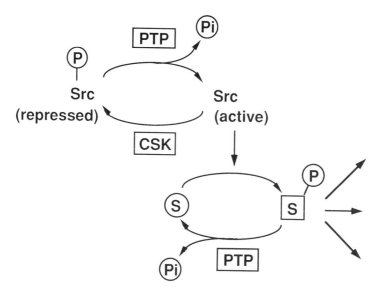

Fig. 13: Possible dual role of tyrosine phosphatases in signal transduction. Upper reaction, activation of src family tyrosine kinases by dephosphorylation of the C-terminal phosphotyrosyl residue. Lower reaction, dephosphorylation of other tyrosine phosphorylated substrates to return the system to its original state. csk is the cellular src kinase that represses enzymatic activity by tyrosine phosphorylation at the C-terminus.

e) If oncogenicity can result from an overexpression of tyrosine kinases, could oncogenicity also result from an underexpression of certain phosphatases?

All the processes Ed Krebs and I have described today have had something in common; they followed a similar pattern at the molecular level. Under the influence of an external stimulus, the state of phosphorylation of a protein or enzyme has been altered. This, in turn, has triggered a given cellular response. The finding that certain oncogenic agents may operate along the same principles may provide some clues as to the very mechanism of cell transformation. And who knows, perhaps with a little luck, a deeper understanding of these signaling pathways may suggest new avenues by which oncogenicity can be brought under control.

ACKNOWLEDGEMENTS

My scientific career has been profoundly marked by two long-standing collaborations, first with the late Eric A. Stein on α-amylases, then with Edwin G. Krebs, with whom I share this Award, on the protein phosphorylation problem. In addition to being the most valuable of colleagues, they have been two of my closest friends. I also owe a debt of gratitude to all those who joined the laboratory over the years, contributing their skills, original ideas and maximum effort before moving on to pursue their own personal academic or research careers. The list would be too long were I to name them all; suffice to recall a few in chronological order: T. Yamamoto, M. Appleman, J. Hedrick, S. Shaltiel, S. Hurd, P. Cohen, L. Heilmeyer, B. Boeker, D. Gratecos, D. Malencik, C. Heizmann, H. Blum, M. Fosset, K. Lerch, J. Demaille, D. Brautigan, E. Villa-Moruzzi, L. Ballou, S. McNall and N. Tonks. They have been superb collaborators; without them and all those I haven't been able to mention by name, including all my present collaborators, nothing that has happened could have happened.

I also owe a debt of gratitude to my wife Beverley for keeping her cool in the midst of recurring crises, whenever I had to prepare last-minute lectures or rush to the airport. Finally, a mountain of thanks goes to my secretary, Carmen Westwater for, time after time, wading through countless drafts of manuscripts, and retrieving lost letters, articles or plane tickets. But those around me exaggerate when they call my office the "Bermuda Triangle".

My indebtedness goes to the National Institute of Diabetes and Digestive and Kidney Diseases, NIH, for supporting my work from day one and the Muscular Dystrophy Association for their unfailing help.

REFERENCES

1. Titani, K., Koide, A., Hermann, J., Ericsson, L. H., Kumar, S., Wade, R. D., Walsh, K. A., Neurath, H., and Fischer, E. H. (1977) *Proc. Natl. Acad. Sci. USA* **74,** 4762–4766.
2. Fischer, E. H., Graves, D. J., Snyder Crittenden, E. R., and Krebs, E. G. (1959) *J. Biol. Chem.* **234,** 1698–1704.
3. Nolan, C., Novoa, W. B., Krebs, E. G., and Fischer, E. H. (1964) *Biochemistry* **3,** 542–551.
4. Kemp, B. E., Graves, D. J., Benjamini, E., and Krebs, E. G. (1977) *J. Biol. Chem.* **252,** 4888–4894.
5. Pearson, R. B. and Kemp, B. E. (1991) *Methods. Enzymol.* **200,** 62–81.
6. Rosell-Perez, M., Villar-Palasi, C., and Larner, J. (1962) *Biochemistry* **1,** 763–768.
7. Friedman, D. L. and Larner, J. (1963) *Biochemistry* **2,** 669–675.
8. Larner, J. and Villar-Palasi, C. (1971) *Curr. Top. Cell Regul.* **3,** 195–236.
9. Smith, C. H., Brown, N. E., and Larner, J. (1971) *Biochim. Biophys. Acta* **3,** 81–88.
10. Cohen, P. (1986) *The Enzymes* **17A,** 461–497.
11. Roach, P. J. (1986) in *Enzymes* (Boyer, P. D. and Krebs, E. G., eds) pp. 499–539, Academic Press, Orlando.

12. Roach, P. J. (1990) *FASEB. J.* **4**, 2961−2968.
13. Krebs, E. G. (1986) *The Enzymes* **17**, 3−18.
14. Edelman, A. M., Blumenthal, D. K., and Krebs, E. G. (1987) *Annu. Rev. Biochem.* **56**, 567−613.
15. Hunter, T. (1991) *Methods. Enzymol.* **200**, 3−37.
16. Seger, R., Ahn, N. G., Posada, J., Munar, E. S., Jensen, A. M., Cooper, J. A., Cobb, M. H., and Krebs, E. G. (1992) *J. Biol. Chem.* **267**, 14373−14379.
17. Pines, J. and Hunter, T. (1990) *New Biol.* **2**, 389−401.
18. Bourret, R. B., Borkovich, K. A., and Simon, M. I. (1991) *Annu. Rev. Biochem.* **60**, 401−441.
19. LaPorte, D. C., Thorness, P. E., and Koshland, D. E., Jr. (1985) *J. Biol. Chem.* **260**, 10563−10568.
20. Hanks, S. K., Quinn, A. M., and Hunter, T. (1988) *Science* **241**, 42−52.
21. Hanks, S. K. and Quinn, A. M. (1991) *Methods. Enzymol.* **200**, 38−62.
22. Walsh, D. A., Perkins, J. P., and Krebs, E. G. (1968) *J. Biol. Chem.* **243**, 3763−3765.
23. Castagna, M., Palmer, W. K., and Walsh, D. A. (1975) *Eur. J. Biochem.* **55**, 193−199.
24. Leiser, M., Rubin, C. S., and Erlichman, J. (1986) *J. Biol. Chem.* **261**, 1904−1908.
25. Bergman, C. B., Bhattacharyya, N., and Rubin, C. S. (1989) *J. Biol. Chem.* **264**, 4648−4656.
26. Carr, D. W., Hausken, Z. E., Fraser, E. D. C., Stofko-Hahn, R. E., and Scott, J. D. (1992) *J. Biol. Chem.* **267**, 13376−13382.
27. Scott, J. D. and Carr, D. W. (1992) *News Phys. Sci.* **7**, 143−148.
28. Takai, Y., Kishimoto, A., Iwasa, Y., Kawahara, Y., Mori, T., and Nishizuka, Y. (1979) *J. Biol. Chem.* **254**, 3692−3695.
29. Nishizuka, Y. (1992) *Science* **258**, 607−614.
30. Mochly-Rosen, D., Khaner, H., Lopez, J., and Smith, B. L. (1991) *J. Biol. Chem.* **266**, 14866−14868.
31. Lee, M. and Nurse, P. (1988) *Trends. Genet.* **4**, 287−290.
32. Nurse, P. (1990) *Nature* **344**, 503−508.
33. Norbury, C. and Nurse, P. (1992) *Annu. Rev. Biochem.* **61**, 441−470.
34. Norbury, C. and Nurse, P. (1992) *Curr. Biol.* **1**, 23−27.
35. Cohen, P. (1989) *Annu. Rev. Biochem.* **58**, 453−508.
36. Cohen, P. and Cohen, P. T. W. (1989) *J. Biol. Chem.* **264**, 21435−21438.
37. Shenolikar, S. and Nairn, A. (1990) in *Advances in Second Messenger and Phosphoprotein Research* (Y. Nishizuka, M. Endo, and C. Tanaka, eds) pp. 1−121, Raven Press, New York, NY.
38. Stralfors, P., Hiraga, A., and Cohen, P. (1985) *Eur. J. Biochem.* **149**, 295−303.
39. Hubbard, M. J. and Cohen, P. (1989) *Eur. J. Biochem.* **180**, 457−465.
40. Chisholm, A. A. and Cohen, P. (1988) *Biochim. Biophys. Acta* **971**, 163−169.
41. DePaoli Roach, A. A. (1989) *Adv. Prot. Phosphatases* **5**, 479−500.
42. Brugge, J. S. and Erikson, R. L. (1977) *Nature* **269**, 346−347.
43. Collett, M. S. and Erikson, R. L. (1978) *Proc. Natl. Acad. Sci. USA* **75**, 2021−2024.
44. Levinson, A. D., Oppermann, H., Levintow, L., Varmus, H. E., and Bishop, J. M. (1978) *Cell* **15**, 561−572.
45. Hunter, T. and Sefton, B. M. (1980) *Proc. Natl. Acad. Sci. USA* **77**, 1311−1315.
46. Collett, M. S., Brugge, J. S., and Erikson, R. L. (1978) *Cell* **15**, 1363.
47. Oppermann, H., Levinson, A. R., Varmus, H. E., Levintow, L., and Bishop, J. M. (1979) *Proc. Natl. Acad. Sci. USA* **76**, 1804−1808.
48. Rohrschneider, L. R., Eisenman, R. N., and Leitch, C. R. (1979) *Proc. Natl. Acad. Sci. USA* **76**, 4479−4483.

49. Czernilofsky, A. P., Levinson, A. D., Varmus, H. E., Bishop, J. M., Tischer, E., and Goodman, H. M. (1980) *Nature* 198 **287**, 198−203.

50. *Oncogenes and the Molecular Origins of Cancer*, (1989) Cold Spring Harbor Laboratory Press, Cold Spring Harbor, NY.

51. Ushiro, H. and Cohen, S. (1980) *J. Biol. Chem.* **255**, 8363−8365.

52. Carpenter, G. (1987) *Annu. Rev. Biochem.* **56**, 881−914.

53. Yarden, Y. and Ullrich, A. (1988) *Annu. Rev. Biochem.* **57,** 443−478.

54. Downward, J., Yarden, Y., Mayes, E., Scrace, G., Totty, N., Stockwell, P., Ullrich, A., Schlessinger, J., and Waterfield, M. D. (1984) *Nature* **307,** 521−527.

55. Ullrich, L., Coussens, L., Hayflick, J. S., Dull, T. J., Gray, A., Tam, A. W., Lee, J., Yarden, Y., Libermann, T. A., Schlessinger, J., Downward, J., Mayes, E. L. V., Whittle, N., Waterfield, M. D., and Seeburg, P. H. (1984) *Nature* **309,** 418−425.

56. Carpenter, G., King, L., and Cohen, S. (1979) *J. Biol. Chem.* **254**, 4884−4891.

57. Sefton, B. M., Hunter, T., Beemon, K., and Eckhart, W. (1980) *Cell* **20**, 807−816.

58. Fischer, E. H., Charbonneau, H., and Tonks, N. K. (1991) *Science* **253**, 401−406.

59. Saito, H. and Streuli, M. (1991) *Cell Growth and Differ.* **2**, 59−65.

60. Charbonneau, H. and Tonks, N. K. (1992) *Annu. Rev. Cell Biol.* **8**, 463−493.

61. Tonks, N. K., Diltz, C. D., and Fischer, E. H. (1988) *J. Biol. Chem.* **263**, 6731−6737.

62. Tonks, N. K., Diltz, C. D., and Fischer, E. H. (1988) *J. Biol. Chem.* **263**, 6722−6730.

63. Charbonneau, H., Tonks, N. K., Kumar, S., Diltz, C. D., Harrylock, M., Cool, D. E., Krebs, E. G., Fischer, E. H., and Walsh, K. A. (1989) *Proc. Natl. Acad. Sci. USA* **86**, 5252−5256.

64. Charbonneau, H., Tonks, N. K., Walsh, K. A., and Fischer, E. H. (1988) *Proc. Natl. Acad. Sci. USA* **85**, 7182−7186.

65. Thomas, M. L. (1989) *Annu. Rev. Immunol.* 7, 339−369.

66. Barnea, G., Silvennoinen, O., Shaanan, B., Honegger, A. M., Canoll, P. D., D'Eustachio, P., Morse, B., Levy, J. B., LaForgia, S., Huebner, K., Musacchio, J. M., Sap, J., and Schlessinger, J. (1992) *Mol. Cell. Biol.* **13**, 1497−1506.

67. Krueger, N. X. and Saito, H. (1992) *Proc. Natl. Acad. Sci. USA* **89**, 7417−7421.

68. Cool, D. E., Tonks, N. K., Charbonneau, H., Walsh, K. A., Fischer, E. H., and Krebs, E. G. (1989) *Proc. Natl. Acad. Sci. USA* **86**, 5257−5261.

69. Cool, D. E., Tonks, N. K., Charbonneau, H., Fischer, E. H., and Krebs, E. G. (1990) *Proc. Natl. Acad. Sci. USA* **87**, 7280−7284.

70. Zander, N. F., Lorenzen, J. A., Cool, D. E., Tonks, N. K., Daum, G., Krebs, E. G., and Fischer, E. H. (1991) *Biochemistry* **30**, 6964−6970.

71. Cool, D. E., Andreassen, P. R., Tonks, N. K., Krebs, E. G., Fischer, E. H., and Margolis, R. L. (1992) *Proc. Natl. Acad. Sci. USA* **89**, 5422−5426.

72. Fujiwara, K. and Pollard, T. D. (1976) *J. Cell Biol.* **71**, 848−875.

73. Sato, N., Yonemura, S., Obinata, T., and Tsukita, S. (1991) *J. Cell Biol.* **113**, 321−330.

74. Zander, N. F., Cool, D. E., Diltz, C. D., Rohrschneider, L. R., Krebs, E. G., and Fischer, E. H. (1993) *Oncogen* **8**, 1175−1182

75. McDonough, S. K., Larsen, S., Brodey, R. S., Stock, N. D., and Hardy, W. D. Jr. (1971) *Cancer Res.* **31**, 953−956.

76. Sherr, C. J. (1988) *Biochim. Biophys. Acta* **948**, 225−243.

77. Kamps, M. L., Buss, J. E., and Sefton, B. M. (1985) *Proc. Natl. Acad. Sci. USA* **82**, 4625−4628.

Derek Walcott

DEREK WALCOTT

Derek Walcott was born in 1930 in the town of Castries in Saint Lucia, one of the Windward Islands in the Lesser Antilles. The experience of growing up on the isolated volcanic island, an ex-British colony, has had a strong influence on Walcott's life and work. Both his grandmothers were said to have been the descendants of slaves. His father, a Bohemian water-colourist, died when Derek and his twin brother Roderick were only a few years old. His mother ran the town's Methodist school. After studying at St. Mary's College in his native island and at the University of the West Indies in Jamaica, Walcott moved in 1953 to Trinidad, where he has worked as theatre and art critic. At the age of 18 he made his debut with 25 *Poems*, but his breakthrough came with the collection of poems *In a Green Night (1962)*. In 1959, he founded the Trinidad Theatre Workshop, which produced many of his early plays.

Walcott has been an assiduous traveller to other countries but has always, not least in his efforts to create an indigenous drama, felt himself deeply rooted in Caribbean society with its cultural fusion of African, Asiatic and European elements. For many years he has divided his time between Trinidad, where he has his home as a writer, and Boston University, where he teaches literature and creative writing.

SELECT BIBLIOGRAPHY

Verse
25 Poems, Port-of-Spain: Guardian Commercial Printery, 1948
Epitaph for the Young, Xll Cantos, Bridgetown: Barbados Advocate, 1949
Poems, Kingston, Jamaica, City Printery, 1951
In a Green Night, Poems 1948—60, London: Cape, 1962
Selected Poems, New York: Farrar Straus Giroux, 1964
The Castaway and Other Poems, London: Cape, 1965
The Gulf and Other Poems, London: Cape,1969
Another Life, New York: Farrar Straus Giroux: London: Cape, 1973
Sea Grapes, London: Cape; New York: Farrar Straus Giroux, 1976
The Star-Apple Kingdom, New York: Farrar Straus Giroux, 1979
Selected Poetry, Ed. by Wayne Brown. London: Heinemann, 1981
The Fortunate Traveller, New York: Farrar Straus Giroux, 1981
The Caribbean Poetry of Derek Walcott, and the Art of Romare Bearden, New York: Limited Editions Club, 1983
Midsummer, New York: Farrar Straus Giroux, 1984
Collected Poems 1948-1984, New York, Farrar Straus Giroux, 1986

The Arkansas Testament, New York, Farrar Straus Giroux, 1987

Omeros, New York: Farrar Straus Giroux, 1990

Drama

Harry Dernier, Bridgetown: Barbados Advocate, 1952

Dream on Monkey Mountain and Other Plays, New York: Farrar Straus Giroux, 1970

The Joker of Seville & O Babylon!, New York: Farrar Straus Giroux, 1978

Remembrance & Pantomime: Two Plays, New York: Farrar Straus Giroux, 1980

Three Plays, New York: Farrar Straus Giroux, 1986

Critical studies

The Art of Derek Walcott, Ed. by Stewart Brown, Bridgend: Seren Books, 1991

THE ANTILLES: FRAGMENTS OF EPIC MEMORY

Nobel Lecture, December 7, 1992

by

Derek Walcott

Trinidad, and Boston University, Boston, MA, USA.

Felicity is a village in Trinidad on the edge of the Caroni plain, the wide central plain that still grows sugar and to which indentured cane cutters were brought after emancipation, so the small population of Felicity is East Indian, and on the afternoon that I visited it with friends from America, all the faces along its road were Indian, which, as I hope to show, was a moving, beautiful thing, because this Saturday afternoon *Ramleela,* the epic dramatization of the Hindu epic the *Ramayana,* was going to be performed, and the costumed actors from the village were assembling on a field strung with different-coloured flags, like a new gas station, and beautiful Indian boys in red and black were aiming arrows haphazardly into the afternoon light. Low blue mountains on the horizon, bright grass, clouds that would gather colour before the light went. Felicity! What a gentle Anglo-Saxon name for an epical memory.

Under an open shed on the edge of the field, there were two huge armatures of bamboo that looked like immense cages. They were parts of the body of a god, his calves or thighs, which, fitted and reared, would make a gigantic effigy. This effigy would be burnt as a conclusion to the epic. The cane structures flashed a predictable parallel: Shelley's sonnet on the fallen statue of Ozymandias and his empire, that "colossal wreck" in its empty desert.

Drummers had lit a fire in the shed and they eased the skins of their tablas nearer the flames to tighten them. The saffron flames, the bright grass, and the hand-woven armatures of the fragmented god who would be burnt were not in any desert where imperial power had finally toppled but were part of a ritual, evergreen season that, like the cane-burning harvest, is annually repeated, the point of such sacrifice being its repetition, the point of the destruction being renewal through fire.

Deities were entering the field. What we generally call "Indian music" was blaring from the open platformed shed from which the epic would be narrated. Costumed actors were arriving. Princes and gods, I supposed. What an unfortunate confession! "Gods, I suppose" is the shrug that embodies our African and Asian diasporas. I had often thought of but never seen *Ramleela,* and had never seen this theatre, an open field, with village

143

children as warriors, princes, and gods. I had no idea what the epic story was, who its hero was, what enemies he fought, yet I had recently adapted the *Odyssey* for a theatre in England, presuming that the audience knew the trials of Odysseus, hero of another Asia Minor epic, while nobody in Trinidad knew any more than I did about Rama, Kali, Shiva, Vishnu, apart from the Indians, a phrase I use pervertedly because that is the kind of remark you can still hear in Trinidad: "apart from the Indians".

It was as if, on the edge of the Central Plain, there was another plateau, a raft on which the *Ramayana* would be poorly performed in this ocean of cane, but that was my writer's view of things, and it is wrong. I was seeing the *Ramleela* at Felicity as theatre when it was faith.

Multiply that moment of self-conviction when an actor, made-up and costumed, nods to his mirror before stopping on stage in the belief that he is a reality entering an illusion and you would have what I presumed was happening to the actors of this epic. But they were not actors. They had been chosen; or they themselves had chosen their roles in this sacred story that would go on for nine afternoons over a two-hour period till the sun set. They were not amateurs but believers. There was no theatrical term to define them. They did not have to psych themselves up to play their roles. Their acting would probably be as buoyant and as natural as those bamboo arrows crisscrossing the afternoon pasture. They believed in what they were playing, in the sacredness of the text, the validity of India, while I, out of the writer's habit, searched for some sense of elegy, of loss, even of degenerative mimicry in the happy faces of the boy-warriors or the heraldic profiles of the village princes. I was polluting the afternoon with doubt and with the patronage of admiration. I misread the event through a visual echo of History—the cane fields, indenture, the evocation of vanished armies, temples, and trumpeting elephants—when all around me there was quite the opposite: elation, delight in the boys' screams, in the sweets-stalls, in more and more costumed characters appearing; a delight of conviction, not loss. The name Felicity made sense.

Consider the scale of Asia reduced to these fragments: the small white exclamations of minarets or the stone balls of temples in the cane fields, and one can understand the self-mockery and embarrassment of those who see these rites as parodic, even degenerate. These purists look on such ceremonies as grammarians look at a dialect, as cities look on provinces and empires on their colonies. Memory that yearns to join the centre, a limb remembering the body from which it has been severed, like those bamboo thighs of the god. In other words, the way that the Caribbean is still looked at, illegitimate, rootless, mongrelized. "No people there", to quote Froude, "in the true sense of the word". No people. Fragments and echoes of real people, unoriginal and broken.

The performance was like a dialect, a branch of its original language, an abridgement of it, but not a distortion or even a reduction of its epic scale. Here in Trinidad I had discovered that one of the greatest epics of the world was seasonally performed, not with that desperate resignation of

144

preserving a culture, but with an openness of belief that was as steady as the wind bending the cane lances of the Caroni plain. We had to leave before the play began to go through the creeks of the Caroni Swamp, to catch the scarlet ibises coming home at dusk. In a performance as natural as those of the actors of the *Ramleela*, we watched the flocks come in as bright as the scarlet of the boy archers, as the red flags, and cover an islet until it turned into a flowering tree, an anchored immortelle. The sigh of History meant nothing here. These two visions, the *Ramleela* and the arrowing flocks of scarlet ibises, blent into a single gasp of gratitude. Visual surprise is natural in the Caribbean; it comes with the landscape, and faced with its beauty, the sigh of History dissolves.

We make too much of that long groan which underlines the past. I felt privileged to discover the ibises as well as the scarlet archers of Felicity.

The sigh of History rises over ruins, not over landscapes, and in the Antilles there are few ruins to sigh over, apart from the ruins of sugar estates and abandoned forts. Looking around slowly, as a camera would, taking in the low blue hills over Port of Spain, the village road and houses, the warrior-archers, the god-actors and their handlers, and music already on the sound track, I wanted to make a film that would be a long-drawn sigh over Felicity. I was filtering the afternoon with evocations of a lost India, but why "evocations"? Why not "celebrations of a real presence"? Why should India be "lost" when none of these villagers ever really knew it, and why not "continuing", why not the perpetuation of joy in Felicity and in all the other nouns of the Central Plain: Couva, Chaguanas, Charley Village? Why was I not letting my pleasure open its windows wide? I was entided like any Trinidadian to the ecstasies of their claim, because ecstasy was the pitch of the sinuous drumming in the loudspeakers. I was entitled to the feast of Husein, to the mirrors and crêpe-paper temples of the Muslim epic, to the Chinese Dragon Dance, to the rites of that Sephardic Jewish synagogue that was once on Something Street. I am only one-eighth the writer I might have been had I contained all the fragmented languages of Trinidad.

Break a vase, and the love that reassembles the fragments is stronger than that love which took its symmetry for granted when it was whole. The glue that fits the pieces is the sealing of its original shape. It is such a love that reassembles our African and Asiatic fragments, the cracked heirlooms whose restoration shows its white scars. This gathering of broken pieces is the care and pain of the Antilles, and if the pieces are disparate, ill-fitting, they contain more pain than their original sculpture, those icons and sacred vessels taken for granted in their ancestral places. Antillean art is this restoration of our shattered histories, our shards of vocabulary, our archipelago becoming a synonym for pieces broken off from the original continent.

And this is the exact process of the making of poetry, or what should be called not its "making" but its remaking, the fragmented memory, the armature that frames the god, even the rite that surrenders it to a final pyre;

the god assembled cane by cane, reed by weaving reed, line by plaited line, as the artisans of Felicity would erect his holy echo.

Poetry, which is perfection's sweat but which must seem as fresh as the raindrops on a statue's brow, combines the natural and the marmoreal; it conjugates both tenses simultaneously: the past and the present, if the past is the sculpture and the present the beads of dew or rain on the forehead of the past. There is the buried language and there is the individual vocabulary, and the process of poetry is one of excavation and of self-discovery. Tonally the individual voice is a dialect; it shapes its own accent, its own vocabulary and melody in defiance of an imperial concept of language, the language of Ozymandias, libraries and dictionaries, law courts and critics, and churches, universities, political dogma, the diction of institutions. Poetry is an island that breaks away from the main. The dialects of my archipelago seem as fresh to me as those raindrops on the statue's forehead, not the sweat made from the classic exertion of frowning marble, but the condensations of a refreshing element, rain and salt.

Deprived of their original language, the captured and indentured tribes create their own, accreting and secreting fragments of an old, an epic vocabulary, from Asia and from Africa, but to an ancestral, an ecstatic rhythm in the blood that cannot be subdued by slavery or indenture, while nouns are renamed and the given names of places accepted like Felicity village or Choiseul. The original language dissolves from the exhaustion of distance like fog trying to cross an ocean, but this process of renaming, of finding new metaphors, is the same process that the poet faces every morning of his working day, making his own tools like Crusoe, assembling nouns from necessity, from Felicity, even renaming himself. The stripped man is driven back to that self-astonishing, elemental force, his mind. That is the basis of the Antillean experience, this shipwreck of fragments, these echoes, these shards of a huge tribal vocabulary, these partially remembered customs, and they are not decayed but strong. They survived the Middle Passage and the *Fatel Rozack*, the ship that carried the first indentured Indians from the port of Madras to the cane fields of Felicity, that carried the chained Cromwellian convict and the Sephardic Jew, the Chinese grocer and the Lebanese merchant selling cloth samples on his bicycle.

And here they are, all in a single Caribbean city, Port of Spain, the sum of history, Trollope's "non-people". A downtown babel of shop signs and streets, mongrelized, polyglot, a ferment without a history, like heaven. Because that is what such a city is, in the New World, a writer's heaven.

A culture, we all know, is made by its cities.

Another first morning home, impatient for the sunrise — a broken sleep. Darkness at five, and the drapes not worth opening; then, in the sudden light, a cream-walled, brown-roofed police station bordered with short royal palms, in the colonial style, back of it frothing trees and taller palms, a pigeon fluttering into the cover of an eave, a rain-stained block of once-modern apartments, the morning side road into the station without traffic. All part of a surprising peace. This quiet happens with every visit to a city that has deepened itself in me. The flowers and the hills are easy, affection for them predictable; it is the architecture that, for the first morning, disorients. A return from American seductions used to make the traveller feel that something was missing, something was trying to complete itself, like the stained concrete apartments. Pan left along the window and the excrescences rear—a city trying to soar, trying to be brutal, like an American city in silhouette, stamped from the same mould as Columbus or Des Moines. An assertion of power, its decor bland, its air conditioning pitched to the point where its secretarial and executive staff sport competing cardigans; the colder the offices the more important, an imitation of another climate. A longing, even an envy of feeling cold.

In serious cities, in grey, militant winter with its short afternoons, the days seem to pass by in buttoned overcoats, every building appears as a barracks with lights on in its windows, and when snow comes, one has the illusion of living in a Russian novel, in the nineteenth century, because of the literature of winter. So visitors to the Caribbean must feel that they are inhabiting a succession of postcards. Both climates are shaped by what we have read of them. For tourists, the sunshine cannot be serious. Winter adds depth and darkness to life as well as to literature, and in the unending summer of the tropics not even poverty or poetry (in the Antilles poverty is poetry with a V, *une vie,* a condition of life as well as of imagination) seems capable of being profound because the nature around it is so exultant, so resolutely ecstatic, like its music. A culture based on joy is bound to be shallow. Sadly, to sell itself, the Caribbean encourages the delights of mindlessness, of brilliant vacuity, as a place to flee not only winter but that seriousness that comes only out of culture with four seasons. So how can there be a people there, in the true sense of the word?

They know nothing about seasons in which leaves let go of the year, in which spires fade in blizzards and streets whiten, of the erasures of whole cities by fog, of reflection in fireplaces; instead, they inhabit a geography whose rhythm, like their music, is limited to two stresses: hot and wet, sun and rain, light and shadow, day and night, the limitations of an incomplete metre, and are therefore a people incapable of the subtleties of contradiction, of imaginative complexity. So be it. We cannot change contempt.

Ours are not cities in the accepted sense, but no one wants them to be. They dictate their own proportions, their own definitions in particular places and in a prose equal to that of their detractors, so that now it is not just St. James but the streets and yards that Naipaul commemorates, its lanes as short and brilliant as his sentences; not just the noise and jostle of Tunapuna but the origins of C.L.R. James's *Beyond a Boundary,* not just Felicity village on the Caroni plain, but Selvon Country, and that is the way it goes up the islands now: the old Dominica of Jean Rhys still very much the way she wrote of it; and the Martinique of the early Césaire; Perse's Guadeloupe, even without the pith helmets and the mules; and what delight and privilege there was in watching a literature—one literature in several imperial languages, French, English, Spanish—bud and open island after island in the early morning of a culture, not timid, not derivative, any more than the hard white petals of the frangipani are derivative and timid. This is not a belligerent boast but a simple celebration of inevitability: that this flowering had to come.

On a heat-stoned afternoon in Port of Spain, some alley white with glare, with love vine spilling over a fence, palms and a hazed mountain appear around a corner to the evocation of Vaughn or Herbert's "that shady city of palm-trees", or to the memory of a Hammond organ from a wooden chapel in Castries, where the congregation sang "Jerusalem, the Golden". It is hard for me to see such emptiness as desolation. It is that patience that is the width of Antillean life, and the secret is not to ask the wrong thing of it, not to demand of it an ambition it has no interest in. The traveller reads this as lethargy, as torpor.

Here there are not enough books, one says, no theatres, no museums, simply not enough to do. Yet, deprived of books, a man must fall back on thought, and out of thought, if he can learn to order it, will come the urge to record, and in extremity, if he has no means of recording, recitation, the ordering of memory which leads to metre, to commemoration. There can be virtues in deprivation, and certainly one virtue is salvation from a cascade of high mediocrity, since books are now not so much created as remade. Cities create a culture, and all we have are these magnified market towns, so what are the proportions of the ideal Caribbean city? A surrounding, accessible countryside with leafy suburbs, and if the city is lucky, behind it, spacious plains. Behind it, fine mountains; before it, an indigo sea. Spires would pin its centre and around them would be leafy, shadowy parks. Pigeons would cross its sky in alphabetic patterns, carrying with them memories of a belief in augury, and at the heart of the city there would be horses, yes, horses, those animals last seen at the end of the nineteenth century drawing broughams and carriages with top-hatted citizens, horses that live in the present tense without elegiac echoes from their hooves, emerging from paddocks at the Queen's Park Savannah at sunrise, when mist is unthreading from the cool mountains above the roofs, and at the centre of the city seasonally there would be races, so that citizens could roar at the speed and grace of these nineteenth-century animals. Its docks, not obscured by smoke or deafened by too much machinery, and above all, it would be so racially various that the cultures of the world — the Asiatic, the Mediterranean, the European, the African — would be represented in it, its humane variety more exciting than Joyce's Dublin. Its citizens would inter-marry as they chose, from instinct, not tradition, until their children find it increasingly futile to trace their genealogy. It would not have too many avenues difficult or dangerous for pedestrians, its mercantile area would be a cacophony of accents, fragments of the old language that would be silenced immediately at five o'clock, its docks resolutely vacant on Sundays.

This is Port of Spain to me, a city ideal in its commercial and human proportions, where a citizen is a walker and not a pedestrian, and this is how Athens may have been before it became a cultural echo.

The finest silhouettes of Port of Spain are idealizations of the craftsman's handiwork, not of concrete and glass, but of baroque woodwork, each fantasy looking more like an involved drawing of itself than the actual building. Behind the city is the Caroni plain, with its villages, Indian prayer flags, and fruit vendors' stalls along the highway over which ibises come like floating flags. Photogenic poverty! Postcard sadnesses! I am not re-creating Eden; I mean, by "the Antilles", the reality of light, of work, of survival. I mean a house on the side of a country road, I mean the Caribbean Sea, whose smell is the smell of refreshing possibility as well as survival. Survival is the triumph of stubbornness, and spiritual stubbornness, a sublime stupidity, is what makes the occupation of poetry endure, when there are so many things that should make it futile. Those things added together can go under one collective noun: "the world".

This is the visible poetry of the Antilles, then. Survival.

If you wish to understand that consoling pity with which the islands were regarded, look at the tinted engravings of Antillean forests, with their proper palm trees, ferns, and waterfalls. They have a civilizing decency, like Botanical Gardens, as if the sky were a glass ceiling under which a colonized vegetation is arranged for quiet walks and carriage rides. Those views are incised with a pathos that guides the engraver's tool and the topographer's pencil, and it is this pathos which, tenderly ironic, gave villages names like Felicity. A century looked at a landscape furious with vegetation in the wrong light and with the wrong eye. It is such pictures that are saddening rather than the tropics itself. These delicate engravings of sugar mills and harbours, of native women in costume, are seen as a part of History, that History which looked over the shoulder of the engraver and, later, the photographer. History can alter the eye and the moving hand to conform a view of itself; it can rename places for the nostalgia in an echo; it can temper the glare of tropical light to elegiac monotony in prose, the tone of judgement in Conrad, in the travel journals of Trollope.

These travellers carried with them the infection of their own malaise, and their prose reduced even the landscape to melancholia and self-contempt. Every endeavor is belittled as imitation, from architecture to music. There was this conviction in Froude that since History is based on achievement, and since the history of the Antilles was so genetically corrupt, so depressing in its cycles of massacres, slavery, and indenture, a culture was inconceivable and nothing could ever be created in those ramshackle ports, those monotonously feudal sugar estates. Not only the light and salt of Antillean mountains defied this, but the demotic vigour and variety of their inhabitants. Stand close to a waterfall and you will stop hearing its roar. To be still in the nineteenth century, like horses, as Brodsky has written, may not be such a bad deal, and much of our life in the Antilles still seems to be in the rhythm of the last century, like the West Indian novel.

By writers even as refreshing as Graham Greene, the Caribbean is looked at with elegiac pathos, a prolonged sadness to which Lévi-Strauss has supplied an epigraph: *Tristes Tropiques*. Their *tristesse* derives from an attitude to the Caribbean dusk, to rain, to uncontrollable vegetation, to the provincial ambition of Caribbean cities where brutal replicas of modern architecture dwarf the small houses and streets. The mood is understandable, the melancholy as contagious as the fever of a sunset, like the gold fronds of diseased coconut palms, but there is something alien and ultimately wrong in the way such a sadness, even a morbidity, is described by English, French, or some of our exiled writers. It relates to a misunderstanding of the light and the people on whom the light falls.

These writers describe the ambitions of our unfinished cities, their unrealized, homiletic conclusion, but the Caribbean city may conclude just at that point where it is satisfied with its own scale, just as Caribbean culture is not evolving but already shaped. Its proportions are not to be measured by the traveller or the exile, but by its own citizenry and architecture. To be told you are not yet a city or a culture requires this response. I am not your city or your culture. There might be less of *Tristes Tropiques* after that.

Here, on the raft of this dais, there is the sound of the applauding surf: our landscape, our history recognized, "at last". *At Last is* one of the first Caribbean books. It was written by the Victorian traveller Charles Kingsley. It is one of the early books to admit the Antillean landscape and its figures into English literature. I have never read it but gather that its tone is benign. The Antillean archipelago was there to be written about, not to write itself, by Trollope, by Patrick Leigh-Fermor, in the very tone in which I almost wrote about the village spectacle at Felicity, as a compassionate and beguiled outsider, distancing myself from Felicity village even while I was enjoying it. What is hidden cannot be loved. The traveller cannot love, since love is stasis and travel is motion. If he returns to what he loved in a landscape and stays there, he is no longer a traveller but in stasis and concentration, the lover of that particular part of earth, a native. So many people say they "love the Caribbean", meaning that someday they plan to return for a visit but could never live there, the usual benign insult of the traveller, the tourist. These travellers, at their kindest, were devoted to the same patronage, the islands passing in profile, their vegetal luxury, their backwardness and poverty. Victorian prose dignified them. They passed by in beautiful profiles and were forgotten, like a vacation.

Alexis Saint-Léger Léger, whose writer's name is Saint-John Perse, was the first Antillean to win this prize for poetry. He was born in Guadeloupe and wrote in French, but before him, there was nothing as fresh and clear in feeling as those poems of his childhood, that of a privileged white child on an Antillean plantation, *"Pour Fêter une Enfance", "Éloges"*, and later *"Images à Crusoe"*. At last, the first breeze on the page, salt-edged and self-renewing as the trade winds, the sound of pages and palm trees turning as "the odour of coffee ascents the stairs".

Caribbean genius is condemned to contradict itself. To celebrate Perse, we might be told, is to celebrate the old plantation system, to celebrate the *bequé* or plantation rider, verandahs and mulatto servants, a white French language in a white pith helmet, to celebrate a rhetoric of patronage and hauteur; and even if Perse denied his origins, great writers often have this folly of trying to smother their source, we cannot deny him any more than we can the African Aimé Césaire. This is not accommodation, this is the ironic republic that is poetry, since, when I see cabbage palms moving their fronds at sunrise, I think they are reciting Perse.

The fragrant and privileged poetry that Perse composed to celebrate his white childhood and the recorded Indian music behind the brown young archers of Felicity, with the same cabbage palms against the same Antillean sky, pierce me equally. I feel the same poignancy of pride in the poems as in the faces. Why, given the history of the Antilles, should this be remarkable? The history of the world, by which of course we mean Europe, is a record of intertribal lacerations, of ethnic cleansings. At last, islands not written about but writing themselves! The palms and the Muslim minarets are Antillean exclamations. At last! the royal palms of Guadeloupe recite *"Eloges"* by heart.

Later, in *"Anabase"*, Perse assembled fragments of an imaginary epic, with the clicking teeth of frontier gates, barren wadis with the froth of poisonous lakes, horsemen burnoosed in sandstorms, the opposite of cool Caribbean mornings, yet not necessarily a contrast any more than some young brown archer at Felicity, hearing the sacred text blared across the flagged field, with its battles and elephants and monkey-gods, in a contrast to the white child in Guadeloupe assembling fragments of his own epic from the lances of the cane fields, the estate carts and oxens, and the calligraphy of bamboo leaves from the ancient languages, Hindi, Chinese, and Arabic, on the Antillean sky. From the *Ramayana* to Anabasis, from Guadeloupe to Trinidad, all that archaeology of fragments lying around, from the broken African kingdoms, from the crevasses of Canton, from Syria and Lebanon, vibrating not under the earth but in our raucous, demotic streets.

A boy with weak eyes skims a flat stone across the flat water of an Aegean inlet, and that ordinary action with the scything elbow contains the skipping lines of the *Iliad* and the *Odyssey,* and another child aims a bamboo arrow at a village festival, another hears the rustling march of cabbage palms in a Caribbean sunrise, and from that sound, with its fragments of tribal myth, the compact expedition of Perse's epic is launched, centuries and archipelagoes apart. For every poet it is always morning in the world. History a forgotten, insomniac night; History and elemental awe are always our early beginning, because the fate of poetry is to fall in love with the world, in spite of History.

There is a force of exultation, a celebration of luck, when a writer finds himself a witness to the early morning of a culture that is defining itself, branch by branch, leaf by leaf, in that self-defining dawn, which is why, especially at the edge of the sea, it is good to make a ritual of the sunrise. Then the noun, the "Antilles" ripples like brightening water, and the sounds of leaves, palm fronds, and birds are the sounds of a fresh dialect, the native tongue. The personal vocabulary, the individual melody whose metre is one's biography, joins in that sound, with any luck, and the body moves like a walking, a waking island.

This is the benediction that is celebrated, a fresh language and a fresh people, and this is the frightening duty owed.

I stand here in their name, if not their image—but also in the name of the dialect they exchange like the leaves of the trees whose names are suppler, greener, more morning-stirred than English—*laurier canelles, bois-flot, bois-canot*—or the valleys the trees mention—*Fond St. Jacques, Mabonya, Forestièr, Roseau, Mahaut*—or the empty beaches—*L'Anse Ivrogne, Case en Bas, Paradis*—all songs and histories in themselves, pronounced not in French—but in patois.

One rose hearing two languages, one of the trees, one of schoolchildren reciting in English:

> I am monarch of all I survey,
> My right there is none to dispute;
> From the centre all round to the sea
> I am lord of the fowl and the brute.
> Oh, solitude! where are the charms
> That sages have seen in thy face?
> Better dwell in the midst of alarms,
> Than reign in this horrible place...

While in the country to the same metre, but to organic instruments, handmade violin, chac-chac, and goatskin drum, a girl named Sensenne singing:

> *Si mwen di 'ous' ça fait mwen la peine*
> *'Ous kai dire ça vrai.*
> (If I told you that caused me pain
> You'll say, "It's true".)
> *Si mwen di 'ous ça pentetrait mwen*
> *'Ous peut dire ça vrai*
> (If I told you you pierced my heart
> You'd say, "It's true".)
> *Ces mamailles actuellement*
> *Pas ka faire l'amour z'autres pour un rien.*
> (Children nowadays
> Don't make love for nothing.)

It is not that History is obliterated by this sunrise. It is there in Antillean geography, in the vegetation itself. The sea sighs with the drowned from the Middle Passage, the butchery of its aborigines, Carib and Aruac and Taino, bleeds in the scarlet of the immortelle, and even the actions of surf on sand cannot erase the African memory, or the lances of cane as a green prison where indentured Asians, the ancestors of Felicity, are still serving time.

That is what I have read around me from boyhood, from the beginnings of poetry, the grace of effort. In the hard mahogany of woodcutters: faces, resinous men, charcoal burners; in a man with a cutlass cradled across his forearm, who stands on the verge with the usual anonymous khaki dog; in the extra clothes he put on this morning, when it was cold when he rose in the thinning dark to go and make his garden in the heights — the heights, the garden, being miles away from his house, but that is where he has his land — not to mention the fishermen, the footmen on trucks, groaning up mornes, all fragments of Africa originally but shaped and hardened and rooted now in the island's life, illiterate in the way leaves are illiterate; they do not read, they are there to be read, and if they are properly read, they create their own literature.

But in our tourist brochures the Caribbean is a blue pool into which the republic dangles the extended foot of Florida as inflated rubber islands bob and drinks with umbrellas float towards her on a raft. This is how the islands from the shame of necessity sell themselves; this is the seasonal erosion of their identity, that high-pitched repetition of the same images of service that cannot distinguish one island from the other, with a future of polluted marinas, land deals negotiated by ministers, and all of this conducted to the music of Happy Hour and the rictus of a smile. What is the earthly paradise for our visitors? Two weeks without rain and a mahogany tan, and, at sunset, local troubadours in straw hats and floral shirts beating "Yellow Bird" and "Banana Boat Song" to death. There is a territory wider than this — wider than the limits made by the map of an island — which is the illimitable sea and what it remembers.

All of the Antilles, every island, is an effort of memory; every mind, every racial biography culminating in amnesia and fog. Pieces of sunlight through the fog and sudden rainbows, *arcs-enciel*. That is the effort, the labour of the Antillean imagination, rebuilding its gods from bamboo frames, phrase by phrase.

Decimation from the Aruac downwards is the blasted root of Antillean history, and the benign blight that is tourism can infect all of those island nations, not gradually, but with imperceptible speed, until each rock is whitened by the guano of white-winged hotels, the arc and descent of progress.

Before it is all gone, before only a few valleys are left, pockets of an older life, before development turns every artist into an anthropologist or folklorist, there are still cherishable places, little valleys that do not echo with ideas, a simplicity of rebeginnings, not yet corrupted by the dangers of change. Not nostalgic sites but occluded sanctities as common and simple as their sunlight. Places as threatened by this prose as a headland is by the bulldozer or a sea almond grove by the surveyor's string, or from blight, the mountain laurel.

One last epiphany: A basic stone church in a thick valley outside Soufrière, the hills almost shoving the houses around into a brown river, a sunlight that looks oily on the leaves, a backward place, unimportant, and one now being corrupted into significance by this prose. The idea is not to

153

hallow or invest the place with anything, not even memory. African children in Sunday frocks come down the ordinary concrete steps into the church, banana leaves hang and glisten, a truck is parked in a yard, and old women totter towards the entrance. Here is where a real fresco should be painted, one without importance, but one with real faith, mapless, Historyless.

How quickly it could all disappear! And how it is beginning to drive us further into where we hope are impenetrable places, green secrets at the end of bad roads, headlands where the next view is not of a hotel but of some long beach without a figure and the hanging question of some fisherman's smoke at its far end. The Caribbean is not an idyll, not to its natives. They draw their working strength from it organically, like trees, like the sea almond or the spice laurel of the heights. Its peasantry and its fishermen are not there to be loved or even photographed; they are trees who sweat, and whose bark is filmed with salt, but every day on some island, rootless trees in suits are signing favourable tax breaks with entrepreneurs, poisoning the sea almond and the spice laurel of the mountains to their roots. A morning could come in which governments might ask what happened not merely to the forests and the bays but to a whole people.

They are here again, they recur, the faces, corruptible angels, smooth black skins and white eyes huge with an alarming joy, like those of the Asian children of Felicity at *Ramleela;* two different religions, two different continents, both filling the heart with the pain that is joy.

But what is joy without fear? The fear of selfishness that, here on this podium with the world paying attention not to them but to me, I should like to keep these simple joys inviolate, not because they are innocent, but because they are true. They are as true as when, in the grace of this gift, Perse heard the fragments of his own epic of Asia Minor in the rustling of cabbage palms, that inner Asia of the soul through which imagination wanders, if there is such a thing as imagination as opposed to the collective memory of our entire race, as true as the delight of that warrior-child who flew a bamboo arrow over the flags in the field at Felicity; and now as grateful a joy and a blessed fear as when a boy opened an exercise book and, within the discipline of its margins, framed stanzas that might contain the light of the hills on an island blest by obscurity, cherishing our insignificance.

154

Rigoberta Menchú

RIGOBERTA MENCHÚ TUM —

A BRIEF BIOGRAPHICAL SKETCH

Rigoberta Menchú was born on 9 January 1959 to a poor Indian peasant family, and raised in the Quiché branch of the Mayan culture. In her early years she helped with the family farm work, either in the northern highlands where her family lived, or on the Pacific coast, where both adults and children went to pick coffee on the big plantations.

Rigoberta Menchú soon became involved in social reform activities through the Catholic Church, and became prominent in the women's rights movement when still only a teenager. Such reform work aroused considerable opposition in influential circles, especially after a guerilla organization established itself in the area. The Menchú family was accused of taking part in guerrilla activities, and Rigoberta's father Vicente was imprisoned and tortured for allegedly having participated in the execution of a local plantation owner. After his release, he joined the recently founded Committee of the Peasant Union (CUC).

In 1979, Rigoberta, too, joined the CUC. That year her brother was arrested, tortured and killed by the army. The following year her father was killed when security forces in the capital stormed the Spanish Embassy, where he and some other peasants were staying. Shortly afterwards, her mother also died after having been arrested, tortured and raped. Rigoberta became increasingly active in the CUC, and taught herself Spanish as well as other Mayan languages than her native Quiché. In 1980, she figured prominently in a strike the CUC organized for better conditions for farm workers on the Pacific coast, and on 1 May 1981 she was active in large demonstrations in the capital. She joined the radical 31st of January Popular Front, in which her contribution chiefly consisted of educating the Indian peasant population in resistance to massive military oppression.

In 1981, Rigoberta Menchú had to go into hiding in Guatemala, and then flee to Mexico. That marked the beginning of a new phase in her life, as the organizer abroad of resistance to oppression in Guatemala and the struggle for Indian peasant peoples' rights. In 1982, she took part in the founding of the joint opposition body the United Representation of the Guatemalan Opposition (RUOG). In 1983, she told her life story to Elisabeth Burgos-Debray. The resulting book, called in English *I, Rigoberta Menchú*, is a gripping human document which attracted considerable international attention. In 1986, Rigoberta Menchú became a member of the National Coordinating Committee of the CUC, and the following year she performed as the narrator in a powerful film called *When the Mountains Tremble*, about the struggles and sufferings of the Maya people. On at least three occasions

Rigoberta Menchú has returned to Guatemala to plead the cause of the Indian peasants, but death threats have forced her to return into exile.

Over the years, Rigoberta Menchú has become widely known as a leading advocate of Indian rights and ethno-cultural reconciliation, not only in Guatemala but in the Western Hemisphere generally, and her work has earned her several international awards.

NOBEL LECTURE

Oslo, December 10, 1992

by

Rigoberta Menchú Tum

Guatemala, and Comité de Unidad Campesina (CUC), Mexico.

Honorables señores del Comité Nobel de la Paz,
Sus majestades los Reyes de Noruega,
Excelentísima señora Primer Ministro,
Excelentísimos miembros de gobiernos y del Cuerpo Diplomático,
Apreciables compatriotas guatemaltecos,
Señoras y señores.

Me llena de emoción y orgullo la distinción que se me hace al otorgarme el Premio Nobel de la Paz 1992. Emoción personal y orgullo por mi Patria de cultura milenaria. Por los valores de la comunidad del pueblo al que pertenezco, por el amor a mi tierra, a la madre naturaleza. Quien entiende esta relación, respeta la vida y exalta la lucha que se hace por esos objetivos.

Considero este Premio, no como un galardón hacia mí en lo personal, sino como una de las conquistas más grandes de la lucha por la paz, por los derechos humanos y por los derechos de los pueblos indígenas, que a lo largo de estos 500 años han sido divididos y fragmentados y han sufrido el genocidio, la represión y la discriminación.

Permítanme expresarles todo lo que para mí significa este Premio.

En mi opinión, el Premio Nobel nos convoca a actuar en función de lo que representa y en función de su gran trascendencia mundial. Es, además de una inapreciable presea, un instrumento de lucha por la paz, por la justicia, por los derechos de los que sufren las abismales desigualdades económicas, sociales, culturales y políticas, propias del orden mundial en que vivimos, y cuya transformación en un nuevo mundo basado en los valores de la persona humana, es la expectativa de la gran mayoría de seres que habitamos este planeta.

Este Premio Nobel significa un portaestandarte para proseguir con la denuncia de la vioiación de los Derechos Humanos, que se cometen contra los pueblos en Guatemala, en América y en el mundo, y para desempeñar un papel positivo en la tarea que más urge en mi país, que es el logro de la paz con justicia social.

El Premio Nobel es un emblema de la Paz y del trabajo en la construcción de una verdadera democracia. Estimulará a los sectores civiles para que, en

159

una sólida unidad nacional, aporten en el proceso de negociaciones en busca de la paz, reflejando el sentir generalizado — aunque algunas veces no expresado por el temor — de la sociedad guatemalteca; el de sentar las bases políticas y jurídicas para darle impulso irreversible a la solución de las causas que dieron origen al conflicto armado interno.

Sin duda alguna, constituye una señal de esperanza para las luchas de los pueblos indígenas en todo el Continente.

También es un homenaje para los pueblos centroamericanos que aún buscan su estabilidad, la conformación de su futuro y el sendero de su desarrollo e integración sobre la base de la democracia civil y el respeto mutuo.

El significado que tiene este Premio Nobel lo demuestran los mensajes de felicitación que llegaron de todas partes, desde jefes de Estado — casi todos los Presidentes de América — hasta las Organizaciones Indígenas y de Derechos Humanos, de todas partes del mundo. De hecho, ellos ven en este Premio Nobel no solamente un galardón y un reconocimiento a una persona, sino un punto de partida de arduas luchas por el logro de esas reivindicaciones que están todavía por cumplirse.

En contraste, paradójicamente, fue precisamente en mi país donde encontré de parte de algunos las mayores objeciones, reservas e indiferencia respecto al otorgamiento del Nobel a esta india quiché. Tal vez porque, en América, sea precisamente en Guatemala en donde la discriminación hacia el indígena, hacia la mujer y la resistencia hacia los anhelos de justicia y paz, se encuentran más arraigadas en ciertos sectores sociales y políticos.

En las actuales circunstancias de este mundo convulso y complejo, la decisión del Comité Noruego del Premio Nobel de la Paz de otorgarme esta honorable distinción, refleja la conciencia de que por ese medio se está dando un gran aliento a los esfuerzos de paz, reconciliación y justicia; a la lucha contra el racismo, la discriminación cultural, para contribuir al logro de la convivencia armónica entre nuestros pueblos.

Con profundo dolor, por una parte, pero con satisfacción por otra, hago del conocimiento de ustedes, que temporalmente el Premio Nobel de la Paz 1992 tendrá que permanecer en la Ciudad de México, en vigilia por la paz en Guatemala. Porque no hay condiciones políticas en mi país que permitan avizorar una pronta y justa solución. La satisfacción y reconocimiento provienen del hecho de que México, nuestro hermano país vecino, que tanto interés y esfuerzo ha puesto en las negociaciones que se realizan para lograr la paz y ha acogido a los refugiados y exiliados guatemaltecos, nos ha otorgado un lugar en el Museo del Templo Mayor (cuna de la memoria milenaria de los Aztecas) para que el Premio Nobel resida, en tanto se crean las condiciones de paz y seguridad para ubicarlo en Guatemala, la tierra del Quetzal.

Al valorar en todo lo que significa el otorgamiento del Premio Nobel, quiero decir algunas palabras en representación de aquellos que no pueden hacer llegar su voz o son reprimidos por expresarla en forma de opinión, de los marginados, de los discriminados, de los que viven en la pobreza, en la miseria, víctimas de la represión y de la violación a los derechos humanos. Sin embargo, ellos que han resistido por siglos, no han perdido la conciencia, la determinación, la esperanza.

Permítanme, señoras y señores, decirles algunas palabras sobre mi país y la Civilización Maya. Los Pueblos Mayas se desarrollaron geográficamente en una extensión de 300 mil kilómetros cuadrados; ocuparon lugares en el Sur de México, Belice, Guatemala y partes de Honduras y El Salvador; desarrollaron una civilización muy rica en los campos de la organización política, en lo social y económico; fueron grandes científicos en lo concerniente a las matemáticas, la astronomía, la agricultura, la arquitectura y la ingeniería; y grandes artistas en la escultura, la pintura, el tejido y el tallado.

Los Mayas descubrieron la categoría matemática CERO, casi al mismo tiempo que ésta fue descubierta en la India y después trasladada a los árabes. Sus previsiones astronómicas basadas en cálculos matemáticos y observaciones científicas, son asombrosos todavía ahora. Elaboraron un calendario más exacto que el Gregoriano, y en la medicina practicaron operaciones quirúrgicas intracraneanas.

En uno de los libros Mayas que escaparon de la destrucción conquistadora, conocido como *Códice de Dresden*, aparecen los resultados de la investigación acerca de los eclipses y contiene una tabla de 69 fechas, en las cuales ocurren eclipses solares en un lapso de 33 años.

Es importante destacar hoy el respeto profundo de la civilización Maya hacia la vida y la naturaleza en general.

¿Quién puede predecir qué otras grandes conquistas científicas y qué desarrollo habrían logrado alcanzar esos pueblos, si no hubieran sido conquistados a sangre y fuego, objetos del etnocidio, que alcanzó casi 50 millones de personas en 50 años?

Este Premio Nobel lo interpreto primero como un homenaje a los pueblos indígenas sacrificados y desaparecidos por la aspiración de una vida más digna, justa, libre, de fraternidad y comprensión entre los humanos. Los que ya no están vivos para albergar la esperanza de un cambio de la situación de pobreza y marginación de los indígenas, relegados y desamparados en Guatemala y en todo el continente americano.

Reconforta esta creciente atención, aunque llegue 500 años más tarde, hacia el sufrimiento, la discriminación, la opresión y explotación que nuestros pueblos han sufrido, pero que gracias a su propia cosmovisión y concepción de la vida han logrado resistir y finalmente ver con perspectivas promisorias. Cómo, de aquellas raíces que se quisieron erradicar, germinan ahora con pujanza, esperanzas y representaciones para el futuro.

Implica también una manifestación del progresivo interés y comprensión internacional por los Derechos los Pueblos originarios, por el futuro de los más de 60 millones de indígenas que habitan nuestra América y su fragor de protesta por los 500 años de opresión que han soportado. Por el genocidio incomparable que han sufrido en toda esta época, del que otros países y las élites en America se han favorecido y aprovechado.

¡Libertad para los indios donde quieran que estén en América y en el mundo, porque mientras vivan vivirá un brillo de esperanza y un pensar original de la vida!

Las manifestaciones de júbilo de las Organizaciones Indígenas de todo el continente y las congratulaciones mundiales recibidas por el otorgamiento del Premio Nobel de la Paz, expresan claramente la trascendencia de esta decisión. Es el reconocimiento de una deuda de Europa para con los pueblos indígenas americanos; es un llamado a la conciencia de la Humanidad para que se erradiquen las condiciones de marginación que los condenó al coloniaje y a la explotación de los no indígenas; y es un clamor por la vida, la paz, la justicia, la igualdad y hermandad entre los seres humanos.

La particularidad de la visión de los pueblos indígenas se manifiesta en las formas de relacionarse. Primero, entre los seres humanos, de manera comunitaria. Segundo, con la tierra, como nuestra madre, porque nos da la vida y no es sólo una mercancía. Tercero, con la naturaleza; pues somos partes integrales de ella y no sus dueños.

La madre tierra es para nosotros, no solamente fuente de riqueza económica que nos da el maíz, que es nuestra vida, sino proporciona tantas cosas que ambicionan los privilegiados de hoy. La tierra es raíz y fuente de nuestra cultura. Ella contiene nuestra memoria, ella acoge a nuestros antepasados y requiere por lo tanto también que nosotros la honremos y le devolvamos con ternura y respeto los bienes que nos brinda. Hay que cuidar y guardar la madre tierra para que nuestros hijos y nuestros nietos sigan percibiendo sus beneficios. Si el mundo no aprende ahora a respetar la naturaleza ¿qué futuro tendrán las nuevas generaciones?

De estos rasgos fundamentales se derivan comportamientos, derechos y obligaciones en el continente americano, tanto para los indígenas como para los no indígenas, sean estos mestizos, negros, blancos o asiáticos. Toda la sociedad tiene la obligación de respetarse mutuamente, de aprender los unos de los otros y de compartir las conquistas materiales y científicas, según su propia conveniencia. Los indígenas jamás han tenido, ni tienen, el lugar que les corresponde en los avances y los beneficios de la ciencia y la tecnología, no obstante que han sido base importante de ellos.

Las civilizaciones indígenas y las civilizaciones europeas de haber tenido intercambios de manera pacífica y armoniosa, sin que mediara la destrucción, explotación, discriminación y miseria, seguramente habrían logrado una conjunción con mayores y más valiosas conquistas para la Humanidad.

No debemos olvidar que cuando los europeos llegaron a América, florecían civilizaciones pujantes. No se puede hablar de descubrimiento de América, porque se descubre lo que se ignora o se encuentra oculto. Pero América y sus civilizaciones nativas se habían descubierto a sí mismas mucho antes de la caída del Imperio Romano y del Medioevo europeo. Los alcances de sus culturas forman parte del patrimonio de la Humanidad y siguen asombrando a sus estudiosos.

Pienso que es necesario que los pueblos indígenas, de los que soy una de sus miembros, aporten su ciencia y sus conocimientos al desarrollo de los humanos, porque tenemos enormes potenciales para ello, intercalando nuestras herencias milenarias con los avances de la civilización en Europa y otras regiones del mundo.

Pero ese aporte, que nosotros entendemos como un rescate del patrimonio natural y cultural, debe de ser en tanto que actores de una planificación racional y consensual del usufructo de los conocimientos y recursos naturales, con garantías de igualdad ante el Estado y la sociedad.

Los indígenas estamos dispuestos a combinar tradición con modernidad, pero no a cualquier precio. No consentiremos que el futuro se nos plantee como posibles guardias de proyectos etnoturísticos a escala continental.

En un momento de resonancia mundial en torno a la conmemoración del V Centenario de la llegada de Cristobal Colón a tierras americanas, el despertar de los pueblos indígenas oprimidos nos exige reafirmar ante el mundo nuestra existencia y la validez de nuestra identidad cultural. Nos exige que luchemos para participar activamente en la decisión de nuestro destino, en la construcción de nuestros estados-naciones. Si con ello no somos tomados en cuenta, hay factores que garantizan nuestro futuro: la lucha y la resistencia; las reservas de ánimo; la decisión de mantener nuestras tradiciones puestas a prueba por tantas dificultades, obstáculos y sufrimientos; la solidaridad para con nuestras luchas por parte de muchos países, gobiernos, organizaciones y ciudadanos del orbe.

Por eso sueño con el día en que la interrelación respetuosa justa entre los pueblos indígenas y otros pueblos se fortalezca, sumando potencialidades y capacidades que contribuyan a hacer la vida en este planeta menos desigual, más distributiva de los tesoros científicos y culturales acumulados por la Humanidad, floreciente de paz y justicia.

Creo que esto es posible en la práctica y no solamente en la teoría. Pienso que esto es posible en Guatemala y en muchos otros países que se encuentran sumidos en el atraso, el racismo, la descriminación y el subdesarrollo.

El día de hoy, en el 47 período de sesiones de la Asamblea General, la Organización de Naciones Unidas — ONU — inaugura 1993 como *Año Internacional de los Pueblos Indios,* en presencia de destacados dirigentes de las organizaciones de los pueblos indígenas y de la coordinación del Movimiento Continental de Resistencia Indígena, Negra y Popular, que participarán protocolariamente en la apertura de labores a fin de exigir que 1993 sea un año con acciones concretas para darle verdaderamente su lugar a los pueblos indígenas en sus contextos nacionales y en el concierto internacional.

La conquista del *Año Internacional de los Pueblos Indígenas* y los avances que representa la elaboración del proyecto de *Declaración Universal* son producto de la participación de numerosos hermanos indígenas, organizaciones no gubernamentales y la gestión éxitosa de los expertos del Grupo de Trabajo asi como la comprensión de varios estados en el seno de la Organización de las Naciones Unidas.

Esperamos que la formulación del proyecto de *Declaración sobre los Derechos de los Pueblos Indígenas* examine y profundice en la contradicción existente entre los avances en materia de derecho internacional y la difícil realidad que en la práctica vivimos los indoamericanos.

Nuestros pueblos tendrán un año dedicado a los problemas que los aquejan y, para ello, se aprestan a llevar a cabo actividades con el objetivo de hacer planteamientos y presionar, mediante las más razonables formas y las argumentaciones más valederas y justas, para la eliminación del racismo, la opresión, la discriminación y la explotación que los ha sumido en la miseria y en el olvido. Para *los condenados de la tierra* también la adjudicación del Premio Nobel representa un reconocimiento, un aliciente y un objetivo.

Desearía que se desarrollara en todos los pueblos un consciente sentido de paz y el sentimiento de solidaridad humana, que puedan abrir nuevas relaciones de respeto e igualdad para el próximo milenio, que deberá ser de fraternidad y no de conflictos cruentos.

En todas partes se está conformando una opinión sobre un fenómeno de actualidad, que a pesar de que se expresa entre guerras y violencia, le plantea a la Humanidad entera la defensa de su validez histórica: la unidad en la diversidad. Y que nos llama a la reflexión para incorporar importantes elementos de cambio y transformación en todos los aspectos de la vida del mundo, en busca de soluciones específicas y concretas a la profunda crisis ética que aqueja a la Humanidad. Esto sin duda tendrá influencias determinantes en la conformación del futuro.

Es posible que algunos centros de poder político y económico, algunos estadistas e intelectuales, todavía no alcancen a comprender el despertar y la configuración promisoria que significa la participación activa de los pueblos indígenas en todos los terrenos de la actividad humana, pero el movimiento amplio y plural desencadenado por las diferentes expresiones políticas e intelectuales amerindias terminará por convencerlos que objetivamente somos parte constituyente de las alternativas históricas que se están gestando a nivel mundial.

Señoras y señores, unas francas palabras sobre mi país.

La atención que con este Premio Nobel de la Paz se centra en Guatemala deberá permitir que internacionalmente se deje de ignorar la violación a los derechos humanos y honrará a todos aquellos que murieron luchando por la igualdad social y la justicia en mi país.

El mundo conoce que el pueblo guatemalteco, mediante su lucha, logró conquistar en octubre de 1944 un periodo de democracia, en que la institucionalidad y los derechos humanos fueron su filosofía esencial. En esa época, Guatemala fue excepcional en el continente americano en su lucha por alcanzar la plena soberanía nacional. Pero en 1954, en una confabulación que unió a los tradicionales centros de poder nacionales, herederos del coloniaje, con poderosos intereses extranjeros, el régimen democrático fue derrocado a través de una invasión armada e impuso de nuevo el viejo sistema de opresión que ha caracterizado la historia de mi país.

La sujeción política, económica y social que se derivó de ese producto de la guerra fría dio origen al conflicto armado interno. La represión contra las organizaciones populares, los partidos democráticos, los intelectuales empezó en Guatemala mucho antes de que se iniciara la guerra. No lo olvidemos.

En el intento de sofocar la rebelión, las dictaduras cometieron las más grandes atrocidades. Se arrasaron aldeas, se asesinaron decenas de miles de campesinos, principalmente indígenas, centenas de sindicalistas y estudiantes, numerosos periodistas por dar a conocer la información, connotados intelectuales y políticos, religiosos y religiosas. Por medio de la persecución sistemática, en aras de la doctrina de seguridad del Estado, se forzó al desplazamiento de un millón de campesinos; a la búsqueda del refugio por parte de 100 mil más en países vecinos. Hay en Guatemala casi 100 mil huérfanos y más de 40 mil viudas. En Guatemala se inventó, como política de Estado, la práctica de los desaparecidos políticos.

Como ustedes saben, yo misma soy sobreviviente de una familia masacrada.

El país se desplomó en una crisis sin precedentes y los cambios en el mundo obligaron e incitaron a los militares a permitir una apertura política que consistió en la elaboración de una nueva Constitución, en una ampliación del juego político y el traspaso del gobierno a sectores civiles. Llevamos ocho años de este nuevo régimen, en el que los sectores populares y medios se han abierto espacios importantes.

No obstante en los espacios abiertos persiste la represión y la violación a los derechos humanos en medio de una crisis económica, que se ha agudizado a tal punto, que el 84% de la población es considerada como pobre y alrededor del 60% como muy pobre. La impunidad y el terror continúan impidiendo la libre manifestación del pueblo por sus necesidades y demandas vitales. Perdura el conflicto armado interno.

La vida política de mi país ha girado en este último tiempo en torno a la búsqueda de una solución política a la crisis global y al conflicto armado que vive Guatemala desde 1962. Este proceso tuvo su origen en el Acuerdo suscrito en esta misma capital, Oslo, entre la Comisión Nacional de Reconciliación con mandato gubernamental, y la Unidad Revolucionaria Nacional Guatemalteca, como un paso necesario para introducir a Guatemala en el espíritu del *Acuerdo de Esquipulas*.

Como consecuencia de este Acuerdo, después de la realización de conversaciones entre la URNG y diversos sectores de la sociedad guatemalteca, se iniciaron durante el régimen del Presidente Serrano negociaciones directas entre el gobierno y la guerrilla, resultado de las cuales han sido ya firmados tres acuerdos. Sin embargo, el tema de los Derechos Humanos ha ocupado bastante tiempo, porque constituye un tema eje de la problemática guatemalteca y alrededor del cual han surgido importantes diferencias. No obstante, se ha avanzado considerablemente también en el mismo.

El proceso de negociaciones busca acuerdos para establecer las bases de una democratización verdadera y la finalización de la guerra. Entiendo que con la buena voluntad de las partes y la participación activa de los sectores civiles, conformando una gran unidad nacional, se podrá rebasar la etapa de los propósitos y sacar a Guatemala de esa encrucijada histórica que ya nos parace eternizarse.

El diálogo y la negociación política son, sin duda, requisitos adecuados para que estos problemas se resuelvan y así ofrecer respuestas valederas y concretas a necesidades vitales y urgentes para la vida y democratización de nuestro pueblo guatemalteco. Pues, estoy convencida de que si los diversos sectores sociales que integran la sociedad guatemalteca encuentran bases de unidad, respetando sus diferencias naturales, podrán hallar conjuntamente una solución a estos problemas y así resolver las causas que condujeron a la guerra que vive Guatemala.

Tanto los sectores civiles guatemaltecos como la comunidad internacional debemos exigir que las negociaciones entre el Gobierno y la URNG sobrepasen el periodo en que se encuentran en la discusión de los Derechos Humanos, y lleguen tan pronto como sea posible, a un acuerdo verificable por la Organización de las Naciones Unidas. Es necesario destacar aquí, en Oslo, que la situación de los Derechos Humanos en Guatemala constituye hoy por hoy el más urgente problema a resolver. Y mi afirmación no es ni casual ni gratuita.

Tal como lo han constatado instituciones internacionales como la Comisión de Derechos Humanos de la ONU, la Comisión Interamericana de Derechos Humanos y otros numerosos organismos humanitarios, Guatemala es uno de los países de América donde se comete el mayor número de violaciones a esos derechos, con la mayor impunidad, y en lo que generalmente están comprometidas de una u otra forma las fuerzas de seguridad. Es imprescindible que la represión y persecución que sufren los sectores populares e indígenas cesen. Que se ponga fin al reclutamiento forzado de jóvenes y a la integración forzada de las Patrullas de Autodefensa Civil, que afecta principalmente a los indígenas.

Urge construir una democracia en Guatemala. Es necesario lograr que se observen los derechos humanos en toda su gama: poner fin al racismo; garantizar la libre organización y locomoción de todos los sectores de la población. En definitiva, es imprescindible abrir el campo a la sociedad civil multiétnica, con todos sus derechos, desmilitarizar el país y sentar las bases para su desarrollo, a fin de sacarlo del atraso y la miseria en que se vive actualmente.

Uno de los más amargos dramas que puedan soportar porcentajes cuantiosos de población es el éxodo forzado. El verse obligados por la fuerza militar y la persecución a abandonar sus poblados, su madre tierra, el sitio de reposo de sus antepasados, su ambiente, la naturaleza que les dio la vida y la diseminación de sus comunidades, que constituyen un coherente sistema de organización social y de democracia funcional.

El caso de los desplazados y refugiados en Guatemala es desgarrador, una parte de ellos condenada al exilio en otros países y la gran mayoría al exilio en su propio país. Forzados a deambular de un lugar para otro, a vivir en barrancos y lugares inhóspitos, algunos desconocidos como ciudadanos guatemaltecos y todos condenados a la miseria y al hambre. No puede haber una democracia verdadera si este problema no se resuelve satisfactoriamente, reintegrando a esta población a sus tierras y poblados.

En la nueva sociedad guatemalteca una reorganización de la tenencia de la tierra es fundamental, para que permita tanto el desarrollo de las potencialidades agrícolas como la restitución a sus legítimos dueños de tierras comunales despojadas. Sin olvidar que este proceso reorganizador debe hacerse con el mayor respeto por la naturaleza, para preservarla y devolverle su vigor y capacidad de generar vida.

No menos distintiva de una democracia es la justicia social. Ella exige la solución de los aterradores índices de mortalidad infantil, de desnutrición, de falta de educacion, de analfabetismo, de salarios de exterminio. Estos problemas aquejan creciente y dolorosamente a la población guatemalteca, sin perspectivas ni esperanza.

Entre los rasgos que caracterizan a la sociedad actual está el papel de la mujer, sin que por ello la emancipación de la mujer haya sido conquistada plenamente en ningún país del mundo.

El desarrollo histórico de Guatemala refleja ahora la necesidad y la irreversibilidad de la contribución activa de la mujer en la configuración del nuevo orden social guatemalteco y, modestamente, pienso que las mujeres indígenas somos ya un claro testimonio de ello. Este Premio Nobel es un reconocimiento a quienes han sido, y todavía lo son en la mayor parte del mundo, las más explotadas de los explotados; las más discriminadas de los discriminados; las más marginadas de los marginados y, sin embargo, productoras de vida de conocimiento, de expresión y de riqueza.

La democracia, el desarrollo y la modernización de un país se hacen imposibles e incongruentes sin la solución de estos problemas.

Igualmente importante es el reconocimiento en Guatemala de la Identidad y los Derechos de los Pueblos Indígenas, que han sido ignorados y despreciados no sólo en el período colonial, sino en la era republicana. No se puede concebir una Guatemala democrática, libre y soberana, sin que la identidad indígena perfile su fisonomía en todos los aspectos de la existencia nacional.

Será indudablemente algo nuevo, inédito, con una fisonomía que en este momento no podemos formular. Pero responderá auténticamente a la Historia y a las características que debe comprender una verdadera nacionalidad guatemalteca. A su perfil verdadero, por tanto tiempo desfigurado.

Esta urgencia y esta vital necesidad, son las que me conducen en este momento, en esta tribuna, a plantear a la opinión nacional y a la comunidad internacional interesarse más activamente en Guatemala.

Tomando en consideración que en relación a mi papel como Premio Nobel en el proceso de negociaciones por la paz en Guatemala se han manejado un abanico de posibilidades, pienso que éste es más bien el de promotora de la paz, la unidad nacional, de la defensa de los derechos indígenas. De tal manera que pueda tomar iniciativas acordes a las que se vayan presentando, evitando de esta manera encasillar el Premio Nobel en un papel.

Convoco a todos los sectores sociales y étnicos que componen el pueblo de Guatemala a participar activamente en los esfuerzos por encontrar una solución pacífica al conflicto armado, forjando una sólida unidad entre los pueblos ladino, negro e indígena, que deben de formar en su diversidad la guatemalidad.

Con ese mismo sentido, yo invito a la comunidad internacional a contribuir con acciones concretas a que las partes superen las diferencias que en este momento mantienen las negociaciones en una situación de expectativa, y así se logre, primero, firmar un acuerdo sobre Derechos Humanos. Para que luego se reanuden las rondas de negociación y se encuentren los puntos de compromiso que permitan que este acuerdo de Paz sea firmado y que la verificación del mismo se haga inmediatamente, pues no me cabe la menor duda de que ésto traería un alivio substancial a la situación existente en Guatemala.

Según mi opinión, también una participación más directa de las Naciones Unidas, que fuera más allá de un papel de observador, podría ayudar substancialmente al proceso a salir del paso.

Señoras y señores, el hecho de que me haya referido preferencialmente a América, y en especial a mi país, no significa que no ocupe un lugar importante en mi mente y corazón la preocupación que viven otros pueblos del mundo en su incesante lucha por defender la paz, el derecho a la vida y todos sus derechos inalienables. La pluralidad de los que nos encontramos reunidos este día es un ejemplo de ello y en tal sentido les doy humildemente las gracias en nombre propio.

Muchas cosas han cambiado en estos años. Grandes transformaciones de carácter mundial han tenido lugar. Dejó de existir la confrontación Este-Oeste y se terminó la Guerra Fría. Estas transformaciones, cuyas modalidades definitivas no se pueden predecir, han dejado vacíos que pueblos del mundo han sabido aprovechar para emerger, luchar y ganar espacios nacionales y reconocimiento internacional.

En la actualidad, luchar por un mundo mejor, sin miseria, sin racismo, con paz en el Oriente Medio y el Sudoeste Asiático, a donde dirijo mi plegaria para la liberación de la señora Aung San Suu Kyi, Premio Nobel de la Paz 1991; por una solución justa y pacífica para los Balcanes; por el fin del apartheid en el Sur de Africa; por la estabilidad en Nicaragua; por el cumplimiento de los Acuerdos de Paz en El Salvador; por el restablecimiento de la democracia en Haití; por la plena soberanía de Panamá; por que todo ello constituye las más altas aspiraciones de justicia en la situación internacional.

Un mundo en paz que le dé coherencia, interrelación y concordancia a las estructuras económicas, sociales y culturales de las sociedades. Que tenga raíces profundas y una proyección robusta.

Tenemos en nuestra mente las demandas más sentidas de la Humanidad entera, cuando propugnamos por la convivencia pacífica y la preservación del medio ambiente.

La lucha que libramos acrisola y modela el porvenir.

168

Nuestra historia es una historia viva, que ha palpitado, resistido y sobrevivido siglos de sacrificios. Ahora resurge con vigor. Las semillas, durante tanto tiempo adormecidas, brotan hoy con certidumbre, no obstante que germinan en un mundo que se caracteriza actualmente por el desconcierto y la imprecisión.

Sin duda que será un proceso complejo y prolongado, pero no es una utopía y nosotros los indígenas tenemos ahora confianza en su realización. Sobre todo, si quienes añoramos la paz y nos esforzamos porque se respeten los derechos humanos en todas partes del mundo donde se violan, y nos oponemos al racismo, encaminamos nuestro empeño en la práctica con entrega y vehemencia.

El Pueblo de Guatemala se moviliza y está consciente de sus fuerzas para construir un futuro digno. Se prepara para sembrar el futuro, para liberarse de sus atavismos, para redescubrirse a sí mismo. Para construir un país con una auténtica identidad nacional. Para comenzar a vivir.

Combinando todos los matices ladinos, garífunas e indígenas del mosaico étnico de Guatemala debemos entrelazar cantidad de colores, sin entrar en contradicción, sin que sean grotescos y antagónicos, dándoles brillo y una calidad superior, como saben tejer nuestros artesanos. Un güipil genialmente integrado, una ofrenda a la Humanidad.

Muchas gracias

NOBEL LECTURE

English translation

Your Majesties, the King and Queen of Norway,
The Honourable Members of the Nobel Peace Committee,
Your Excellency, the Prime Minister,
Your Excellencies, members of the Government and the Diplomatic Corps,
Dear Guatemalan countrymen and women,
Ladies and Gentlemen,

I feel a deep emotion and pride for the honour of having been awarded the Nobel Peace Prize for 1992. A deep personal feeling and pride for my country and its very ancient culture. For the values of the community and the people to which I belong, for the love of my country, of Mother Nature. Whoever understands this respects life and encourages the struggle that aims at such objectives.

I consider this Prize, not as an award to me personally, but rather as one of the greatest conquests in the struggle for peace, for Human Rights and for the rights of the indigenous people who, for 500 years, have been split, fragmented, as well as the victims of genocides, repression and discrimination.

Please allow me to convey to you all, what this Prize means to me.

In my opinion, the Nobel Peace Price calls upon us to act in accordance with what it represents, and the great significance it has worldwide. In addition to being a priceless treasure, it is an instrument with which to fight for peace, for justice, for the rights of those who suffer the abysmal economical, social, cultural and political disparities, typical of the order of the world in which we live, and where the conversion into a new world based on the values of the human being, is the expectation of the majority of those who live on this planet.

This Nobel Prize represents a standard bearer that encourages us to continue denouncing the violation of Human Rights, committed against the people in Guatemala, in America and in the world, and to perform a positive role in respect of the most pressing task in my country, i.e. to achieve peace and social justice.

The Nobel Prize is a symbol of peace, and of the efforts to build up a real democracy. It will stimulate the civil sectors so that through a solid national unity, these may contribute to the process of negotiations that seek peace, reflecting the general feeling — although at times not possible to express because of fear — of Guatemalan society: to establish political and legal grounds that will give irreversible impulses to a solution to what initiated the internal armed conflict.

There is no doubt whatsoever that it constitutes a sign of hope in the struggle of the indigenous people in the entire Continent.

It is also a tribute to the Centro-American people who are still searching for their stability, for the structuring of their future, and the path for their development and integration, based on civil democracy and mutual respect.

The importance of this Nobel Prize has been demonstrated by all the congratulations received from everywhere, from Heads of Government — practically all the American Presidents — to the organizations of the indigenous people and of Human Rights, from all over the world. In fact, what they see in this Nobel Peace Price is not only a reward and a recognition of a single person, but a starting point for the hard struggle towards the achievement of those issues that remain to be complied with.

As a contrast, and paradoxically, it was actually in my own country where I met, on the part of some people, with the strongest objections, reserve and indifference, for the award of the Nobel Peace Prize. Perhaps because in Latin America, it is precisely in Guatemala where the discrimination towards natives, towards women, and the repression of the longing for justice and peace, are more deeply rooted in certain social and political sectors.

Under the present circumstances, in this disordered and complex world, the decision of the Norwegian Nobel Peace Prize Committee to award this honourable distinction to me, reflects the awareness of the fact that, in this way, courage and strength is given to the struggle for peace, reconciliation and justice; to the struggle against racism, cultural discrimination, and hence contributes to the achievement of harmonious co-existence between our people.

With deep pain, on one side, but with satisfaction on the other, I have to inform you that the Nobel Peace Prize 1992 will have to remain temporarily in Mexico City, in a kind of wake — waiting for peace in Guatemala. Because there are no political conditions in my country that would indicate or make me foresee a prompt and just solution. The satisfaction and gratitude are due to the fact that Mexico, our wonderful neighbour country, that has been so dedicated and interested, that has made such great efforts in respect of the negotiations that are being conducted to achieve peace, that has received and admitted so many refugees and exiled Guatemalans, has given us a place in the Museo del Templo Mayor (the cradle of the ancient Aztecas) so that the Nobel Prize may remain there, until peaceful and safe conditions are established in Guatemala to place it there, in the land of the Quetzal.

When evaluating the overall significance of the award of the Peace Prize, I would like to say some words on behalf of all those whose voice cannot be heard or who have been repressed for having spoken their opinions, of all those who have been marginalized, who have been discriminated, who live in poverty, in need, of all those who are the victims of repression and violation of human rights. Those who, nevertheless, have endured through centuries, who have not lost their conscience, the quality of determination and hope.

Please allow me, ladies and gentlemen, to say some words about my country and the civilization of the Mayas. The Maya people developed and spread geographically through some 300,000 square km; they occupied parts of the South of Mexico, Belice, Guatemala, as well as Honduras and El Salvador; they developed a very rich civilization in the area of political organization, as well as in social and economic fields; they were great scientists in the fields of mathematics, astronomy, agriculture, architecture and engineering; they were great artists in the fields of sculpture, painting, weaving and carving.

The Mayas discovered the zero value in mathematics, at about the same time that it was discovered in India and later passed on to the Arabs. Their astronomic forecasts based on mathematical calculations and scientific observations were amazing, and still are. They prepared a calendar more accurate than the Gregorian, and in the field of medicine they performed intracranial surgical operations.

One of the Maya books, saved from destruction by the conquerors, known as *Códice de Dresden,* contains the results of an investigation on eclipses as well a table of 69 dates, in which solar eclipses occur in a lapse of 33 years.

Today, it is important to emphasize the deep respect that the Maya civilization had towards life and nature in general.

Who can predict what other great scientific conquests and developments these people could have achieved, if they had not been conquered by blood and fire, and subjected to an ethnocide that affected nearly 50 million people in the course of 500 years.

I would describe the meaning of this Nobel Peace Prize, in the first place as a tribute to the Indian people who have been sacrified and have disappeared because they aimed at a more dignified and just life with fraternity and understanding among human beings. To those who are no longer alive to keep up the hope for a change in the situation in respect of poverty and marginalization of the Indians, of those who have been banished, of the helpless in Guatemala as well as in the entire American Continent.

This growing concern is comforting, even though it comes 500 years later, to the suffering, the discrimination, the oppression and the exploitation that our peoples have been exposed to, but who, thanks to their own cosmovision — and concept of life, have managed to withstand and finally see some promising prospects. How those roots, that were to be eradicated, now begin to grow with strength, hope and visions of the future!

It also represents a sign of the growing international interest for, and understanding of the original Rights of the People, of the future of more than 60 million Indians that live in our Americas, and their outcry because of the 500 years of oppression that they have endured. For the genocides beyond comparison that they have had to suffer, and from which other countries and the elite of the Americas have profited and taken advantage.

Let there be freedom for the Indians, wherever they may be in the

American Continent or elsewhere in the world, because while they are alive, a glow of hope will be alive as well as the true concept of life.

The expressions of great happiness by the Indian Organizations in the entire Continent and the worldwide congratulations received for the award of the Nobel Peace Prize, clearly indicate the great importance of this decision. It is the recognition of the European debt to the American indigenous people; it is an appeal to the conscience of Humanity so that those conditions of marginalization that condemned them to colonialism and exploitation may be irradicated; it is a cry for life, peace, justice, equality and fraternity between human beings.

The peculiarities of the vision of the Indian people are expressed according to the way in which they are related to each other. First, between human beings, through communication. Second, with the earth, as with our mother, because she gives us our lives and is not mere merchandise. Third, with nature, because we are an integral part of it, and not its owners.

To us mother Earth is not only a source of economic riches that give us the maize, which is our life, but she also provides so many other things that the privileged ones of today strive for. The Earth is the root and the source of our culture. She keeps our memories, she receives our ancestors and she, therefore, demands that we honour her and return to her, with tenderness and respect, those goods that she gives us. We have to take care of her so that our children and grandchildren may continue to benefit from her. If the world does not learn now to show respect to nature, what kind of future will the new generations have?

From these basic features derive behaviour, rights and obligations in the American Continent, for Indians as well as for non-Indians, whether they be racially mixed, blacks, whites or Asian. The whole society has an obligation to show mutual respect, to learn from each other and to share material and scientific achievements, in the most convenient way. The Indians never had, and still do not have, the place that they should have occupied in the progress and benefits of science and technology, although they represented an important basis for this development.

If the Indian civilizations and the European civilizations could have made exchanges in a peaceful and harmonious manner, without destruction, exploitation, discrimination and poverty, they could, no doubt, have achieved greater and more valuable conquests for Humanity.

Let us not forget that when the Europeans came to America, there were flourishing and strong civilizations there. One cannot talk about a "discovery of America", because one discovers that which one does not know about, or that which is hidden. But America and its native civilizations had discovered themselves long before the fall of the Roman Empire and Medieval Europe. The significance of its cultures form part of the heritage of humanity and continue to astonish the learned.

I think it is necessary that the Indian people, of which I am a member, should contribute with science and knowledge to human development, because we have enormous potential and we could combine our very ancient heritage with the achievements of European civilization as well as with civilizations in other parts of the world.

But this contribution, that to our understanding is a recovery of the natural and cultural heritage, must take place based on a rational and consensus basis in respect of the right to make use of knowledge and natural resources, with guarantees for equality between Government and society.

We the Indians are willing to combine tradition with modernism, but not at any cost. We will not tolerate nor permit that our future be planned as possible guardians of ethno-touristic projects on a continental level.

At a time when the commemoration of the Fifth Centenary of the arrival of Columbus in America has repercussions all over the world, the revival of hope for the Indian people demands that we reassert our existence to the world and the value of our cultural identity. It demands that we endeavour to actively participate in the decisions that concern our destiny, in the building-up of our countries/nations. Should we, in spite of all, not be taken into consideration, there are factors that guarantee our future: struggle and endurance courage the decision to maintain our traditions that have been exposed to so many perils and sufferings solidarity towards our struggle on the part of numerous countries, governments, organizations and citizens of the world.

That is why I dream of the day when the relationship between the indigenous peoples and other peoples is strengthened; when they can combine their potentialities and their capabilities and contribute to make life on this planet less unequal.

Today, in the 47th period of sessions of the General Assembly, the United Nations (UN) will proclaim 1993 as the *International Year of the Indian People,* in the presence of well-known chiefs of the organizations of the Indian people and the Continental Resistance Movement of Indians, blacks and other peoples. They will all formally participate in the opening of the working sessions in order to make 1993 a year of specific actions to truly place the Indian peoples within their national contexts and to make them part of mutual international agreements.

The achievement of the *International Year of the Indian People* and the progress represented by the preparation of the project for the *Universal Declaration,* are the result of the participation of numerous Indian brothers, nongovernmental organizations and the successful efforts of the experts in the Working Group, in addition to the comprehensiveness shown by many countries in the United Nations.

We hope that the formulation of the project in respect of the *Declaration on the Rights of the Indian People* will examine and go deeply into the existing contradictions between the progress in terms of international rights and the difficult reality that we, the Indo-Americans, experience.

Our people will have a year dedicated to the problems that afflict them and, in this respect, are now getting ready to carry out different activities with the purpose of presenting proposals and putting pressure on action plans. All this will be conducted in the most reasonable way and with the most convincing and justified arguments for the elimination of racism, oppression, discrimination and the exploitation of those who have been dragged into poverty and oblivion. Also for those who have been doomed, the award of the Nobel Peace Prize represents a recognition, an encouragement and an objective for the future.

I wish that a conscious sense of peace and a feeling of human solidarity would develop in all peoples, which would open new relationships of respect and equality for the next millennium, to be ruled by fraternity and not by cruel conflicts.

Opinion is being formed everywhere today, that in spite of wars and violence, calls upon the entire human race to protect its historical values and to form unity in diversity. And this calls upon us all to reflect upon the incorporation of important elements of change and transformation in all aspects of life on earth, in the search for specific and definite solutions to the deep ethical crisis that afflicts Humanity. This will, no doubt have decisive influence on the structure of the future.

There is a possibility that some centers of political and economic power, some statesmen and intellectuals, have not yet managed to see the advantages of the active participation of the Indian peoples in all the fields of human activity. However, the movement initiated by different political and intellectual "Amerindians" will finally convince them that, from an objective point of view, we are a constituent part of the historical alternatives that are being discussed at the international level.

Ladies and gentlemen, allow me to say some candid words about my country.

The attention that this Nobel Peace Prize has focused on Guatemala, should imply that the violation of the human rights is no longer ignored internationally. It will also honour all those who died in the struggle for social equality and justice in my country.

It is known throughout the world that the Guatemalan people, as a result of their struggle, succeeded in achieving, in October 1944, a period of democracy where institutionality and human rights were the main philosophies. At that time, Guatemala was an exception in the American Continent, because of its struggle for complete national sovereignty. However, in 1954, a conspiracy that joined the traditional national power centers, inheritors of colonialism, with powerful foreign interests, overthrew the democratic regime as a result of an armed invasion, thereby re-imposing the old system of oppression which has characterized the history of my country.

The economic, social and political subjection that derived from the Cold War, was what initiated the internal armed conflict. The repression against the organizations of the people, the democratic parties and the intellectuals, started in Guatemala long before the war started. Let us not forget that.

In the attempt to crush rebellion, dictatorships have committed the greatest atrocities. They have levelled villages, and murdered thousands of farmers particularly Indians, hundreds of trade union workers and students, outstanding intellectuals and politicians, priests and nuns. Through this systematic persecution in the name of the safety of the nation, 1 million farmers were removed by force from their lands; 100,000 had to seek refuge in neighbouring countries. In Guatemala, there are today almost 100,000 orphans and more than 40,000 widows. The practice of "missing" politicians was invented in Guatemala, as a government policy.

As you know, I am myself a survivor of a massacred family.

The country collapsed into a crisis never seen before and the changes in the world forced and encouraged the military forces to permit a political opening that consisted in the preparation of a new Constitution, in an expansion of the political field, and in the transfer of the government to civil sectors. We have had this new regime for eight years and in certain fields there have been some openings of importance.

However, in spite of these openings, repression and violation of human rights persist in the middle of an economic crisis, that is becoming more and more acute, to the extent that 84% of the population is today considered as poor, and some 60% are considered as very poor. Impunity and terror continue to prevent people from freely expressing their needs and vital demands. The internal armed conflict still exists.

The political life in my country has lately centered around the search for a political solution to the global crisis and the armed conflict that has existed in Guatemala since 1962. This process was initiated by the Agreement signed in this City of Oslo, between the Comisión Nacional de Reconciliación (National Commission for Reconciliation) with government mandate, and the Unidad Revolucionaria Nacional Guatemalteca—URNG—(The Guatemalan National Revolutionary Unity), as a necessary step to introduce to Guatemala the spirit of the Agreement of Esquipulas.

As a result of this Agreement and conversations between the URNG and different sectors of Guatemalan society, direct negotiations were initiated under the government of President Serrano, between the government and the guerrilla, as a result of which three agreements have already been signed. However, the subject of Human Rights has taken long time, because this subject constitutes the core of the Guatemalan problems, and around this core important differences have arisen. Nevertheless, there has been considerable progress.

The process of negotiations aims at reaching agreements in order to establish the basis for a real democracy in Guatemala and for an end to the war. As far as I understand, with the goodwill of the parties concerned and the active participation of the civil sectors, adapting to a great national unity, the phase of purposes and intentions could be left behind so that Guatemala could be pulled out of the crossroads that seem to have become eternal.

Dialogues and the political negotiations are, no doubt, adequate means to solve these problems, in order to respond in a specific way to the vital and urgent needs for life and for the implementation of democracy for the Guatemalan people.

176

It is necessary to point out, here in Oslo, that the issue of Human Rights in Guatemala constitutes, at present, the most urgent problem that has to be solved. My statement is neither incidental nor unjustified.

As has been ascertained by international institutions, such as The United Nations Commission on Human Rights, The Interamerican Commission of Human Rights and many other humanitarian organizations, Guatemala is one of the countries in America with the largest number of violations of these rights, and the largest number of cases of impunity where security forces are generally involved. It is imperative that the repression and persecution of the people and the Indians be stopped. The compulsory mobilization and integration of young people into the Patrols of Civil Self Defense, which to a great extent affects the Indian people, must also be stopped.

Democracy in Guatemala must be built-up as soon as possible. It is necessary that Human Rights agreements be fully complied with, i.e. an end to racism; guaranteed freedom to organize and to move within all sectors of the country. In short, it is imperative to open all fields to the multi-ethnic civil society with all its rights, to demilitarize the country and establish the basis for its development, so that it can be pulled out of today's underdevelopment and poverty.

Among the most bitter dramas that a great percentage of the population has to endure, is the forced exodus. Which means, to be forced by military units and persecution to abandon their villages, their mother Earth, where their ancestors rest, their environment, the nature that gave them life and the growth of their communities, all of which constituted a coherent system of social organization and functional democracy.

The case of the displaced and of refugees in Guatemala is heartbreaking; some of them are condemned to live in exile in other countries, but the great majority live in exile in their own country. They are forced to wander from place to place, to live in ravines and inhospitable places, some not recognized as Guatemalan citizens, but all of them are condemned to poverty and hunger. There cannot be a true democracy as long as this problem is not satisfactorily solved and these people are reinstated on their lands and in their villages.

In the new Guatemalan society, there must be a fundamental reorganization in the matter of land ownership, to allow for the development of the agricultural potential, as well as for the return of the land to the legitimate owners. This process of reorganization must be carried out with the greatest respect for nature, in order to protect her and return to her, her strength and capability to generate life.

No less characteristic of a democracy is social justice. This demands a solution to the frightening statistics on infant mortality, of malnutrition, lack of education, analfabetism, wages insufficient to sustain life. These problems have a growing and painful impact on the Guatemalan population and imply no prospects and no hope.

Among the features that characterize society today, is that of the role of women, although female emancipation has not, in fact, been fully achieved so far by any country in the world.

The historical development in Guatemala reflects now the need and the irreversibility of the active contribution of women to the configuration of the new Guatemalan social order, of which, I humbly believe, the Indian women already are a clear testimony. This Nobel Peace Prize is a recognition to those who have been, and still are in most parts of the world, the most exploited of the exploited; the most discriminated of the discriminated, the most marginalized of the marginalized, but still those who produce life and riches.

Democracy, development and modernization of a country are impossible and incongruous without the solution of these problems.

In Guatemala, it is just as important to recognize the identity and the rights of the indigenous peoples, that have been ignored and despised not only during the colonial period, but also in during the Republic. It is not possible to conceive a democratic Guatemala, free and independent, without the indigenous identity shaping its character into all aspects of national existence.

It will undoubtedly be something new, a completely new experience, with features that, at the moment, we cannot describe. But it will authentically respond to history and the characteristics of the real Guatemalan nationality. The true profile that has been distorted for such a long time.

This urgency of this vital need, are the issues that urge me, at this moment, from this rostrum, to urge national opinion and the international community, to show a more active interest in Guatemala.

Taking into consideration that in connection with my role as a Nobel Prize Winner, in the process of negotiations for peace in Guatemala many possibilities have been handled, but now I think that this role is more likely to be the role of a promotor of peace, of national unity, for the protection of the rights of the indigenous peoples. In such a way, that I may take initiatives in accordance with the needs, and thereby prevent the Peace Prize from becoming on a piece of paper that has been filed.

I call upon all the social and ethnic sectors that constitute the people of Guatemala to participate actively in the efforts to find a peaceful solution to the armed conflict, to build-up a sound unity between the "ladinos" (of Indian and Spanish descent), the blacks and the Indians, all of whom must create within their diverse groups, a "Guatemality".

Along these same lines, I invite the international community to contribute with specific actions so that the parties involved may overcome the differences that at this stage keep negotiations in a wait-and-see state, so that they will succeed, first of all, in signing an agreement on Human Rights. And then, to re-initiate the rounds of negotiation and identify those issues on which to compromise, to allow for the Peace Agreement to be signed and immediately ratified, because I have no doubt that this will bring about great relief in the prevailing situation in Guatemala.

Ladies and gentlemen, the fact that I have given preference to the American Continent, and in particular to my country, does not mean that I do not have an important place in my mind and in my heart for the concern of other peoples of the world and their constant struggle in the defense of peace, of the right to a life and all its inalienable rights. The majority of us who are gathered here today, constitute an example of the above, and along these lines I would humbly extend to you my gratitude.

Many things have changed in these last years. There have been great changes of worldwide character. The East-West confrontation has ceased to exist and the Cold War has come to an end. These changes, the exact forms of which cannot yet be predicted, have left gaps that the people of the world have known how to make use of in order to come forward, struggle and win national terrain and international recognition.

Today, we must fight for a better world, without poverty, without racism, with peace in the Middle East and in Southeast Asia, to where I address a plea for the liberation of Mrs. Aung San Suu Kyi, winner of the Nobel Peace Prize 1991; for a just and peaceful solution in the Balkans; for the end of the apartheid in South Africa; for the stability in Nicaragua, that the Peace Agreement in El Salvador be observed; for the re-establishment of democracy in Haiti; for the complete sovereignty of Panama; because all of these constitute the highest aims for justice in the international situation.

A world at peace that could provide consistency, interrelations and concordance in respect of the economic, social and cultural structures of the societies would indeed have deep roots and a sound influence.

We have in our mind the deepest felt demands of the entire human race, when we strive for peaceful co-existence and the preservation of the environment.

The struggle we fight purifies and shapes the future.

Our history is a living history, that has throbbed, withstood and survived many centuries of sacrifice. Now it comes forward again with strength. The seeds, dormant for such a long time, break out today with some uncertainty, although they germinate in a world that is at present characterized by confusion and uncertainty.

There is no doubt that this process will be long and complex, but it is no Utopia and we, the Indians, we have new confidence in its implementation.

The peoples of Guatemala will mobilize and will be aware of their strength in building up a worthy future. They are preparing themselves to sow the future, to free themselves from atavisms, to rediscover their heritage. To build up a country with a genuine national identity. To start a new life.

By combining all the shades and nuances of the "ladinos", the "garífunas" and Indians in the Guatemalan ethnic mosaic, we must interlace a number of colours without introducing contradictions, without a becoming grotesque nor antagonistic, but we must give them brightness and a superior quality, just the way our weavers weave a typical "güipil" shirt, brilliantly composed, a gift to Humanity.

Thank you very much.

THE PRIZE IN ECONOMIC SCIENCES
IN MEMORY OF ALFRED NOBEL

THE INSTITUTION

On the occasion of its tercentenary, in 1968, Sveriges Riksbank (Bank of Sweden) made a donation to the Nobel Foundation for the purpose of awarding, through the Royal Swedish Academy of Sciences, *The Sveriges Riksbank (Bank of Sweden) Prize in Economic Sciences in Memory of Alfred Nobel.*

The statutes for the distribution of the Prize are, *mutatis mutandis,* the same as those for the Nobel Prizes. The presentation of the Prize is to take place at the Nobel Ceremony on December 10 at the same time as that of the Nobel Prizes.

The amount of the Prize is the same as that of the Nobel Prizes for the year. A special diploma and a gold medal are presented on this occasion.

In 1992, the Committee responsible for preparing matters was composed of the following members:

ASSAR LINDBECK, Professor of International Economics at Stockholm University, *Chairman of the Committee;* LARS WERIN, Professor of Economics at Stockholm University; INGEMAR STÅHL, Professor of Economics at Lund University; KARL-GÖRAN MÄLER, Professor of Economics at the Stockholm School of Economics; BENGT-CHRISTER YSANDER, Professor of Economics at Uppsala University; *Secretary of the Committee:* LARS E. O. SVENSSON, Professor of International Economics at Stockholm University; *adjoint members:* LENNART JÖRBERG, Professor of Economic History at Lund University; BERTIL NÄSLUND, Professor of Economics at the Stockholm School of Economics.

THE PRIZE-WINNERS AND CITATION

THE ROYAL SWEDISH ACADEMY OF SCIENCES
decided on October 13, 1992, to award the Sveriges Riksbank (Bank of Sweden) Prize in Economic Sciences in Memory of Alfred Nobel to

GARY S. BECKER
University of Chicago, USA

for having extended the domain of microeconomic analysis to a wide range of human behavior and interaction, including nonmarket behavior.

The number of candidates formally proposed was 144.

THE INSIGNIA AND THE AMOUNT OF THE PRIZE

The Prize-Winner received a *diploma*, a *medal* and a *document* indicating the amount of the Prize which was, like that of the Nobel Prizes, 6,500,000 Swedish kronor.

The diploma presented to the Prize-Winner was designed by the Swedish artist Philip von Schantz. Calligraphy by Annika Rücker.

THE SVERIGES RIKSBANK (BANK OF SWEDEN) PRIZE IN ECONOMIC SCIENCES IN MEMORY OF ALFRED NOBEL

Speech by Professor Assar Lindbeck of the Royal Swedish Academy of Sciences.
Translation from the Swedish text.

Your Majesties, Your Royal Highnesses, Ladies and Gentlemen,

Gary Becker has made it his task to extend the analytical domain of what he calls "an economic approach" to various social issues. Now it is important to bear in mind that what Becker calls "an economic approach" does *not* mean that individuals are assumed to strive solely for economic gain. Non-pecuniary, and indeed also altruistic, aspects are part of Becker's analysis alongside of pecuniary aspects. Therefore, the analysis should perhaps more appropriately be characterized as a theory of rational choice, i.e. of *purposeful behavior,* rather than as a traditional "economic approach."

Such a concept of research might perhaps, when looked at superficially, seem trivial. But that is precisely what it is *not.* Human behavior in the areas where Becker has conducted his studies has hitherto often been assumed to be unexplained, *habitual* behavior, rather than founded on rational calculations. Moreover, had Becker's approach been trivial, it would hardly have given rise to the amount of criticism and protest it was plagued with when first launched.

An important application of Becker's model of analysis is his studies of education and on-the-job training, i.e. investments in human capital, as they are now called. With the aid of this concept, Becker has developed, and empirically tested, an explicit theory of the wage structure in society and its development over time. Researchers after Becker have used the same method of analysis, to explain among other things, such as diverse phenomena as economic growth, the composition of trade, and investment in the sphere of health.

Another of Becker's important contributions is his analysis of the role of the family, or the household, in society. In traditional theory, the household was supposed to have a choice between income, and by means of this income, consumption of purchased consumer goods on the one hand, and leisure on the other hand. Becker's basic idea is rather to look upon the household as "a small factory" producing services for the members of the household with an input of time and purchased consumer goods, the latter being regarded as intermediate inputs in the production process taking place in the household.

This analysis is an interesting example of how a *new* angle to an old question can lead to completely new insights. In the context of this alternative approach, a wage rise for example, leads to a shift to less time-consuming production of the services produced within the household. Rising wages on the open market make it more costly to have one member of the family specializing in household production (e.g. child care). Therefore, parts of the earlier social and economic functions of the family are moved to other institutions such as businesses, schools, day care centers for children and various public institutions. This development constitutes a stimulus to work outside the home, a stimulus that also makes parents choose to have fewer children, investing rather in more education for the children they choose to have. Becker uses his theory to explain the historical decline of fertility in the industrialized countries, and the differences in fertility between countries, and between urban and rural areas.

Becker has also applied his theory to the area of "crime and punishment." He assumes that, except for a limited number of psychopaths, individuals who behave criminally react in predictable ways to different stimuli in the form of benefits and costs of criminal activities. This theory seems to provide realistic predictions about what groups of citizens can be expected to commit specific types of crime. The empirical studies conducted in connection with this theory also indicate that an increase in the probability of being convicted has a more discouraging effect on criminality than has the harshness of the punishment.

Yet another application concerns discrimination, with regard to race and sex, on the job and housing markets. Becker shows that such behavior works, purely analytically, as a "tax wedge," i.e. a marginal tax, between social and private economic returns. Discrimination, therefore, tends to harm economically, not only the party subjected to discrimination but also the party carrying our discrimination.

I now turn to you, Professor Becker: You have always chosen important *social* issues for your research agenda, such as population growth, the role of the family in society, the importance of education and on-the-job training, crime and punishment, and discrimination. You have, thanks to your creative and often provocative research strategy, widened the domain of models of "rational choice." It is a pleasure to convey to you the warmest congratulations from the Royal Swedish Academy of Sciences and to ask you to receive, from the hands of His Majesty the King, the 1992 Prize in Economic Sciences in Memory of Alfred Nobel.

Gary S Becker

GARY S. BECKER

I was born in Pottsville, Pennsylvania, a little coal mining town in Eastern Pennsylvania, where my father owned a small business. He had first gone into business for himself after leaving Montreal and his family for the United States when he was only sixteen-years-old. He moved many times in the eastern United States before settling in Pottsville in the mid-1920s. My two sisters, Wendy and Natalie, and brother, Marvin, were also born there. However, when I was four or five we moved to Brooklyn, New York, where my father became a partner in another business.

I went to elementary school and high school in Brooklyn. I was a good student, but until age sixteen was more interested in sports than intellectual activities. At that time I had to decide between being on the handball and math teams since they met during the same time period. It was indicative of my shift in priorities that I chose math, although I was better at handball.

My father had left school in Montreal after the 8th grade because he was eager to make money. My mother — whose family emigrated from Eastern Europe to New York City when she was six months old — also left after the 8th grade because girls were not expected to get much education. There were only a few books in our house, but my father kept up with the political and financial news, and my older sister read a lot. After my father lost most of his sight I had the task of reading him stock quotations and other reports on financial developments. Perhaps that stimulated my interest in economics, although I was rather bored by it.

We had many lively discussions in the house about politics and justice. I believe this does help explain why by the time I finished high school, my interest in mathematics was beginning to compete with a desire to do something useful for society. These two interests came together during my freshman year at Princeton, when I accidentally took a course in economics, and was greatly attracted by the mathematical rigor of a subject that dealt with social organization. During the following summer I read several books on economics.

To be financially independent more quickly, I decided at the end of my first year to graduate in three years, a seldom used option at Princeton. I had to take a few extra courses during the next year, and I chose reading courses in modern algebra and differential equations for the summer afterwards. For the equations course, I was given a set of unpublished lectures that emphasized existence proofs and uniqueness of solutions to differential equations. I learned a lot about such proofs, but very little about actually solving one of these equations. Still, my heavy investment in mathematics at Princeton prepared me well for the increasing use of mathematics in economics.

I began to lose interest in economics during my senior (third) year because it did not seem to deal with important social problems. I contemplated transferring to sociology, but found that subject too difficult. Fortunately, I decided to go to the University of Chicago for graduate work in economics. My first encounter in 1951 with Milton Friedman's course on microeconomics renewed my excitement about economics. He emphasized that economic theory was not a game played by clever academicians, but was a powerful tool to analyze the real world. His course was filled with insights both into the structure of economic theory and its application to practical and significant questions. That course and subsequent contacts with Friedman was had a profound effect on the direction taken by my research.

While Friedman was clearly the intellectual leader, Chicago had a first class group of economists who were doing innovative research. Especially important to me were Gregg Lewis's use of economic theory to analyze labor markets, T.W. Schultz's pioneering research on human capital, Aaron Director's applications of economics to anti-trust problems, and industrial organization more generally, and L.J. Savage's research on subjective probability and the foundation of statistics.

I published two articles in 1952, based on my research at Princeton. But I realized shortly after arriving in Chicago that I had to begin to learn again what economics is all about. I published nothing else until an article written with Friedman and a book based on my Ph.D. dissertation came out in 1957. The book contains the first systematic effort to use economic theory to analyze the effects of prejudice on the earnings, employment and occupations of minorities. It started me down the path of applying economics to social issues, a path that I have continued to follow.

The book was very favorably reviewed in a few major journals, but for several years it had no visible impact on anything. Most economists did not think racial discrimination was economics, and sociologists and psychologists generally did not believe I was contributing to their fields. However, Friedman, Lewis, Schultz, and others at Chicago were confident I had written an important book. Support by the people I respected so highly was crucial to my willingness to persevere in the face of much hostility.

After my third year of graduate study I became an assistant professor at Chicago. I had a light teaching load and could concentrate mainly on research. However, I felt that I would become intellectually more independent if I left the nest and had to make it on my own. After three years in that position, I turned down a much larger salary from Chicago to take a similar appointment at Columbia combined with one at the National Bureau of Economic Research, then also located in Manhattan. I have always believed this was the correct decision, for I developed greater independence and self-confidence than seems likely if I remained at Chicago.

For twelve years I divided my time between teaching at Columbia and doing research at the Bureau. My book on human capital was the outgrowth of my first research project for the Bureau. During this period I also wrote frequently cited articles on the allocation of time, crime and punishment, and irrational behavior.

At Columbia I began a workshop on labor economics and related subjects — anything that interested us was "related." This involved transplanting the workshop system of supervising doctoral research from Chicago — where it originated. After a few years, Jacob Mincer joined the Columbia department and became co-director of the workshop. We had a very exciting atmosphere and attracted most of the best students at Columbia. Both Mincer and I were doing research on human capital before this subject was adequately appreciated in the profession at large, and the students found it fascinating. We were also working on the allocation of time, and other subjects in the forefront of research.

I married for the first time in 1954, and have two daughters from that marriage, Judy and Catherine. To provide a better family atmosphere I lived in the suburbs and commuted to Columbia and the Bureau. Eventually, I began to tire of commuting and decided either to move into New York or to leave Columbia for another university. I also was beginning to feel intellectually stale.

My decision to leave was hastened by the student riots in 1968. I believed that Columbia should take a firm hand and uphold the right to free inquiry without student intimidation. The central administration wanted to do this, but it was incompetent, and was opposed by many faculty who behaved no better than the students.

In 1970, I returned to Chicago, and found the atmosphere there very stimulating. The department was still powerful, especially after it had added George Stigler and Harry Johnson. Stigler and I soon became close friends, and he had a very large effect on my subsequent intellectual development. We wrote two influential papers together: a controversial one on the stability of tastes, and an early treatment of the principle-agent problem. Stigler also renewed my interest in the economics of politics; I had published a short paper on this subject in 1958. In the 1980s I published two articles that developed a theoretical model of the role of special interest groups in the political process.

But mainly I worked on the family after returning to Chicago. I had much earlier used economic theory to try to understand birth rates and family size. I now began to consider the whole range of family issues: marriage, divorce, altruism toward other members, investments by parents in children, and long term changes in what families do. A series of articles in the 1970s culminated in 1981 in *A Treatise on the Family*. Since I continued to work on this subject, a greatly expanded edition was published in 1991. I have tried not only to understand the determinants of divorce, family size, and the like, but also the effects of changes in family composition and structure on inequality and economic growth. Most of my research on the family and that by students and faculty at Chicago and elsewhere was presented at the Workshop in Applications of Economics that Sherwin Rosen and I run.

For a long time my type of work was either ignored or strongly disliked by most of the leading economists. I was considered way out and perhaps not really an economist. But younger economists were more sympathetic. They may disagree with my analysis, but accept the kind of problems, studied as perfectly legitimate. During the past ten years I have received much tangible evidence of this shift in professional opinion, including the presidency of the American Economic Association, the Seidman Award, and the first social science Award of Merit from the National Institute of Health.

In 1983, the sociology department at Chicago offered me a joint appointment. I was happy to accept because this was an outstanding department. Its invitation to me gave a signal to the sociology profession that the rational choice approach was a respectable theoretical paradigm. James Coleman and I shortly thereafter began an interdisciplinary faculty seminar on rational choice in the social sciences that has been far more successful than we anticipated.

Until 1985, I had published only technical books and technical articles in professional journals. At that time, I was surprised by being asked to write a monthly column for *Business Week* magazine. Since I feared that I could not write for a general audience, I was inclined to turn the offer down. Finally, however, I agreed to do some columns on an experimental basis. It was a wise decision, for I was forced to learn how to write about economic and social issues without using technical jargon, and in about 800 words per column. Doing this has enormously improved my capacity to discuss important subjects briefly and in simple language. The pressure of having to do a column every month also makes me stay abreast of many subjects that interest the business and professional readers of the magazine.

I married for the second time in 1980 to Guity Nashat — my first wife died in 1970. This gave me two stepsons, Michael and Cyrus, to go with two daughters. Guity is the one who overcame my reluctance to do the Business Week columns. She is an historian of the Middle East with professional interests that overlap my own: on the role of women in economic and social life, and the causes of economic growth. The personal and professional compatibility she provides has made my life so much better.

THE ECONOMIC WAY OF LOOKING AT LIFE*

Nobel Lecture, December 9, 1992

by

GARY S. BECKER

Department of Economics, University of Chicago, Chicago, IL. 60637, USA

1. *The Economic Approach*

My research uses the economic approach to analyze social issues that range beyond those usually considered by economists. This lecture will describe the approach, and illustrate it with examples drawn from past and current work.

Unlike Marxian analysis, the economic approach I refer to does not assume that individuals are motivated solely by selfishness or gain. It is a *method* of analysis, not an assumption about particular motivations. Along with others, I have tried to pry economists away from narrow assumptions about self interest. Behavior is driven by a much richer set of values and preferences.

The analysis assumes that individuals maximize welfare *as they conceive it*, whether they be selfish, altruistic, loyal, spiteful, or masochistic. Their behavior is forward-looking, and it is also consistent over time. In particular, they try as best they can to anticipate the uncertain consequences of their actions. Forward-looking behavior, however, may still be rooted in the past, for the past can exert a long shadow on attitudes and values.

Actions are constrained by income, time, imperfect memory and calculating capacities, and other limited resources, and also by the available opportunities in the economy and elsewhere. These opportunities are largely determined by the private and collective actions of other individuals and organizations.

Different constraints are decisive for different situations, but the most fundamental constraint is limited time. Economic and medical progress have greatly increased length of life, but not the physical flow of time itself, which always restricts everyone to twenty-four hours per day. So while goods and services have expended enormously in rich countries, the total time available to consume has not.

Thus, wants remain unsatisfied in rich countries as well as in poor ones.

---

* This lecture is dedicated to the memory of George J. Stigler, who died almost exactly one year ago. Nobel Laureate, outstanding economist, very close friend and mentor, he would be as happy as I am had he lived to see me deliver the 1992 Nobel Lecture in Economics.

For while the growing abundance of goods may reduce the value of additional goods, time becomes more valuable as goods become more abundant. Utility maximization is of no relevance in a Utopia where everyone's needs are fully satisfied, but the constant flow of time makes such a Utopia impossible. These are some of the issues analyzed in Becker [1965], and Linder [1970].

The following sections illustrate the economic approach with four very different subjects. To understand discrimination against minorities, it is necessary to widen preferences to accommodate prejudice and hatred of particular groups. The economic analysis of crime incorporates into rational behavior illegal and other antisocial actions. The human capital approach considers how the productivity of people in market and non-market situations is changed by investments in education, skills, and knowledge. The economic approach to the family interprets marriage, divorce, fertility, and relations among family members through the lens of utility-maximizing forward-looking behavior.

2. *Discrimination Against Minorities*

Discrimination against outsiders has always existed, but with the exception of a few discussions of the employment of women (see Edgeworth [1922], and Faucett [1918]), economists wrote little on this subject before the 1950s. I began to worry about racial, religious, and gender discrimination while a graduate student, and used the concept of discrimination coefficients to organize my approach to prejudice and hostility to members of particular groups.

Instead of making the common assumptions that employers only consider the productivity of employees, that workers ignore the characteristics of those with whom they work, and that customers only care about the qualities of the goods and services provided, discrimination coefficients incorporate the influence of race, gender, and other personal characteristics on tastes and attitudes. Employees may refuse to work under a woman or a black even when they are well paid to do so, or a customer may prefer not to deal with a black car salesman. It is only through *widening* of the usual assumptions that it is possible to begin to understand the obstacles to advancement encountered by minorities.

Presumably, the amount of observable discrimination against minorities in wages and employment depends not only on tastes for discrimination, but also on other variables, such as the degree of competition and civil rights legislation. However, aside from the important theory of compensating differentials originated by Adam Smith, and a few major studies like Myrdal's *American Dilemma* [1944], there was little else available in the 1950s to build on to analyze how prejudice and other variables interact. I spent several years working out a theory of how actual discrimination in earnings and employment is determined by tastes for discrimination, along with the degree of competition in labor and product markets, the distribution of discrimination coefficients among members of the majority group, the

192

access of minorities to education and training, the outcome of median voter and other voting mechanisms that determine whether legislation favors or is hostile to minorities, and other considerations. Since there was so much to be done in this field, my advisors encouraged me to convert my doctoral dissertation (Becker [1955]) into a book (Becker [1957]).

The actual discrimination in the market place against a minority group depends on the combined discrimination of employers, workers, consumers, schools, and governments. The analysis shows that sometimes the environment greatly softens, while at other times it magnifies, the impact of a given amount of prejudice. For example, the discrepancy in wages between equally productive blacks and whites, or women and men, would be much smaller than the degree of prejudice against blacks and women when many companies can efficiently specialize in employing mainly blacks or women.

Indeed, in a world with constant returns to scale in production, two segregated economies with the same distribution of skills would completely bypass discrimination and would have equal wages and equal returns to other resources, regardless of the desire to discriminate against the segregated minorities. Therefore, discrimination by the majority in the marketplace is effective because minority members cannot provide various skills in sufficient quantities to companies that would specialize in using these workers.

When the majority is very large compared to the minority — in the United States whites are nine times as numerous and have much more human and physical capital per capita than blacks — market discrimination by the majority hardly lowers their incomes, but may greatly reduce the incomes of the minority. However, when minority members are a sizable fraction of the total, discrimination by the majority injures them as well.

This proposition can be illustrated with an analysis of discrimination in South Africa, where blacks are four to five times as numerous as whites. Discrimination against blacks has also significantly hurt whites, although some white groups have benefitted (see Becker [1971, pages 30−31], and Hutt [1964]). Its sizable cost to whites suggests why apartheid and other blatant forms of Afrikaaner discrimination eventually broke down.

A literature has developed on whether discrimination in the marketplace due to prejudice disappears in the long run. Whether employers who do not want to discriminate will eventually compete away all discriminating employers depends not only on the distribution of tastes for discrimination among potential employers, but critically also on the nature of firm production functions.

Of greater significance empirically is the long run discrimination by employees and customers, who are far more important sources of market discrimination than employers. There is no reason to expect discrimination by these groups to be competed away in the long run unless it is possible to have enough efficient segregated firms and effectively segregated markets for goods.

A novel theoretical development in recent years is the analysis of the consequences of stereotyped reasoning or statistical discrimination (see Phelps [1972], and Arrow [1973]). This analysis suggests that the *beliefs* of employers, teachers, and other influential groups that minority members are less productive *can* be self-fulfilling, for these beliefs may cause minorities to underinvest in education, training, and work skills, such as punctuality. The underinvestment does make them less productive (see a good recent analysis by Loury [1992]).

Evidence from many countries on the earnings, unemployment, and occupations of blacks, women, religious groups, immigrants, and others has expanded enormously during the past twenty-five years. This evidence more fully documents the economic position of minorities and how that changes in different environments. However, the evidence has not dispelled some of the controversies over the source of lower incomes of minorities (see Cain's [1986] good review of both the theoretical literature and empirical analysis.)

3. *Crime and Punishment*

I began to think about crime in the 1960s after driving to Columbia University for an oral examination of a student in economic theory. I was late and had to decide quickly whether to put the car in a parking lot or risk getting a ticket for parking illegally on the street. I calculated the likelihood of getting a ticket, the size of the penalty, and the cost of putting the car in a lot. I decided it paid to take the risk and park on the street. (I did not get a ticket.)

As I walked the few blocks to the examination room, it occurred to me that the city authorities had probably gone through a similar analysis. The frequency of their inspection of parked vehicles and the size of the penalty imposed on violators should depend on their estimates of the type of calculations potential violators like me would make. Of course, the first question I put to the hapless student was to work out the optimal behavior of both the offenders and the police, something I had not yet done.

In the 1950s and 1960s, intellectual discussions of crime were dominated by the opinion that criminal behavior was caused by mental illness and social oppression, and that criminals were helpless "victims." A book by a well-known psychiatrist was entitled *The Crime of Punishment* (see Menninger [1966]). Such attitudes began to exert a major influence on social policy, as laws changed to expand criminals' rights. These changes reduced the apprehension and conviction of criminals, and provided less protection to the law-abiding population.

I was not sympathetic to the assumption that criminals had radically different motivations from everyone else. I explored instead the theoretical and empirical implications of the assumption that criminal behavior is rational (see the early pioneering work by Bentham [1931] and Beccaria [1986]), but again "rationality" did not necessarily imply narrow materialism. It recognized that many people are constrained by moral and ethical

194

considerations, and did not commit crimes even when they were profitable and there was no danger of detection.

However, police and jails would be unnecessary if such attitudes always prevailed. Rationality implied that some individuals become criminals because of the financial rewards from crime compared to legal work, taking account of the likelihood of apprehension and conviction, and the severity of punishment.

The amount of crime is determined not only by the rationality and preferences of would-be criminals, but also by the economic and social environment created by public policies, including expenditures on police, punishments for different crimes, and opportunities for employment, schooling, and training programs. Clearly, the type of legal jobs available as well as law, order, and punishment are an integral part of the economic approach to crime.

Total public spending on fighting crime can be reduced, while keeping the mathematically expected punishment unchanged, by offsetting a cut in expenditures on catching criminals with a sufficient increase in the punishment to those convicted. However, risk-preferring individuals are more deterred from crime by a higher probability of conviction than by severe punishments. Therefore, optimal behavior by the State would balance the reduced spending on police and courts from lowering the probability of conviction against the preference of risk-preferring criminals for a lesser certainty of punishment. The State should also consider the likelihood of punishing innocent persons.

In the early stages of my work on crime, I was puzzled by why theft is socially harmful since it appears merely to redistribute resources, usually from wealthier to poorer individuals. I resolved the puzzle (Becker [1968, fn. 3] by recognizing that criminals spend on weapons and on the value of the time in planning and carrying out their crimes, and that such spending is socially unproductive — it is what is now called "rent-seeking" — because it does not create wealth, only forcibly redistributes it. The social cost of theft was approximated by the number of dollars stolen since rational criminals would be willing to spend up to that amount on their crimes. (I should have added the resources spent by potential victims protecting themselves against crime.)

One reason why the economic approach to crime became so influential is that the same analytic apparatus can be used to study enforcement of all laws, including minimum wage legislation, clean air acts, insider trader and other violations of security laws, and income tax evasions. Since few laws are self-enforcing, they require expenditures on conviction and punishment to deter violators. The United States Sentencing Commission has explicitly used the economic analysis of crime to develop rules to be followed by judges in punishing violators of Federal statutes (United States Sentencing Commission [1988]).

Studies of crime that use the economic approach have become common during the past quarter century. These include analysis of the optimal marginal punishments to deter increases in the severity of crimes — for example, to deter a kidnapper from killing his victim (the modern literature starts with Stigler [1970]), and the relation between private and public enforcement of laws (see Becker and Stigler [1974], and Landes and Posner [1975]).

Fines are preferable to imprisonment and other types of punishment because they are more efficient. With a fine, the punishment to offenders is also revenue to the State. The early discussions of the relations between fines and other punishments have been clarified and considerably improved (see, e.g., Polinsky and Shavell [1984], and Posner [1986]).

Empirical assessments of the effects on crime rates of prison terms, conviction rates, unemployment levels, income inequality, and other variables have become more numerous and more accurate (the pioneering work is by Ehrlich [1973], and the subsequent literature is extensive). The greatest controversies surround the question of whether capital punishment deters murders, a controversy that is far from being resolved (see, e.g., Ehrlich [1975], and National Research Council [1978]).

4. *Human Capital*

Until the 1950s economists generally assumed that labor power was given and not augmentable. The sophisticated analyses of investments in education and other training by Adam Smith, Alfred Marshall, and Milton Friedman were not integrated into discussions of productivity. Then T. W. Schultz and others began to pioneer the exploration of the implications of human capital investments for economic growth and related economic questions.

Human capital analysis starts with the assumption that individuals decide on their education, training, medical care, and other additions to knowledge and health by weighing the benefits and costs. Benefits include cultural and other non-monetary gains along with improvement in earnings and occupations, while costs usually depend mainly on the foregone value of the time spent on these investments.

Human capital is so uncontroversial nowadays that it may be difficult to appreciate the hostility in the 1950s and 1960s toward the approach that went with the term. The very concept of *human* capital was alleged to be demeaning because it treated people as machines. To approach schooling as an investment rather than a cultural experience was considered unfeeling and extremely narrow. As a result, I hesitated a long time before deciding to call my book *Human Capital*, and hedged the risk by using a long subtitle. Only gradually did economists, let alone others, accept the concept of human capital as a valuable tool in the analysis of various economic and social issues.

My work on human capital began with an effort to calculate both private and social rates of return to men, women, blacks, and other groups from investments in different levels of education. After a while it became clear that the analysis of human capital could help explain many regularities in

196

labor markets and the economy at large. It seemed possible to develop a more general theory of human capital that includes firms as well as individuals, and that could consider its macro-economic implications.

The empirical analysis tried to correct data on the higher earnings of more educated persons for the fact that they are abler: they have higher I.Q.s and score better on other aptitude tests. It also considered the effects on rates of return to education of mortality, income taxes, foregone earnings, and economic growth. Ability corrections did not seem very important, but large changes in adult mortality and sizeable rates of economic growth did have big effects.

The empirical study of investments in human capital received a major boost from Mincer's classic work [see 1974]. He extended a simple regression analysis that related earnings to years of schooling (Becker and Chiswick [1966]) to include a crude but very useful measure of on-the-job training and experience − years after finishing school; he used numerous individual observations rather than grouped data, and he carefully analyzed the properties of residuals from earnings-generating equations. There are now numerous estimated rates of return to education and training for many countries (for a summary of some of this literature, see Psacharopoulos [1975]).

The accumulating evidence on the economic benefits of schooling and training also promoted the importance of human capital in policy discussions. This new faith in human capital has reshaped the way governments approach the problem of stimulating growth and productivity, as was shown by the emphasis on human capital in the recent presidential election in the United States.

One of the most influential theoretical concepts in human capital analysis is the distinction between general and specific training or knowledge (see Becker [1962], and Oi [1962]). By definition, firm-specific knowledge is useful only in the firms providing it, whereas general knowledge is useful also in other firms. Teaching someone to operate an IBM-compatible personal computer is general training, while learning the authority structure and the talents of employees in a particular company is specific knowledge. This distinction helps explain why workers with highly specific skills are less likely to quit their jobs and are the last to be laid off during business downturns. It also explains why most promotions are made from within a firm rather than through hiring − workers need time to learn about a firm's structure and "culture" − and why better accounting methods would include the specific human capital of employees among the principle assets of most companies.

Firm-specific investments produce rents that must be shared between employers and employees, a sharing process that is vulnerable to "opportunistic" behavior because each side may try to extract most of the rent after investments are in place. Rents and opportunism due to specific investments play a crucial role in the modern economic theory of organizations (see Williamson [1985]), and in many discussions of principal-agent problems (see, for example, Grossman and Hart [1983]). The implications of specific capital for sharing and turnover have also been used in analyzing marriage "markets" to explain divorce rates and bargaining within a marriage (see Becker, Landes and Michael [1977], and McElroy and Horney [1981]), and in analyzing political "markets" to explain the low turnover of politicians (see Cain, Ferejohn and Firoina [1987]).

The theory of human capital investment relates inequality in earnings to differences in talents, family background, and bequests and other assets (see Becker and Tomes [1986]). Many empirical studies of inequality also rely on human capital concepts, especially differences in schooling and training (see Mincer [1974]). The sizeable growth in earnings inequality in the United States during the 1980s that has excited so much political discussion is largely explained by higher returns to the more educated and better trained (see, e.g., Murphy and Welch [1992]).

Human capital theory gives a provocative interpretation of the so-called "gender gap" in earnings. Traditionally, women have been far more likely than men to work part-time and intermittently partly because they usually withdrew from the labor force for a while after having children. As a result, they had fewer incentives to invest in education and training that improved earnings and job skills.

During the past twenty years all this changed. The decline in family size, the growth in divorce rates, the rapid expansion of the service sector where most women are employed, the continuing economic development that raised the earnings of women along with men, and civil rights legislation encouraged greater labor force participation by women, and hence greater investment in market-oriented skills. In practically all rich countries, these forces significantly improved both the occupations and relative earnings of women.

The United States' experience is especially well-documented. The gender gap in earnings among full-time men and women remained at about 35 percent from the mid-fifties to the mid-seventies. Then women began the steady economic advance which is still continuing; it narrowed the gap to under 25 percent. Women are flocking to business, law, and medical schools, and are working at skilled jobs that they formerly shunned, or were excluded from.

Schultz and others (see, e.g., Schultz [1963], and Denison [1962]) early on emphasized that investments in human capital were a major contributor to economic growth. But after a while the relation of human capital to growth was neglected, as economists became discouraged about whether the available growth theory gave many insights into the progress of different countries. The revival of more formal models of endogenous growth has brought human capital once again to the forefront of the discussions (see e.g., Romer [1986], Lucas [1988], Barro and Sala-i-Martin [1992], and Becker, Murphy and Tamura [1990]).

198

5. *Formation, Dissolution, and Structure of Families*

The rational choice analysis of family behavior builds on maximizing behavior, investments in human capital, the allocation of time, and discrimination against women and other groups. The rest of the lecture focuses on this analysis since it is still quite controversial.

Writing *A Treatise on the Family* is the most difficult sustained intellectual effort I have undertaken. The family is arguably the most fundamental and oldest of institutions — some authors trace its origin to more than 50,000 years ago. The *Treatise* tries to analyze not only modern Western families, but also those in other cultures and the changes in family structure during the past several centuries.

Trying to cover this broad subject required a degree of mental commitment over more than six years, during many nighttime as well as daytime hours, that left me intellectually and emotionally exhausted. In his autobiography, Bertrand Russell says that writing the *Principia Mathematica* used up so much of his mental powers that he was never again fit for really hard intellectual work. It took about two years after finishing the *Treatise* to regain my intellectual zest.

The analysis of fertility has a long and honorable history in economics, but until recent years marriage and divorce, and the relations between husbands, wives, parents, and children had been largely neglected by economists (although see the important study by Mincer [1962]). The point of departure of my work on the family is the assumption that when men and women decide to marry or have children or divorce, they attempt to maximize their utility by comparing benefits and costs. So they marry when they expect to be better off than if they remained single, and they divorce if that is expected to increase their welfare.

People who are not intellectuals are often surprised when told that this approach is controversial since it seems obvious to them that individuals try to raise their welfare by marriage and divorce. The rational choice approach to marriage and other behavior is in fact often consistent with the instinctive economics "of the common man" (Farrell and Mandel [1992]).

Still, intuitive assumptions about behavior is only the *starting point* of systematic analysis, for alone they do not yield many interesting implications. The rational choice approach embeds them in a framework that combines maximizing behavior with analysis of marriage and divorce markets, specialization and the division of labor, old-age support, investments in children, and legislation that affects families. The implications of the full model are often not so obvious, and sometimes run sharply counter to received opinion.

For example, contrary to a common belief about divorce among the rich, the economic analysis of family decisions shows that wealthier couples are *less* likely to divorce than poorer couples. According to this theory, richer couples tend to gain a lot from remaining married, whereas many poorer couples do not. A poor woman may well doubt whether it is worth staying married to someone chronically unemployed. Empirical studies for many countries do indicate that the marriages of richer couples are much more stable (see Becker, Landes and Michael [1977]).

Efficient bargaining between husbands and wives implies that the trend in Europe and the United States toward no-fault divorce during the past two decades would not raise divorce rates,and, therefore, that contrary to many claims, it could not be responsible for the rapid rise in these rates. However, the theory does indicate that no-fault divorce hurts women with children whose marriages are broken up by their husbands. Households headed by unmarried women with children now comprise about one-fifth of all households with children in the United States and other advanced countries.

Economic models of behavior have been used to study fertility ever since Malthus's classic essay; the great Swedish economist, Knut Wicksell, was attracted to economics by his belief in the Malthusian predictions of over-population. But Malthus's conclusion that fertility would rise and fall as incomes increased and decreased was contradicted by the large decline in birth rates after some countries became industrialized during the latter part of the nineteenth century and the early part of this century.

The failure of Malthus's simple model of fertility persuaded economists that family-size decisions lay beyond economic calculus. The neo-classical growth model reflects this belief, for in most versions it takes population growth as exogenous and given (see, for example, Cass [1965], or Arrow and Kurz [1970]).

However, the trouble with the Malthusian approach is not its use of economics per se, but an economics inappropriate for modern life. It neglects that the time spent on child care becomes more expensive as countries become more productive. The higher value of time raises the cost of children, and thereby reduces the demand for large families. It also fails to consider that the greater importance of education and training in industrialized economies encourages parents to invest more in the skills of their children, which also raises the cost of large families. The growing value of time and the increased emphasis on schooling and other human capital explain the decline in fertility as countries develop, and many features of birth rates in modern economies.

Why in almost all societies have married women specialized in bearing and rearing children and in certain agricultural activities, whereas married men have done most of the fighting and market work? The explanation, presumably, is a combination of biological differences between men and women — especially differences in their innate capacities to bear and rear children — and discrimination against women in market activities, partly through cultural conditioning. Large and highly emotional differences of opinion exist over the relative importance of biology and discrimination in generating the traditional division of labor in marriages (see, for example, Boserup [1970]).

The economic analysis of this division of labor does not determine the relative importance of biology and discrimination, but it shows how sensitive the division is to *small* differences in either. Since the return from investing in a skill is greater when more time is spent utilizing the skill, a married couple could gain a lot from a sharp division of labor because the husband could specialize in some types of human capital and the wife in others. Given such a large gain from specialization within a marriage, only a *little* discrimination against women or *small* biological differences in child-rearing skills would cause the division of labor between household and market tasks to be systematically related to gender. The sensitivity to small differences explains why the empirical evidence cannot readily choose between biological and "cultural" interpretations. This theory also explains why many women entered the labor force as families became smaller, divorce more common, and earning opportunities for women improved.

Relations among family members differ radically from those among employees of firms and members of other organizations. The interactions between husbands, wives, parents, and children are more likely to be motivated by love, obligation, guilt, and a sense of duty than by self-interest narrowly interpreted.

It was demonstrated about twenty years ago that altruism within families enormously alters how they respond to shocks and public policies that redistribute resources among members. Becker [1974] showed that exogenous redistributions of resources from an altruist to her beneficiaries (or vice-versa) may not affect the welfare of anyone because the altruist would try to reduce her gifts by the amount redistributed. Barro [1974] derived this result in an intergenerational context, which cast doubt on the common assumption that government deficits and related fiscal policies have real effects on the economy.

The "Rotten-Kid Theorem" — the name is very popular even when critics disagree with the result — carries the analysis of altruism further, for it shows how the behavior of selfish individuals is affected by altruism. Under some conditions, even selfish beneficiaries — of course, most parents believe that the best example of this is selfish children with altruistic parents — are induced to act *as if* they are altruistic toward their benefactors because that raises their own selfish welfare. They act this way because otherwise gifts from their benefactors would be reduced enough to make them worse off (see Becker [1974], and the elaboration and qualifications to the analysis in Lindbeck and Weibull [1987], Bergstrom [1989], and Becker [1991, pp. 9 – 13]).

The Bible, Plato's *Republic*, and other early writings discussed the treatment of young children by their parents, and of elderly parents by adult children. Both the elderly and children need care — in one case because of declining health and energy, and in the other because of biological growth and dependency. A powerful implication of the economic analysis of relations within families is that these two issues are closely related.

Parents who leave sizable bequests do not need old-age support because instead they help out their children. I mentioned earlier one well-known implication of this: under certain conditions, budget deficits and social security payments to the elderly have no real effects because parents simply offset the bigger taxes in the future on their children through larger bequests.

It is much less appreciated that altruistic parents who leave bequests also tend to invest more in their children's skills, habits, and values. For they gain from financing all investments in the education and skills of children that yield a higher rate of return than the return on savings. They can indirectly save for old age by investing in children, and then reducing bequests when elderly. Both parents and children would be better off when parents make all investments in children that yield a higher return than that on savings, and then adjust bequests to the efficient level of investment (see section 1 of the Appendix for a formal demonstration).

Even in rich countries many parents do not plan on leaving bequests. These parents want old-age support, and they "underinvest" in their children's education and other care. They underinvest because they cannot compensate themselves for greater spending on children by reducing bequests since they do not plan on leaving any.

Both the children and parents would be better off if the parents agreed to invest more in the children in return for a commitment by the children to care for them when they need help. But how can such a commitment be enforced? Economists and lawyers usually recommend a written contract to insure commitment, but it is absurd to contemplate that a society will enforce contracts between adults and ten-year-olds or teenagers.

Part of my current research considers an indirect way to generate commitments when promises and written agreements are not binding. I will describe briefly some of this new work because it carries the economic approach to the family unto uncharted ground related to the rational formation of preferences within families.

Parental attitudes and behavior have an enormous influence on their children. Parents who are alcoholic or are addicted to crack create a bizarre atmosphere for impressionable youngsters, whereas parents with stable values who transmit knowledge and inspire their children favorably influence both what their children are capable of and what they want to do. The economic approach can contribute insights into the formation of preferences through childhood experiences without necessarily adopting the Freudian emphasis on the primacy of what happened during the first few months of life.

Again, I am trying to model a common sense idea; namely, that the attitudes and values of adults are enormously influenced by their childhood experiences. An Indian doctor living in the United States may love curry because he acquired a strong taste for it while growing up in India, or a woman may forever fear men because she was sexually abused as a child.

Through its assumption of forward-looking behavior, the economic point of view implies that parents try to anticipate the effect of what happens to children on their attitudes and behavior when adults. These effects help determine the kind of care parents provide. For example, parents worried about old-age support may try to instill in their children feelings of guilt, obligation, duty, and filial love that indirectly, but still very effectively, can "commit" children to helping them out.

Economists have too narrow a perspective on commitments. "Manipulating" the experiences of others to influence their preferences may appear to be inefficient and fraught with uncertainty, but it can be the most effective way to obtain commitment. Economic theory needs to incorporate guilt, affection, and related attitudes into preferences in order to have a deeper understanding of when commitments are "credible" (see section 2 of the appendix for a formal discussion).

Parents who do not leave bequests may be willing to make their children feel guiltier precisely because they gain more utility from greater old-age consumption than they lose from an equal reduction in children's consumption. This type of behavior may be considerably more common than suggested by the number of families that leave bequests, for parents with young children often do not know whether they will be financially secure when they are old. They may try to protect themselves against ill health, unemployment, and other hazards of old age by instilling in their children a willingness to help out if that becomes necessary.

This analysis of the link between childhood experiences and adult preferences is closely related to work on rational habit formation and addictions (see Becker and Murphy [1988]). The formation of preferences is rational in the sense that parental spending on children partly depends on the anticipated effects of childhood experiences on adult attitudes and behavior. I do not have time to consider the behavior of children — such as crying and acting "cute" — that tries in turn to influence the attitudes of parents.

Many economists, including myself, have excessively relied on altruism to tie together the interests of family members. Recognition of the connection between childhood experiences and future behavior reduces the need to rely on altruism in families. But it does not return the analysis to a narrow focus on self-interest, for it partially replaces altruism by feelings of guilt, obligation, anger, and other attitudes usually neglected by models of rational behavior.

If parents anticipate that children will help out in old age — perhaps because of guilt or related motivations — even parents who are not very loving toward their children would invest more in the children's human capital, and save less to provide for their old age. (For a proof, see section 3 of the Appendix.)

Equation (12) of the Appendix shows that parents always prefer small increases in their own consumption to equal increases in their children's *if* the only way they can get greater consumption is by making children feel guiltier. This means that altruistic parents who take steps to make their children feel guiltier always underinvest in the children's human capital. This shows directly why creating guilt has costs and is not fully efficient.

Altruistic family heads who do not plan to leave bequests try to create a "warm" atmosphere in their families, so that members are willing to come to the assistance of those experiencing financial and other difficulties. This conclusion is relevant to discussions of so-called "family values," a subject that received attention during the recent presidential campaign in the United States. Parents help determine the values of children — including their feelings of obligation, duty, and love — but what parents try to do can be greatly affected by public policies and changes in economic and social conditions.

Consider, for example, a program that transfers resources to the elderly, perhaps especially to poorer families who do not leave bequests, that reduces the elderly's dependence on children. According to the earlier analysis, parents who do not need support when they become old do not try as hard to make children more loyal, guiltier, or otherwise feel as well-disposed toward their parents. This means that programs like social security that significantly help the elderly would encourage family members to drift apart emotionally, not by accident but as maximizing responses to those policies.

Other changes in the modern world which have altered family values include increased geographical mobility, the greater wealth that comes with economic growth, better capital and insurance markets, higher divorce rates, smaller families, and publicly-funded health care. These developments have generally made people better off, but they also weakened the personal relations within families between husbands and wives, parents and children, and among more distant relatives, partly by reducing the incentives to invest in *creating* closer relations.

6. *Concluding Comments*

An important step in extending the traditional analysis of individual rational choice is to incorporate into the theory a much richer class of attitudes, preferences, and calculations. This step is prominent in all the examples that I consider. The analysis of discrimination includes in preferences a dislike of — prejudice against — members of particular groups, such as blacks or women. In deciding whether to engage in illegal activities, potential criminals are assumed to act as if they consider both the gains and the risks — including the likelihood they will be caught and severity of punishments. In human capital theory, people rationally evaluate the benefits and costs of activities, such as education, training, expenditures on health, migration, and formation of habits that radically alter the way they are. The economic approach to the family assumes that even intimate decisions like marriage, divorce, and family size are reached through weighing the advantages and disadvantages of alternative actions. The weights are determined by preferences that critically depend on the altruism and feelings of duty and obligation toward family members.

Since the economic, or rational choice, approach to behavior builds on a theory of individual decisions, criticisms of this theory usually concentrate on particular assumptions about how these decisions are made. Among other things, critics deny that individuals act consistently over time, and question whether behavior is forward-looking, particularly in situations that differ significantly from those usually considered by economists — such as those involving criminal, addictive, family, or political behavior. This is not the place to go into a detailed response to the criticisms, so I simply assert that no approach of comparable generality has yet been developed that offers serious competition to rational choice theory.

While the economic approach to behavior builds on a theory of individual choice, it is not mainly concerned with individuals. It uses theory at the micro level as a powerful tool to derive implications at the group or macro level. Rational individual choice is combined with assumptions about technologies and other determinants of opportunities, equilibrium in market and nonmarket situations, and laws, norms, and traditions to obtain results concerning the behavior of groups. It is mainly because the theory derives implications at the macro level that it is of interest to policymakers and those studying differences among countries and cultures.

None of the theories considered in this lecture aims for the greatest generality; instead, each tries to derive concrete implications about behavior that can be tested with survey and other data. Disputes over whether punishments deter crime, whether the lower earnings of women compared to men are mainly due to discrimination or lesser human capital, or whether no-fault divorce laws increase divorce rates all raise questions about the empirical relevance of predictions derived from a theory based on individual rationality.

A close relation between theory and empirical testing helps prevent both the theoretical analysis and the empirical research from becoming sterile. Empirically oriented theories encourage the development of new sources and types of data, the way human capital theory stimulated the use of survey data, especially panels. At the same time, puzzling empirical results force changes in theory, as models of altruism and family preferences have been enriched to cope with the finding that parents in Western countries tend to bequeath equal amounts to different children.

I have been impressed by how many economists want to work on social issues rather than issues forming the traditional core of economics. At the same time, specialists from fields that do consider social questions are often attracted to the economic way of modelling behavior because of the analytical power provided by the assumption of individual rationality. Thriving schools of rational choice theorists and empirical researchers are active in sociology, law, political science, history, anthropology, and psychology. The rational choice model provides the most promising basis presently available for a unified approach to the analysis of the social world by scholars from the social sciences.

APPENDIX

1. To show this formally, suppose that each person lives for three periods: youth (y), middle age (m), and old age (o), and has one child at the beginning of period m. A child's youth overlaps his parents' middle age, and a child's

middle age overlaps his parents' old age. The utility parents get from altruism is assumed to be separable from the utilities produced by their own consumption.

A simple utility function of parents (V_p) incorporating these assumptions is

$$V_p = u_{mp} + \beta u_{op} + \beta a V_c, \tag{1}$$

where β is the discount rate. Selfish parents have an a = 0, while the degree of altruism rises with a. I do not permit parents to be sadistic toward children (a < 0), although the analysis is easily generalized to include sadists.

Each person works and earns income only during middle age. It is possible to save then to provide consumption for old age (Z_{op}) by accumulating assets with a yield of R_k. Parents influence children's earnings by investing in their human capital. The marginal yield on investments in human capital (R_h) is defined as

$$R_h = \frac{dE_c}{dh}, \tag{2}$$

where E_c is the earnings of children at middle age. This yield is assumed to decline as more is invested in children: $dR_h/dh \leq 0$, where h is the amount invested.

Parents must also decide whether to leave bequests, denoted by k_c. If parents can consume at different ages, leave bequests, or invest in the child's human capital, their budget constraint is

$$Z_{mp} + h + \frac{Z_{op}}{R_k} + \frac{k_c}{R_k} = A_p, \tag{3}$$

where A is the present value of resources.

One first order condition to maximize parental utility determines their optimal consumption at middle and old age

$$u'_{mp} = \beta R_k u'_{op} = \lambda_p, \tag{4}$$

where λ_p is the parents' marginal utility of wealth. Another condition determines whether they give bequests,

$$\beta a V'_c \leq \frac{\lambda_p}{R_k} = \beta u'_{op}; \tag{5}$$

and the last determines investments in the human capital of children

$$R_h \beta a V'_c = \lambda_p. \tag{6}$$

Equation (6) assumes that the first order condition for investment in human capital is a strict equality; that some human capital is always invested in children. This can be justified with an Inada-type condition that small investments in human capital yield very high rates of return. In rich economies like Sweden or the United States, investments in basic knowledge and

206

nutrition of children presumably do yield a very good return. As long as parents are not completely selfish — as long as a > 0 — then such a condition does always imply positive investment in human capital. For completely selfish parents, equation (6) would be an inequality.

Equation (4) determines the accumulation of assets to finance old-age consumption. Whether parents leave bequests or want old-age support from their children is determined by the inequality in (5). If this is a strict inequality, parents want support and would not leave bequests.

That inequality can be written in a more revealing way. If children also maximize their utility, then the envelope theorem implies that

$$au'_{mc} < u'_{op} \text{ whenever } aV'_c < u'_{op} \text{ since } V'_c = u'_{mc}. \tag{7}$$

Equation (7) has the intuitive interpretation that parents do not give bequests when the utility they get from their children consuming a dollar more at middle age is less than the utility they get from a dollar more of their own consumption at old age. Obviously, such an inequality holds for completely selfish parents since the left-hand side of equations (5) and (7) are zero when a is zero. The weaker the altruism (the smaller a) the more parents want from children.

Combining equations (5) and (6) gives

$$\frac{\lambda_p}{R_h} \leq \frac{\lambda_p}{R_k}, \text{ or } R_h \geq R_k. \tag{8}$$

Equation (8) implies that the marginal rate of return on human capital equals the return on assets when parents give bequests, and it is greater than the asset return when parents do not give bequests. Parents can help children either by investing in their human capital or by leaving them assets. Since they want to maximize the advantage to children, given the cost to themselves — parents are not sadistic — they help in the most efficient form.

Consequently, if strict inequality holds in equation (8), they would not give bequests, for the best way to help children when the marginal return on human capital exceeds that on assets is to invest only in human capital. Parents leave bequests only when they get the same marginal return on both (some of these results have been derived in Becker and Tomes [1986]).

2. To analyze in a simple way the influence of parents over the formation of children's preferences, suppose parents can take actions x and y when children are young that affect children's preferences when adults. I use the assumption of separability to write the utility function of middle-aged children as

$$V_c = u_{mc} + H(y) - G(x,g) + \beta u_{oc} + \dots. \tag{9}$$

I assume that $H' > 0$ and $G_x > 0$, which means that an increase in y raises the utility of children, but an increase in x lowers their utility. For concreteness, interpret H as "happiness," and G as the "guilt" children feel toward their parents, so that greater x makes children feel guiltier. The question is: why would non-sadistic parents want to make their children feel guilty?

The variable g is the key to understanding why. This measures the contribution of children to the old-age support of parents; let us assume that children feel less guilty when they contribute more ($G_g < 0$). If $G_{gx} > 0$, then greater x both raises children's guilt and stimulates more giving by them.

The budget constraint of parents becomes:

$$Z_{mp} + h + x + y + \frac{Z_{op}}{R_k} + \frac{k_c}{R_k} = A_p + \frac{g}{R_k}. \tag{10}$$

The first-order condition for the optimal y is

$$\beta a H' \leq \lambda_p. \tag{11}$$

Since $H' > 0$, it is easy to understand why an altruistic parent may try to affect children's preferences through y since an increase in y makes children happier.

The first order condition for x is more interesting, for even altruistic parents may want to make their children feel guilty if that sufficiently raises old-age support. This first order condition can be written as

$$\frac{dV_p}{dx} = \frac{dg}{dx}\beta(u'_{op} - au'_{mc}) - \beta a \frac{dG}{dx} \leq \lambda_p, \tag{12}$$

where dG/dx incorporates the induced change in g. The second term in the middle expression is negative to altruistic parents because greater x does raise children's guilt, which lowers the utility of these parents (a > 0). However, guilt also induces children to increase old-age support, as given by dg/dx. The magnitude of this response determines whether it is worthwhile for parents to make children feel guiltier.

Increased old-age support from children has two partially offsetting effects on the welfare of altruistic parents. On the one hand, it raises their old-age consumption and utility, as given by u'_{op}. On the other hand, it lowers children's consumption, and hence the utility of altruistic parents, as given by $-au'_{mc}$. This means that altruistic parents who leave bequests never try to make children feel guiltier, for $u'_{op} = au'_{mc}$ for these parents. Since dG/dx > 0, they must be worse off when their children feel guiltier.

3. Combine the first order conditions in Equations (5) and (6) to get

$$\frac{u'_{op}}{au'_{mc}} = \frac{R_h}{R_k}. \tag{13}$$

Both sides of this equation exceed unity when parents do not give bequests. Since greater old-age support from children lowers the left-hand side by lowering the numerator and raising the denominator, the right-hand side must also fall to be in a utility maximizing equilibrium. But since R_k is given by market conditions, the right-hand side can fall only if R_h falls, which implies greater investment in children when parents expect greater old-age support from children. Even completely selfish parents (a=0) might invest in children if that would sufficiently increase the expected old-age support from guilty children.

BIBLIOGRAPHY

Arrow, Kenneth J., (1973) "The Theory of Discrimination," in Orley Ashenfelter and Albert Rees, eds., *Discrimination in Labor Markets* (Princeton NJ: Princeton University Press), pp. 3 – 33.

Arrow, Kenneth J. and Kurz, Mordecai, (1970) *Public Investment, the Rate of Return, and Optimal Fiscal Policy* (Baltimore: Published for Resources for the Future by Johns Hopkins University Press).

Barro, Robert J., (1974) "Are Government Bonds Net Wealth?" *Journal of Political Economy* 82: 1095 – 1117.

Barro, Robert J. and Sala-i-Martin, X., (1992) "Convergence," *Journal of Political Economy* 100: 223 – 51.

Beccaria, Cesare, marchese di, (1986) *On Crimes and Punishment*, 1st ed., translation of *Dei Delith e delle Pene* (Indianapolis: Hackett Publishing Co.).

Becker, Gary S., (1955) "Discrimination in the Market Place," Ph.D. dissertation, University of Chicago.

Becker, Gary S., (1957) *The Economics of Discrimination*, 1st ed. (Chicago: University of Chicago Press).

Becker, Gary S., (1962) "Investment in Human Capital: A Theoretical Analysis," *Journal of Political Economy* LXX: 9 – 49.

Becker, Gary S., (1964) *Human Capital*, 1st ed. (New York: Columbia University Press for the National Bureau of Economic Research).

Becker, Gary S., (1965) "A Theory of the Allocation of Time," *Economic Journal* 75 (299): 493 – 517.

Becker, Gary S., (1968) "Crime and Punishment: An Economic Approach," *Journal of Political Economy* 76: 169 – 217.

Becker, Gary S., (1971) *The Economics of Discrimination*, 2nd ed. (Chicago: University of Chicago Press).

Becker, Gary S., (1974) "A Theory of Social Interactions," *Journal of Political Economy* 82: 1063 – 93.

Becker, Gary S., (1991) *A Treatise on the Family*, expanded ed. (Cambridge MA: Harvard University Press).

Becker, Gary S. and Chiswick, Barry, (1966) "Education and the Distribution of Earnings," *American Economic Review* LVI: 358 – 69.

Becker, Gary S., Landes, Elisabeth M., and Michael, Robert T., (1977) "An Economic Analysis of Marital Instability," *Journal of Political Economy* 85: 1141 – 87.

Becker, Gary S. and Murphy, Kevin M., (1988) "The Family and the State," *Journal of Law and Economics* 31: 1 – 18.

Becker, Gary S., Murphy, Kevin M., and Tamura, Robert, (1990) "Human Capital, Fertility, and Economic Growth," *Journal of Political Economy* 98: S12 – 37.

Becker, Gary S. and Stigler, George J., (1974) "Law Enforcemnt, Malfeasance, and Compensation of Enforcers," *Journal of Legal Studies* 3: 1 – 18.

Becker, Gary S. and Tomes, Nigel, (1986) "Human Capital and the Rise and Fall of Families," *Journal of Labor Economics* 4: S1-S39.

Bentham, Jeremy, (1931) *Theory of Legislation* (New York: Harcourt, Brace).

Bergstrom, Theodore, (1989) "A Fresh Look at the Rotten-Kid Theorem – And Other Household Mysteries," *Journal of Political Economy* 97: 1138 – 59.

Boserup, Ester, (1970) *Women's Role in Economic Development* (London: Allen and Unwin).

Cain, Bruce E., Ferejohn, John, and Fiorina, Morris, (1987) *The Personal Vote: Constituency Service and Electoral Independence* (Cambridge MA: Harvard University Press).

Cain, Glen G., (1986) "The Economic Analysis of Labor Market Discrimination: A Survey," in O. Ashenfelter and R. Layard, eds., *Handbook of Labor Economics*, Handbooks in Labor Economics Series, no. 5 (New York: Elsevier Science): 693–785.

Cass, David, (1965) "Optimal Growth in an Aggregative Model of Capital Accumulation," *Review of Economic Studies* 32: 233–240.

Denison, Edward F., (1962) *Sources of Economic Growth in the United States* (Washington, D.C.: Committee for Economic Development).

Edgeworth, F. Y., (1922) "Equal Pay to Men and Women for Equal Work" *Economic Journal* XXXII: 431–57.

Ehrlich, Isaac, (1973) "Participation in Illegitimate Activities: A Theoretical and Empirical Investigation," *Journal of Political Economy* 81: 521–65.

Ehrlich, Isaac, (1975) "The Deterrent Effect of Capital Punishment: A Question of Life and Death," *American Economic Review* 85: 397–417.

Farrell, C. and Mandel, M., "Uncommon Sense," *Business Week*, October 26, 1992, pp. 36–37.

Faucett, M., (1918) "Equal Pay for Equal Work," *Economic Journal* XXVIII: 1–6.

Grossman, Sanford J. and Hart, Oliver D., (1983) "An Analysis of the Principal-Agent Problem," *Econometrica* 51: 7–45.

Hutt, William H., (1964) *The Economics of the Colour Bar: A Study of the Economic Origins and Consequences of Racial Segregation in South Africa* (London: Published for the Institute of Economic Affairs by A. Deutsch).

Landes, William M. and Posner, Richard A., (1975) "The Private Enforcement of Law," *Journal of Legal Studies* 4: 1–46.

Lindbeck, Assar and Weibull, Jorgen W., (1988) "Strategic Interaction with Altruism: The Economics of Fait Accompli," *Journal of Poltical Economy* 96: 1165–82. University of Stockholm.

Linder, Staffan Burenstam, (1970) *The Harried Leisure Class* (New York: Columbia University Press).

Loury, Glenn C., (1992) "Incentive Effects of Affirmative Action," *Annals of the American Academy of Political and Social Science* 523: 19–29.

Lucas, Robert E., Jr., (1988) "On the Mechanics of Economic Development," *Journal of Monetary Economics* 22: 3–42.

McElroy, Marjorie B. and Horney, Mary Jean, (1981) "Nash-Bargained Household Decisions: Toward a Generalizaton of the Theory of Demand," *International Economic Review* 22: 333–49.

Menninger, Karl, (1966) *The Crime of Punishment* (New York: The Viking Press).

Mincer, Jacob, (1962) "Labor Force Participation of Married Women," in *Aspects of Labor Economics*, a conference of the Universities – National Bureau Committee for Economic Research (Princeton NJ: Princeton University Press for the National Bureau of Economic Research).

Mincer, Jacob, (1974) *Schooling, Experience, and Earnings* (New York: Columbia University Press for the National Bureau of Economic Research).

Murphy, Kevin M. and Welch, Finis, (1992) "The Structure of Wages," *Quarterly Journal of Economics* 107: 285–326.

Myrdal, Gunnar, (1944) *An American Dilemma: The Negro Problem and Modern Democracy*, 2 vols. (New York: Random House).

National Research Council (U.S.), Panel of Research on Deterrent and Incapacitative Effects, (1978) *Deterrence and Incapacitation: Estimating the Effects of Criminal Sanctions on Crime Rates*, Alfred Blumstein, Jacqueline Cohen, and Daniel Nagin, eds. (Washington, D.C.: National Academy of Sciences).

Oi, Walter Y., (1962) "Labor as a Quasi-Fixed Factor," *Journal of Political Economy* 70: 538–55.

Phelps, Edmund S., (1972) "The Statistical Theory of Racism and Sexism," *American Economic Review* 62: 659–61.

Polinsky, A. Mitchell and Shavell, Steven, (1984) "The Optimal Use of Fines and Imprisonment," *Journal of Public Economics* 24: 89–99.

Posner, Richard A., (1986) *Economic Analysis of Law*, 3rd ed. (Boston: Little, Brown).

Psacharopoulos, George, (1975) *Earnings and Education in OECD Countries* (Paris: Organization for Economic Co-operation; Washington, D.C.: OECD Publications Center).

Romer, Paul M., (1986) "Increasing Returns and Long Run Growth," *Journal of Political Economy* 94: 1002–37.

Schultz, Theodore W., (1963) *The Economic Value of Education* (New York: Columbia University Press).

Stigler, George J., (1970) "The Optimum Enforcement of Laws," *Journal of Political Economy* 78: 526–36.

United States Sentencing Commission (1988) "Discussion Draft of Sentencing Guidelines and Policy Statement for Organizations: Proposed Chapter 8 for the Guidelines Manual."

Williamson, Oliver E., (1985) *The Economic Institutions of Capitalism: Firms, Markets, Relational Contracting* (New York: Free Press; London: Collier Macmillan).

ACKNOWLEDGEMENTS

I have had valuable comments from James Coleman, Richard Posner, Sherwin Rosen, Raaj Sah, Jose Scheinkman, Richard Stern, and Stephen Stigler.